China's Economic Modernisation and Structural Changes

Essays in Honour of John Wong

EAI Series on East Asia

ISSN: 2529-718X

Series Editors: WANG Gungwu
(East Asian Institute, National University of Singapore)

ZHENG Yongnian
(East Asian Institute, National University of Singapore)

About the Series

EAI Series on East Asia was initiated by the East Asian Institute (EAI) (http://www.eai.nus.edu.sg). EAI was set up in April 1997 as an autonomous research organisation under a statute of the National University of Singapore. The analyses in this series are by scholars who have spent years researching on their areas of interest in East Asia, primarily, China, Japan and South Korea, and in the realms of politics, economy, society and international relations.

Published:

China's Economic Modernisation and Structural Changes:
Essays in Honour of John Wong
    edited by ZHENG Yongnian and Sarah Y TONG

The Rise of the Regulatory State in the Chinese Health-care System
    by QIAN Jiwei

Contemporary South Korean Economy: Challenges and Prospects
    by CHIANG Min-Hua

China's Economy in Transformation under the New Normal
    edited by Sarah Y TONG and WAN Jing

China's Development: Social Investment and Challenges
    by ZHAO Litao

Politics, Culture and Identities in East Asia: Integration and Division
    edited by LAM Peng Er and LIM Tai Wei

*The complete list of the published volumes in the series can also be found at
http://www.worldscientific.com/series/eaisea

EAI Series on
East Asia

China's Economic Modernisation and Structural Changes

Essays in Honour of John Wong

Editors

ZHENG Yongnian

East Asian Institute
National University of Singapore
Singapore

Sarah Y TONG

East Asian Institute
National University of Singapore
Singapore

World Scientific

:W JERSEY · LONDON · SINGAPORE · BEIJING · SHANGHAI · HONG KONG · TAIPEI · CHENNAI · TOKYO

Published by

World Scientific Publishing Co. Pte. Ltd.
5 Toh Tuck Link, Singapore 596224
USA office: 27 Warren Street, Suite 401-402, Hackensack, NJ 07601
UK office: 57 Shelton Street, Covent Garden, London WC2H 9HE

Library of Congress Cataloging-in-Publication Data
Names: Wong, John, 1939–   honoree. | Zheng, Yongnian, editor. |
    Tong, Sarah Y. (Sarah Yueting), editor.
Title: China's economic modernisation and structural changes : essays in honour of John Wong /
    edited by Yongnian Zheng (East Asian Institute, National University of Singapore, Singapore),
    Sarah Y. Tong (East Asian Institute, National University of Singapore, Singapore).
Description: New Jersey : World Scientific, [2019] | Series: EAI series on East Asia; Volume 6 |
    Includes index.
Identifiers: LCCN 2019003716| ISBN 9789811203619 (hc : alk. paper)
Subjects: LCSH: Economic development--China. | China--Economic policy--1949– |
    China--Economic conditions--1949–
Classification: LCC HC427.95 .C456185 2019 | DDC 330.951--dc23
LC record available at https://lccn.loc.gov/2019003716

British Library Cataloguing-in-Publication Data
A catalogue record for this book is available from the British Library.

For any available supplementary material, please visit
https://www.worldscientific.com/worldscibooks/10.1142/11365#t=suppl

Desk Editors: Anthony Alexander/Lixi Dong

Typeset by Stallion Press
Email: enquiries@stallionpress.com

Printed in Singapore

Prologue: Remembering Professor John C.H. Wong

A Special Tribute by Y.Y. KUEH

I have known Professor John Wong for over half a century. In June this year, when Professor Aline Wong sent the bad news from Singapore, it was a bolt from the blue. Amidst tears of grief, we could only lament the impermanence of life.

It was not more than three months before, at 10 am of the Saturday on 3 March, when Mr and Mrs Wong personally drove to Pan Pacific Hotel to pick up my wife Wang Xiaohu and I for a breakfast at Singapore's Tanglin Club. It was also only 28 October of last year, during their short visit to Hong Kong, when I invited them to my house to renew acquaintances and to dine at San Xi Lou. I specially chose this famous Sichuan cuisine restaurant because they have long resided in Singapore, and would probably enjoy dishes similar to that of the spicy dishes of Southeast Asia, even though they might not have fully comprehend what "San Xi" refers to. It is actually a name that came from Emperor Qianlong's private study, called the Three Treasures Hall or San Xi Tang.

After dinner, the four of us took the elevator to the basement carpark of Coda Plaza, the building where the restaurant is located. Just when we were about to board the car, Professor Aline Wong accidently tripped over a little stone step, a dent less than two inches, and fell.

It frightened all of us, but fortunately she had no major injuries. The carpark was brightly lighted at that moment, so it was a mystery how she tripped. To think about it, I had brought along with us a few bottles of German beer during dinner, because I thought it would help ease the spiciness of the super spicy chicken dish, but there was no other strong liquor. Moreover, it was basically Professor John Wong and I who were drinking. Aline and Xiaohu were happily chatting about family affairs most of the time and hardly drank any beer. They were definitely not drunk, but Aline still unexpectedly missed that step. It seems that John was more used to the spiciness of Southeast Asia, so much so that he could also handle the Sichuan spiciness effortlessly.

Mentioning about German beer, it reminds me of the first time when I met John. It was the autumn of 1967. I was invited to an academic seminar, held at the University of Hong Kong sponsored by the Leverhulme Foundation, where I submitted my first paper written in English about "The Debate on Economic Policy between Mao Zedong and Liu Shaoqi". John was there too, and he jokingly commented that I have a strong German accent after listening to my presentation in English. I also playfully replied that after indulging in German beer for six years, neither had my Teochew accent changed nor my hair turned white, and such were qualities of a hero. This interesting conversation has also been recounted in my book *You xue jiang hu liu shi zai: xin ying, yi qu, fan si* (World Scientific Publishing, August 2017, p. 230).

The year before that, which was the end of 1966, I had just completed my PhD in Germany and returned to teach at the New Asia College (the Chinese University of Hong Kong was established in 1963 and New Asia College was one of the constituent colleges). In earlier part of the same year, John had also obtained his PhD from the University of London, and was employed as a lecturer for Economics at his alma mater, the University of Hong Kong. He demonstrated an extraordinary command of the English language, and it was very impressive.

Even though it was hard to communicate between English and German, John and I were like fellow students considering our similarity in age and educational background. Not to mention, we shared the same interests and aspirations in focusing research on political economic issues of contemporary China. In fact, John was younger than me by two years. During my 80th birthday last year, I had warmly invited John and Aline to Hong Kong for the birthday banquet. Among the guests were many Shaolin-level "Gongfu Pandas" who are also friends of John. It is a pity that John had to fly to mainland China for academic visits and to give lectures.

Talking about "Gongfu Panda", it deeply and sadly reminds me of John's talents. When Aline informed us of the terrible news, she had attached a short essay written by John on his sickbed before his death. In the essay, it actually touched upon my above-mentioned memoir *You xue jiang hu liu shi zai*, and translated the title to *Gongfu Panda Roaming Around for 60 Years*. I thought it was a brilliant and intriguing translation. That piece of short essay was also John's last words, written during his hospitalisation in the middle of March this year. It is a paper he was invited to write, by the East Asian Institute (EAI) that he founded, for the International Conference on 25 May to discuss about "China's Economic Modernisation and Structural Change". Coincidently, the purpose of this conference held by EAI was to mark, pay respect to and commemorate Professor John Wong as a notable scholar, as well as his thorough knowledge of both the western and Chinese studies and his research on the political economy of China. It is saddening for fate to play such a trick, just like Beethoven's Symphony No. 5 "Destiny"; it is almost impossible to forget the whole list of John's papers on "China Research", for the texts he wrote resemble the resounding Symphony No. 3 "Hero". It is heartrending to lose all chances of hearing these pieces play again.

I would like to borrow an online music critics' comment on Beethoven's Symphony No. 5 to describe John's style and achievements in academics. This critic commented that, "this symphony piece is most representative of Beethoven's artistic style, for it is rigorously structured, skillfully concise, explicitly organised, and artistically contagious. Beethoven's sense towards music is so extraordinary precise that is not an exaggeration to dub him 'the saint of music'." I think it is perfectly appropriate to replace "Beethoven" in this statement with "John Wong". John's papers on China's unanticipated economic growth are "grandeur and smooth like drifting clouds and flowing water" — certainly comparable to Beethoven's Symphony No. 3.

Honestly, after I began my teaching career and started to give lectures for the course on "Economy of China", the first book that I read cover to cover was John's book on *Land Reform in The People's Republic of China: Institutional Transformation in Agriculture* published in 1973. This is also mentioned in my memoir *You xue jiang hu liu shi zai* (pp. 414–415). For the few decades after John's family moved to Singapore in 1971, I was greatly inspired and benefited from reading all the books and papers that he wrote after his establishment of EAI, as well as his policy recommendations to the Singapore government in the form of executive summaries and background briefs (please see p. 410). John had published a huge collection of books, and his works on the Chinese economy are remarkable in terms of both quality and quantity. While I wish he had stayed, I had also been asking myself if he would still attain such outstanding achievements if he had remained in Hong Kong (please see p. 415).

Coming back to the recent years, one of the last articles that John had written was the commentary published in Singapore's *Straits Times* (on 7 March 2017), titled "The myths of a China-led global order". This article mentioned that, "Mr Trump's presidency might just mark the turning point for the decline of the American economy." When I saw this, I had just completed a long paper that was about to be submitted to the first "Dialogue of Civilizations" held in Penang (25–26 March 2017) organised by Penang state of Malaysia. My paper was titled "The Belt and Road Grand Strategy and the Wisdom of 'Befriending Distant States and Attacking Neighboring Ones' from the Spring and Autumn Period — also discussing on the position of ASEAN and possible impacts on President Trump's new Asia-Pacific policy". When I read John's perspective, I was elated to find that we had unintentionally come to hold the same views (please see p. 400).

As Trump launched the China–US trade war this year with great arrogance and magnitude, I see this as pretending to appear fierce, but in fact weak and frightened on the inside. Recently, Trump had also called for the United States' exit from the World Trade Organisation, risking a danger of disrupting the order of the world's free trade and investments. Apparently, this shows that the global competitiveness of this world bully is never like before, and is beginning to decline. This kind of global (or overlooking the whole of China) perspective on the political economy has been consistent throughout all of John's work, and it can be identified as one of his academic styles and features.

Similarly, John and I are both unfamiliar and uncommitted to the application of complicated western-style econometric models in the analysis and observation of real-life problems that arise during China's economic development and reform. We also consider it as a shame to cooperate with so-called "current affair experts", who drift away from the political economy, social or institutional level to talk extravagantly on the rights and wrongs of Chinese economy (please see p. 425). Regarding this problem, Professor Shin Chuei-Ling from the Department of Political Economy, National Sun Yat-sen University of Taiwan, has written a comprehensive overview of Professor John Wong's academic methodology and achievements, which is well worth a read.

I believe that all scholars and experts who have the chance to browse through the various papers written by John will be amazed by his incisive and unique insights, as well as his fluent and powerful language. You will probably think it was written by an energetic young man, and you can never expect that he would pass away so suddenly. Thinking about the present again brings my thoughts back to 50 years ago, which was during the autumn of 1967 — the seminar on "China's Economic Problems" when we first met, and we already felt like old friends. At that time, however, we had yet to become confidants. Nevertheless, John and Aline had, on the eve of their departure to Singapore in 1971, warmly welcomed us to their farewell banquet held in their residence along Robinson Road of the Mid-Levels region in Hong Kong. This scene is still fresh in my memory, and I can only revisit it with tears and sorrow.

Written on 20 October 2018
English translation by Chen Juan

Note: The Chinese original is attached as an appendix at the end of this volume.

Biography

 **John Wong** was a professorial fellow and academic adviser of the East Asian Institute (EAI), National University of Singapore and former research director of EAI, and director of the Institute of East Asian Political Economy (IEAPE). He taught Economics at the University of Hong Kong during 1966–1970 and at the National University of Singapore from 1971 to 1990.

He was a short-term academic visitor at the Fairbank Centre of Harvard University, Economic Growth Centre of Yale University, St Antony College of Oxford University and Economics Department of Stanford University. He had held the ASEAN Chair at the University of Toronto.

He had written/edited 40 books, and published over 400 articles and papers on China, and development in East Asia and ASEAN. His first book was *Land Reform in the People's Republic of China* (New York, Praeger, 1973) and his most recent book was *Zhu Rongji and China's Economic Take-Off* (London, Imperial College Press, 2016). In addition, he had written numerous policy-related reports on development in China for the Singapore government. He received his PhD from the University of London.

Professor Wong passed away in June 2018. For over three decades, Professor Wong had followed and provided insightful analyses on the remarkable transformation of China's economy.

List of Contributors

CAO Cong holds a PhD in sociology from Columbia University and is now a Professor in innovation studies at the University of Nottingham Ningbo China. As a scholar of social studies of science, technology and innovation in China, Dr Cao has studied China's scientific elite, human resources in science and technology, research and entrepreneurship in nanotechnology and biotechnology, and the reform of the science and technology system. His research has been supported by the U.S. National Science Foundation, European Union's Framework Program (FP) 7, and the National Natural Science Foundation of China, among others.

Sarah CHAN is a Research Fellow at the East Asian Institute, National University of Singapore. She obtained her PhD from the Nanyang Technological University. Previously, she was a Consultant for the Asian Development Bank and a Senior Economist at the Monetary Authority of Singapore. Her research interests include China's economic and financial developments as well as trade and investment in East Asia. She has published in refereed journals, namely, *Asian Survey, Asia Pacific Business Review, East Asia: An International Quarterly, China Economic Policy Review* and *Post-Communist Economies*.

CHEN Juan is a Research Assistant at the East Asian Institute, National University of Singapore. She graduated with a Bachelor's degree in International Politics from Peking University, China. Her research interests include China's political development and foreign policy, and mass political behaviour, and she has written on topics including Chinese cyber nationalism, Chinese Communist Youth League and neo-nationalism in Japan. Prior to university, she received her education in Singapore.

CHEN Kang is a Professor of Economics at the Lee Kuan Yew School of Public Policy, National University of Singapore. He has published widely on issues relating to China's economic reform and development in professional journals, including *Journal of Comparative Economics, China Economic Review, European Journal of Political Economy, Economic Systems Research* and *Economic Modelling.* He served as the Head of the Economics Division at Nanyang Technological University, Vice President of the Economic Society of Singapore and Director of the East Asian Economic Association. He currently serves on the editorial board of the *European Journal of Political Economy.*

KONG Tuan Yuen is a Visiting Research Fellow at the East Asian Institute, National University of Singapore. He received his PhD in Industrial Economics from the National Central University, Taiwan. His research interests include China's industry development, especially that of strategic emerging industries, and China–ASEAN relations. He had published his works in *Review of Global Politics, Applied Econometrics and International Development* and *Journal of Overseas Chinese and Southeast Asian Studies.*

Y. Y. KUEH is a retired Professor of Economics based in Hong Kong. He formerly taught at the Chinese University of Hong Kong (as a Senior Lecturer), Lingnan University (Dean of Social Science) and Macquarie University in Sydney, Australia (Founding Director of the Centre for Chinese Political Economy). He is currently a Senior College Tutor (honorary title) of New Asia College, CUHK. His research interests and publications (more than 100 articles in various international journals and over 10 specialist books — mostly by Oxford Clarendon Press) cover a wide range of topics, virtually all in the field of Chinese economic studies.

LI Bingqin is the SHARP Associate Professor and Director of Chinese Social Policy Program at the Social Policy Research Centre at the University of New South Wales, Australia. Her research is on social policy and governance. She has particular expertise on China, and China in a comparative perspective. Her current projects include housing policy, urban governance, delivering Sustainable Development Goals in China and the impact of technological innovations on social development. Her research has been published in academic journals in social policy and urban studies, such as *Urban Studies, Environment & Urbanisation, Social Policy & Administration and Public Administration and Development*. She has consulted for multiple international organisations.

LIN Shuanglin is a Professor of the National School of Development, Director of China Center for Public Finance, Peking University. He has been a Noddle Distinguished Professor at the University of Nebraska Omaha. His research concentrates on public economics, economic growth and China's public finance. He has published extensively in academic journals, including *Journal of Economic Theory* and *Journal of Public Economics*, and completed many research projects for the Ministry of Finance of China, the World Bank, and the United Nations. He was the President of the Chinese Economists Society during the period 2002–2003 and Chair of the Department of Public Finance at Peking University from 2005 to 2013.

LU Ding graduated from Fudan University (China) in 1983 and received a PhD in economics from Northwestern University, USA in 1991. He is currently a Professor and the Vice Dean of School of Entrepreneurship and Management, ShanghaiTech University, China. He was a Tenured Professor at the University of the Fraser Valley,

Canada from 2008 to 2018 and Sophia University, Japan from 2005 to 2008. His academic career also consists of affiliations with National University of Singapore (1992–2005) and University of Nebraska at Omaha (1991–1992). His research published works cover regional economic development, international trade and investment, and comparative economic systems, with a focus on China's development.

Barry NAUGHTON is the So Kwanlok Professor at the School of Global Policy and Strategy, University of California, San Diego. Naughton's work on the Chinese economy focuses on market transition, industry and technology, foreign trade, and political economy. His first book, *Growing Out of the Plan*, won the Ohira Prize in 1996, and a new edition of his popular survey and textbook, *The Chinese Economy: Adaptation and Growth*, appeared in 2018. Naughton received his PhD in Economics from Yale University in 1986.

QIAN Jiwei is Senior Research Fellow at the East Asian Institute, National University of Singapore. He is also a Co-Editor of the book series *Social Policy and Development Studies in East Asia* (Palgrave Macmillan). His research on health economics, health policy and social policy has been published in publications such as *The China Quarterly, Health Economics, Policy and Law, Journal of European Social Policy, Journal of Mental Health Policy and Economics, Journal of Social Policy, Land Use Policy, Public Administration and Development, Public Choice, Singapore Economic Review* and *Social Policy & Administration*. He is also on the editorial board of *China: An International Journal* and *East Asian Policy*.

Jim SHEN Huangnan is currently a PhD candidate in development economics and international development at the School of African and Oriental Studies, University of London. He holds a BSc in Management from the London School of Economics and Political Science (LSE) and MSc in Economics and Management from LSE as well. He is a member of international econometric society, development studies association, Chinese Economists Society, Royal Atlantic Economic Society, Forum for Research in Empirical International Trade and World Interdisciplinary

Network for Institutional Research. He is also one of the research team members at Tsinghua Modern SOE Research Institute. He has published extensively on the topics of large SOE reforms in China as well as the global supply chains. He has published more than 15 papers including working papers. His work appears on *Structural Change and Economic Dynamics, Fudan Journal of Humanities and Social Science* and so on. He is on the editorial board of the journal *Modern Management Forum*.

TIAN Zhilei is an Assistant Professor at the China Institute for Educational Finance Research, Peking University. He received his PhD in Economics from Beijing Normal University. His research interests encompass economics of education, education finance, technical vocational education and training, and policy evaluation methodology. He has been frequently consulted by the Chinese government on technical vocational education and training policies.

Sarah Y TONG is a Senior Research Fellow at the East Asian Institute, National University of Singapore. Her research interests concentrate on the recent development and transformation of Chinese Economy. Her work appeared in journals such as the *Journal of International Economics, Global Economic Review, China: An International Journal, Review of Development Economics, China and the World Economy, Comparative Economic Studies* and *China Economic Review*. In addition to contributing chapters to numerous books on contemporary China, she edited and co-edited several books including *Trade, Investment and Economic Integration* (2014), *China's Evolving Industrial Policies and Economic Restructure* (2014), *China's Great Urbanization* (2017) and *China's Economic Transformation under the New Normal* (2017).

WANG Rong is the Director and a Professor of the China Institute for Educational Finance Research, Peking University and the Founding Chairwoman of the China National Research Association for Education Financing. She is also the youngest member of China's State Education Advisory Committee. She completed her BS and MA from Peking University and PhD in education from the University of California,

Berkeley. Professor Wang is recognised as one of the most important scholars in the field of education finance in China for her role in designing the free rural compulsory education policy and several other important education finance policies since 2005.

WU Yanrui is a Professor and the Head of Economics, University of Western Australia. He specialises in development economics, energy and environment, and applied econometrics. His research interests include the Asian economies (particularly China, India and Indonesia), productivity and efficiency analysis, economic growth, resource and environmental economics. He has published extensively in his fields. His work is widely cited by the profession (with about 5,000 cites, a h-index of 31 and i10-index of 78 according to Google Scholars). He has provided consultancy for governments, NGOs and MNCs. He is the sole author of several books such as *Productive Performance in Chinese Enterprises* (Macmillan, 1996), *China's Consumer Revolution* (Edward Elgar Publishing, 1999), *The Macroeconomics of East Asian Growth* (Edward Elgar Publishing, 2002), *China's Economic Growth* (Routledge, 2004), *Productivity, Efficiency and Economic Growth in China* (Palgrave Macmillan, 2008) and *Understanding Economic Growth in China and India* (World Scientific Publishing, 2012). Professor Wu is an Associate Editor of *China Economic Review*, a member of the editorial board of *Journal of Chinese Economic and Business Studies* (Routledge, UK), *China Agricultural Economic Review* (Emerald, UK) and *East Asian Policy* (National University of Singapore).

XING Yuqing is a Professor of Economics of the National Graduate Institute for Policy Studies in Tokyo. He served as the Director of the Capacity Building and Training Department of the Asian Development Bank Institute from 2011 to 2014. He also held positions such as Sabbatical Fellow at the World Institute for Development Economics Research and Visiting Professor of the Institute of Advanced Studies, both at the United Nations University; Visiting Research Fellow of the Bank of Finland and Visiting Senior Research Fellow of the East Asian

Institute at the National University of Singapore. He provided consulting services to Asian Development Bank, the International Monetary Fund and the Japan International Cooperation Agency. Dr Xing's research focuses on international trade, foreign direct investments, exchange rates and global value chains. He is a leading expert on global value chains. His research on the iPhone and the China–US trade balance has been discussed widely in the global mainstream media, challenging conventional views on bilateral trade statistics and instigating a reform of trade statistics. Dr Xing received his bachelor's and master's degrees from Peking University and a PhD in economics from the University of Illinois at Urbana–Champaign.

ZHANG Jun is a University Professor of Economics and currently serves as the Dean of School of Economics, Fudan University, Shanghai, China. He is also the Founding Director of the China Center for Economic Studies, a Shanghai-based think tank for the Chinese economy. His recent contributions have been to *The World Economy, China Economic Review, Economic Systems, Comparative Economic Studies, Journal of Asian Economics, Journal of the Asia Pacific Economy* and so on. He is the recipient of the Bergson Prize by the American Association for Comparative Economic Studies for his paper published in *Comparative Economic Studies* in 2015. Over the past 25 years, he has authored or edited numerous books including *Economic Transition with Chinese Characteristics: Thirty Years of Reform and Opening Up* (McGill-Queen University Press, 2008), *Transformation of the Chinese Enterprises* (Cengage Learning, 2009), *Unfinished Reforms of the Chinese Economy* (World Scientific Publishing Ltd, 2013) and *End of Hyper Growth In China* (Palgrave Macmillan, 2016).

ZHENG Yongnian is a Professor and the Director of the East Asian Institute, National University of Singapore. He received his BA and MA degrees from Beijing University and his PhD at Princeton University. He is the Editor of the series on *Contemporary China* (World Scientific Publishing) and Editor of *China Policy* series (Routledge). He is also the Editor of *China: An International Journal* and *East Asian*

Policy. His papers have appeared in internationally refereed journals such as *Comparative Political Studies, Political Science Quarterly, Third World Quarterly* and *China Quarterly.* He is the author of a few dozen books, including *Market in State: The Political Economy of Domination in China, Contemporary China, The Chinese Communist Party as Organizational Emperor, Technological Empowerment, De Facto Federalism in China, Discovering Chinese Nationalism in China* and *Globalization and State Transformation in China,* and Editor of many books on China and its foreign relations including the latest volumes *China Entering the Xi Era* (2014), *China and the New International Order* (2008) and *China and International Relations* (2010).

Contents

Introduction

ZHENG Yongnian and Sarah Y TONG

This publication of collected essays on China's economic modernisation and structural changes is dedicated to the memory of Professor John Wong who unexpectedly passed away on 11 June 2018.

Professor Wong has been an instrumental and seminal figure at the East Asian Institute (EAI) of the National University of Singapore. The EAI was set up in April 1997 as an autonomous research organisation under a statute of the National University of Singapore. It is the successor of the former Institute of East Asian Political Economy (IEAPE), which was itself the successor of the Institute of East Asian Philosophies (IEAP), originally established by Dr Goh Keng Swee in 1983 for the study of Confucianism. The main mission of EAI is to promote academic and policy-oriented research on contemporary China and other East Asian economies. Professor Wong was a key figure whose earlier work was intertwined with the foundational origins of EAI. Professor Wong became the Director of IEAP in 1990, and then the Director of IEAPE, and then the Research Director of EAI. Under his directorship, IEAP started on its documentary accumulation of knowledge through building up an inventory of official yearbooks, books and journals on contemporary China, which today has become the largest and most comprehensive library in this subject in Southeast Asia. This achievement propelled Singapore to become a major centre of contemporary China studies in the region.

In addition to being an effective administrator, his profound knowledge of contemporary China studies plus his training as a development economist had significantly oriented the institute's research towards policy relevance, providing significant insights into the rise of China. Indeed, his administration and research experience had become synonymous with the institute itself. There are so many memories of Professor Wong, but what has made EAI distinctive among research institutes in the region are the following aspects of his legacy.

First of all, as an experienced economist and a prolific scholar with a passion for Sinology, Professor Wong's work covers a wide range of areas, from earlier writings on China's agricultural and rural development to China's external economic relations, and more recently to important issues concerning China's economic growth and sustainable development such as income inequality and technological advancement.

Second, Professor Wong approached the field of China studies from a more holistic approach rather than a narrowly defined economics perspective. In addition to leveraging on his deep knowledge of China's past, Professor Wong understood how the cultural, historical and social trends in China had shaped its economy. Professor Wong's writings incorporate his analytical understanding of a professional economist with additional insights of an area studies specialist who looked into various non-economic elements.

Third, Professor Wong always stressed the importance of writing short, clear and concise policy papers for EAI's stakeholders. Indeed, Professor Wong distilled the conceptual foundations of EAI's Background Briefs, policy reports written for the Singaporean ministries with crisp and unambiguous language, taking after the genetic imprints of the late Dr Goh Keng Swee' ideas. Through his professional and meticulous reviews of Background Brief drafts by EAI researchers, Professor Wong communicated with and taught younger scholars on gaining insights about contemporary China and acquiring skills to conduct effective policy research. By focusing on the practical dimensions of the subject matters, these EAI Background Briefs distinguish themselves from more conventional academic writings and have become a defining symbol of EAI output.

Perhaps Professor Wong's most important legacy over the decades is his mentoring of younger scholars at the institute. He spent much time and efforts in coaching younger scholars on their writing and analytical skills. In addition to stressing the importance of writing well and in a concise manner, Professor Wong encouraged younger scholars to read widely and not merely confine themselves to a particular area of specialisation. He believed that reading beyond one's specific areas of specialisation would enable one to see the bigger picture, developing new interest and new areas to write on, and to expand one's scope and depth of knowledge.

The loss to EAI from Professor Wong's demise is immense. We believe, however, scores of younger scholars have grown and matured through years of guidance and wise counsel from Professor Wong. They are prepared and keen to carry on the good work done by Professor Wong and others during the years he was with EAI. As China rises to be a great power and countries around the globe become increasingly interdependent, the study of China and its transformation is more than ever important for Singapore, as well as for the region and the world at large.

In this collection of essays, we included the papers presented at the conference in honour of Professor Wong, held in late May 2018, less than two weeks before his unexpected demise. Other contributors include scholars who have worked with Professor Wong and no doubt benefited from his guidance and advice.

The collection starts with a prologue by Professor Kueh Yak Yeow (郭益耀) of Lingnan University's School of Social Sciences and a long-time friend of Professor Wong. Professor Kueh remembers emotionally his numerous encounters with Professor Wong and Dr Aline Wong. He also highlights their shared passion on China studies and his appreciation for Professor's holistic and policy-oriented approach in reading and interpreting China.

The year 2018 marked the 40th anniversary of China's economic reform and opening up. China's economy has grown significantly larger and increasingly more complex, making it impossible to cover all the aspects in this collection. The chapters in this volume are divided into four parts, each of which deals with one important aspect of China's economy.

The five chapters in the first part focus on overall structural changes and issues concerning macroeconomic management. Chapter 1 examines the structural changes in the Chinese economy, including both its recent dynamics and the challenges the country faces. In particular, the author examines the changing importance of consumption and investment in driving growth, the evolution of income inequality, and the comparative development of the state and the non-state sector in the economy. The author foresees that, under changing domestic and global economic conditions, the task of steering the economy towards quality growth is challenging. The government has to strike a delicate balance between short-term growth objectives and long-term sustainable development.

The topic of Chapter 2 is the economic role of government in China's economy. It is a revisit to an issue that the author researched upon with Professor Wong over two decades ago. The chapter concludes that, while China's economic landscape has changed profoundly since the early 1990s, the government's involvements in the economy are as deep and wide-ranging as before. Furthermore, the author finds that the relative power between the state and the market varies across sectors and areas. On one hand, state-owned firms and financial institutions are used to implement the government's development agenda. On the other, markets for goods and services are relatively developed, compared to factor markets, especially for land.

Chapter 3 examines the dynamics of China's fiscal management. The author first reviews the development of China's growth-promoting fiscal reforms and rapid growth of recent decades. More importantly, the chapter emphasises the challenges faced by China's fiscal system, including income inequality, environmental degradation and high local government debt. The author provides useful suggestions to enhance quality growth, such as increasing environmental and resource taxes, personal income tax reforms, and increasing government spending on public goods. The author also argues that it is essential to curtail local government debt and to stimulate growth through corporate income tax reduction.

Chapter 4 focuses on the issue of capital account liberalisation in China. The author reviews that, while China achieved full current account convertibility in as early as late 1996, capital account liberalisation has been carefully sequenced, gradual and heavily managed by the authorities. She also highlights the difficulties and challenges a more open exchange policy entails for the Chinese government in conducting monetary policies. In particular, the author asserts that convertibility for capital account transactions can be a double-edged sword for developing the economy. It could improve capital allocation efficiency on one hand and possibly disable the economy on the other. The risks are higher in circumstances such as underdeveloped financial institutions and financial markets.

Chapter 5 examines the evolution of competition policy in China, an important aspect for developing a comprehensive regulatory framework. The author highlights several features of China's competition policy and its implementation. First, cases are under different government agencies, depending on the types of violating behaviour. Second, while the relevant law was introduced only 10 years ago, the implementation seemed quite prolific as large numbers of cases have been reported, reviewed and adjudicated. Third, there exist various concerns regarding the enforcement, including the lack of capacity and expertise in the government, a possible conflict of interests among institutions between the implementation of industrial policies and the enforcement of completion policy, and the lack of transparency in case proceedings.

The second part has three chapters which examine issues relevant to sustainable development and certain new trends in the economy. These include science and technology and innovation, education system, and e-commerce. In Chapter 6, the author first provides an overview of China's achievement while making its innovation system more responsive to the domestic and international challenges. Furthermore, the author discusses the underlying factors that have contributed to the phenomenal progress as well as the problems that may derail China's efforts to become an innovation-oriented nation and a global leader in science and technology. Speculation on China's future direction is also offered.

Chapter 7 focuses on China's education financing of the past four decades, especially development since 2005. First, the authors highlight the difficulties in education financing before 2005, including ill-defined responsibilities among different levels of governments and inadequate budget associated with fiscal restructuring of the mid-1990s and rural tax-for-fee reforms in the early 2000s. The authors then examine the government's efforts and policy changes since 2005 that led to the rapid growth of fiscal funding for education and an improved education financing system, such as setting a numeral target for education spending, an overhaul of education financing system and a rapid expansion in central governments' fiscal responsibility.

Chapter 8 looks at the recent rapid expansion of e-commerce in China, which has become an increasingly important new driving force for growth. Supported by a convenient payment technology and efficient logistic arrangement, e-commerce has not only surged quickly in volume but also expanded widely, from urban to rural areas and from domestic to cross-border trade. Led by several internet giant companies and supported by the governments' accommodating policies, the Chinese e-commerce sector has created innovative new methods to promote online business activities, attracting growing numbers of producers, consumers and market intermediaries.

Part three includes three chapters that examine China's large state sector and its transformation. In Chapter 9, the author argues that changes in the governance of China's state firms since 2013 have resulted in the sector being increasingly "financialised". However, the author stresses that such "financialisation" has taken place in a rather particular context, where the government has begun to reemphasise the primacy of government-defined national goals after market-oriented economic reforms between 1978 and the mid-2000s. The outcome, the author declares, has been an increasingly interventionist government, steering increasingly important state firms through various financial instruments.

Chapter 10 reviews China's state-owned enterprise (SOE) reforms and restructuring since the late 1970s, focusing on the latest round since 2013. In particular, the author examines the several policy directives announced by the government and discusses their useful elements for reinvigorating the transformation of the state sector. These include the categorisation of SOEs into different classes, the transformation of government's role from asset management to capital management, and the encouragement of SOE ownership diversification. While reform experiments have been carried out in many SOEs and at various localities, the author cautions that contradictions and ambiguities remain. These include, for example, the interplay between state and the market in sectors with SOEs.

Chapter 11 studies an important issue concerning China's large SOEs, namely the role of party committee within these large organisations. Through theoretical investigation, the authors illustrate why effective functioning of party committees within large SOEs might help mitigate certain inefficiencies, such as preventing "empire-building" activities by CEOs through monitoring. Meanwhile, the authors also show that imposing party committee control within large SOEs could also undermine the effect of incentives for the CEOs and SOE managers to exert full efforts. To balance the two effects, the authors suggest that the party committee's authority should be set at a level where part of the benefit of following party direction is accrued to the CEOs as a way of incentivising these managers.

The three chapters in the last part examine China's regional development and trade development. In Chapter 12, the author describes the shifts of fiscal power across China's provincial economies in the context of changing developmental convergence. Analysis using data from 1995 to 2016 show that distribution of provincial contributions to the central government's tax revenue has become less concentrated in the last 10 years, similar to the pattern of changes in the distribution of local economic sizes. Measured in net fiscal positions of provincial economies, however, the cross-region distribution of fiscal power has become more concentrated since 2005, which may have important implications on intergovernmental political–economy relationship.

In Chapter 13, the author reviews the evolution of China's housing policies during the past four decades of reform, placing special attention on the issue of affordable housing. While housing reform has been an important element of China's overall transition towards market economy, concerns over housing affordability arose as housing turned into financial assets and income from land use right transfer an essential source of local government revenues, both leading to rising house prices. The government has developed a multilayered housing system that provides subsidised rental housing and home ownership to the urban unemployed and to lower and lower middle-income groups. However, the implementations of such programs may encounter serious difficulties when local governments have little incentives and limited financial capability. Further reforms in regulatory framework and financial governance are needed.

In Chapter 14, the author examines the rapid expansion of China's trade over the last 40 years, with a particular focus on the importance of the global value chains (GVCs). The author accepts that many factors identified by other scholars have been significant, such as abundant labour endowment, domestic institutional reforms and trade liberalisation, favourable exchange policies, and the large amount of inward foreign direct investment. Nonetheless, the author argues that GVCs have functioned as a vehicle for Chinese exports entering international markets, particularly those of high-income countries. By successfully plugging into GVCs, Chinese firms have been able to bundle their low-skilled labour services with globally recognised brands and advanced technologies of multinational enterprise, and sell their products to consumers of international markets. Continuous technology innovations, aggressive promotions of a brand and the worldwide development of distribution networks by lead firms of GVCs help expand old demand and create new demand, which in turn lift the demand for tasks performed by Chinese firms integrated with supply chains and eventually enhance China's exports.

While China is one of the oldest civilisations in the world, issues and problems identified and discussed in the volume are new. In economics of development, China's experience is unique due to its unique political economy system. There are no ready answers to so many changes that the country faces today. What made Professor Wong a distinguished professional economist on China was his creative thinking on China's economy. If there is no answer that one can find in conventional textbooks, then one has to search for a new one by learning from practice. This is the spirit that we should inherit from Professor Wong. This is also the meaning of this volume in memory of Professor Wong.

Part 1

Structural Changes
and Macroeconomic Management

Chapter 1

Structural Changes in Chinese Economy: Progress and Challenges

WU Yanrui*

C hina has enjoyed high growth for about four decades. However, the changing domestic and global conditions have led to the urgency for major structural transformation. This is well recognised by Chinese policymakers who adopted the term "new normal" economic growth. The new normal growth implies slow sustainable growth which is steering profound structural changes in the Chinese economy. How far have structural changes gone? What will be the challenges faced by policymakers in the future? These are some of the questions to be explored in this chapter.

The rest of the chapter provides a brief introduction to current economic conditions in China. This is followed by an examination of the changing role of consumption and investment in the economy, the evolution of inequality in China and the comparative development of the state and non-state sectors. This chapter then discusses the balance between short-term goals and long-term growth. Finally, the challenges ahead are investigated.

---

*WU Yanrui is a Professor and Head of Department of Economics, Business School, University of Western Australia. Work on this chapter benefitted from the financial support of EAI and comments from Dr Sarah Tong and participants of "China's Economy: Modernisation and Structural Changes", a conference in honour of Professor John Wong, 25 May 2018.

China's "New Normal" Growth

China's economic growth has slowed down from its recent peak rate of 14.2% in 2007 to 6.9% in 2017 (see Figure 1). This slow growth trend is officially called the "new normal" growth and is projected to remain the same in the coming decade.[1] On the one hand, global economic recovery is slow and China's population dividends are disappearing. These factors imply modest economic growth in China in the future. On the other hand, the reduced rate of growth is still significant relative to the average growth rate of OECD economies and in terms of the size of the Chinese economy. Even if China's growth rate in 2017 was much lower than the average rate in the last four decades, Chinese economy's contribution to the world's newly added gross domestic product (GDP)

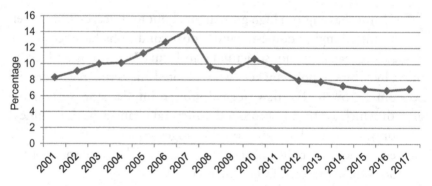

Figure 1:   China's Economic Growth Rates, 2001–2017

Source: Author's own work by using data from *China Statistical Yearbook 2017* and Statistical Communique 2018, China National Statistics Bureau, Beijing.

---

[1] The term "new normal" was formally used for the first time by Mohamed A El-Erian, Head of Pacific Investment Management Company, in a speech titled "*Navigating the New Normal in Industrial Countries*", International Monetary Fund and Per Jacobsson Foundation, 2010; *China Economic Update: Investing in High-quality Growth*, Washington, DC, World Bank Group, 2018, at <http://documents.worldbank.org/curated/en/510581527687140906/China-economic-update-investing-in-high-quality-growth> (accessed June 2018); and *Asian Development Outlook: How Technology Affects Jobs*, Manila, Asian Development Bank, 2018, at <http://dx.doi.org/10.22617/FLS189310-3> (accessed June 2018).

was 31.7%, which is much greater than the United States' contribution of 13.2% in the same year.[2]

While the Chinese economy is already the largest globally in purchasing power parity terms, China's GDP in US dollar terms is only 60.1% of the United States' GDP in 2016. With an annual rate of growth of 6.5%, China's total GDP is expected to overtake the United States' GDP by around 2034. By then, China's GDP per capita will still be 23.6% of the United States'.[3] Thus, the process of catch up with the advanced world will last a long time. For this reason, sustainable growth is important for China in the coming decades. An important factor underlying this growth is the structural transformation of the economy.

Evidence of Consumption-driven Growth

The concept of structural change was originally associated with the Lewis model which focuses on the trend of economic activities moving from agriculture with low productivity to industry and then services with high productivity.[4] This process is called structural change or transformation. In the case of the Chinese economy in the 21st century, structural changes are more complicated and can be investigated in different perspectives. Some economists defined China's structural changes as "triple imbalances", namely growth shift towards domestic demand, structural change to reduce income disparities, and balance between short-term growth and long term sustainability. Other authors emphasised the importance of the growth of the private sector. Hence,

---

[2] Unless stated otherwise, these percentage shares and other statistics in this chapter are calculated by using statistics from the World Development Indictors, The World Bank, at <https://data.worldbank.org/products/wdi> (accessed June 2018).

[3] These predictions are made by using statistics from the World Development Indictors, The World Bank, at <https://data.worldbank.org/products/wdi> (accessed June 2018), and assuming that the American economy will grow at an average rate of 3.5% per annum and Chinese economy at a rate of 6.5% per annum.

[4] W Arthur Lewis, "Economic Development with Unlimited Supplies of Labour", *The Manchester School*, vol. 22, no. 2, 1954, pp. 139–191.

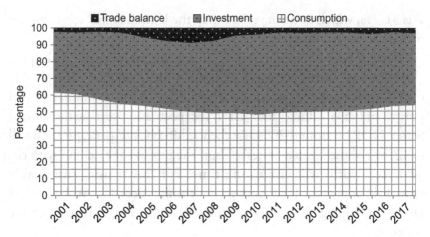

Figure 2: Composition of China's GDP, 2001–2017

Source: Author's own work by using data from *China Statistical Yearbook 2017* and Statistical Communique 2018, China National Statistics Bureau, Beijing.

the Chinese economy needs restructuring to accommodate the development of the private sector. Thus, economic structural changes refer to restructuring of the economy in several dimensions.[5]

Consumption, investment (or capital formation) and trade balance are important components of GDP. The shares of these components over GDP demonstrate the pattern of growth in an economy. For decades, China's economic growth has been investment-driven. In the 21st century, the role of consumption increased, and consumption maintained its dominant share over GDP among the three components (see Figure 2).

Though consumption share declined slightly at the beginning years of the new century, it has recovered gradually since the onset of the global financial crisis. During this period, investment share was

---

[5] Barry Naughton, "Restructuring and Reform: China 2016", in *Structural Change in China: Implications for Australia and the World*, conference papers and discussions, Reserve Bank of Australia, 2016, at <https://www.rba.gov.au/publications/confs/2016/> (accessed June 2018). Nicholas Lardy, *Markets over Mao: The Rise of Private Business in China*, Washington, DC, Peterson Institute for International Economics, 2014.

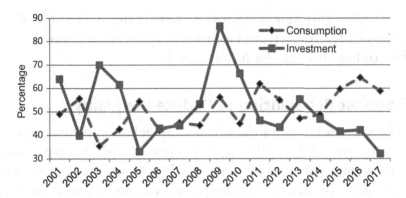

Figure 3: Consumption and Investment Changes over Newly Added GDP
Source: Author's own work by using data from *China Statistical Yearbook 2017* and Statistical Communique 2018, China National Statistics Bureau, Beijing.

relatively stable. Thus, in terms of growth drivers shifting towards consumption, China's structural change was very modest in the past decade, or even negligible according to some authors.

However, if one looks at the shares of investment and consumption changes over newly added GDP, the shift from investment to consumption is clearly evident in Figure 3, particularly in the last three years. As for the role of trade, Figure 2 shows clearly a one-off shock to GDP during the years when China's WTO accession was fully implemented. After that, China's trade balance or net trade as a share of GDP remains unchanged and is compatible with those in other major economies. For example, according to the latest data available, trade balance over GDP in 2016 was 1.05% in Japan, 2.23% in China and 7.97% in Germany.[6]

Associated with the declining role of investment is the rise of services in the Chinese economy. In 2012, China's service sector overtook the manufacturing sector to become the largest contributor towards GDP growth. It has maintained a steady growth trend since then. In 2017, according to the Statistical Communique 2018 published by the China

---

[6] These shares are calculated using statistics from World Development Indicators, The World Bank, at <https://data.worldbank.org/products/wdi> (accessed June 2018).

National Statistics Bureau, Beijing, services accounted for 51.6% of the country's GDP, which is not high relative to developed economies and thus has huge potential for further growth.

Economic Rebalancing to Reduce Inequality

China's development in the past decades followed the doctrine of "let some get rich first" (让一部分人先富起来), which was proposed by the former leader Deng Xiaoping in the 1980s. The consequence of this policy is the deteriorating inequality as economic growth took off in the country. Therefore, the main task of economic restructuring is to reduce inequality. There is some evidence of falling inequality in recent years. A report by the Organisation for Economic Cooperation and Development (OECD) shows that China's Gini coefficient, a popular measure of inequality, peaked with a value of 0.491 in 2008 and has since followed a declining trend. It reached 0.465 in 2016.[7]

Further analysis illustrates that the decline in inequality is mainly due to rising income shares of the vast majority of Chinese households with middle income (or the middle class) (see Table 1). This trend is observed among both urban and rural households. In addition, China's urban–rural gap peaked a decade ago and has since maintained a modest declining trend. However, the poorest rural households tend to lose their income share or remain at the same level (see Table 1). The 19th Congress of the Communist Party of China (held on 18 October 2017) formally endorsed the policy of "targeted poverty alleviation" (精准扶贫). Hopefully, this policy may help narrow the gap between the poorest households and other families in the country.

There is also regional disparity. In general, households in the coastal provinces have the highest per capita income, followed by those in turn in the northeast, central and western regions. In recent years, the

---

[7] "2017 OECD Economic Survey of China: More Resilient and Inclusive Growth", OECD, 21 March 2017, at <www.oecd.org/eco/surveys/economic-survey-china.htm> (accessed June 2018). Litao Zhao, "High Inequality Levelling Off in China", EAI Background Brief No. 1346, East Asian Institute, National University of Singapore, 2018.

Table 1:   Income Shares by Category, 2013–2017

	Bottom	L-middle	Middle	U-middle	Top
Year	20%	20%	20%	20%	20%
Urban households					
2013	6.97	12.41	17.01	22.96	40.66
2017	**7.06**	**12.63**	**17.38**	**23.24**	39.68
Rural households					
2013	5.71	11.83	16.74	23.43	42.29
2017	4.59	11.62	16.67	**23.57**	**43.55**

Note: Values in bold indicate that income shares of the middle-income group rose.

Source: Author's own calculation by using data from *China Statistics Yearbook 2017*, China National Statistics Bureau, Beijing.

income gap between the coastal provinces and northeast regions is widening, while the central and western regions have narrowed their income gap with the coastal provinces. These changes in regional disparity may reflect the success of the "western development program" launched in 1999 and the "central rising" policy implemented in 2005. In addition, the central and western regions may also benefit from industrial upgrading in the coastal areas which led to the relocation of some economic activities. However, the "northeast revitalisation" program has been less effective so far, and thus the northeast provinces are lagging behind in terms of economic growth.

Private Economy vs State Sectors

A major task of economic restructuring is to balance the development of the state sector vs the private sector. Due to four decades economic reform, state ownership has retreated, shrinking the state sector. Figure 4 demonstrates that in the past decade the state sector employment number was stable but its share over total urban employment shows a declining trend. Thus, the state sector is still substantial but is shrinking relative to the non-state sector.

Figure 4 also shows that the declining trend of the state sector was temporarily interrupted following the implementation of the

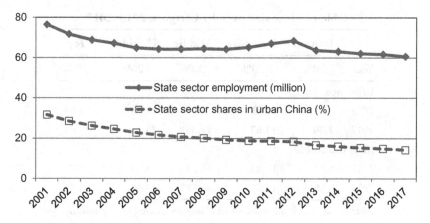

Figure 4: The State Sector Employment in China

Source: Author's own calculation by using data from *China Statistics Yearbook 2017*, China National Statistics Bureau, Beijing.

four trillion renminbi economic stimulus program in 2008. This phenomenon triggered the debate about the so-called "state sector advances and private sector retreats" (国进民退) at that time. Empirical evidence does not however support this argument. In terms of the number of firms, state-owned enterprises (SOEs) only account for about 5% but their overall share in assets is close to 40% (see Figure 5). These shares are pretty stable in recent years. However, their revenue share is steadily declining.

It can be concluded that SOEs in China still control substantial resources, but their efficiency keeps falling. Some authors reckon that the private sector may be underestimated according to official statistics.[8]

Short-term vs Long-term Development

While China's high economic growth for four decades is unprecedented, this growth has a serious environmental consequence. An important

---

[8] Nicholas Lardy, *Markets over Mao: The Rise of Private Business in China*.

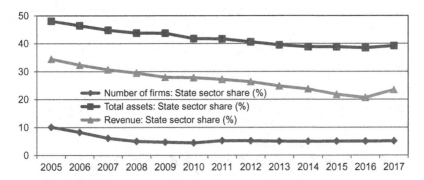

Figure 5: State Sector in China

Source: Author's own calculation by using data from *China Statistics Yearbook 2017*, China National Statistics Bureau, Beijing.

goal of structural change is to balance the short-term growth with long-term development so that growth becomes sustainable. A key indicator of monitoring environmental quality is energy intensity, which is defined as energy consumption per unit of GDP in an economy or a sector. In the past two decades, China's energy intensity maintained a declining trend (see Figure 6). This may reflect improvement in energy use efficiency, changes in fuel mixes and technological progress.

Furthermore, empirical evidence shows that energy-intensive sectors tend to grow slowly (see Figure 7). For example, the steel making and processing sector is the largest consumer of energy and recorded negative growth in 2017. The tobacco sector is an exception which is not energy-intensive and had a negative growth rate in 2017.

In addition, the latest statistics show that China's service sector accounted for 51.6% of the economy in 2017 and recorded a growth rate of 8.0%, which is much higher than the growth rates in agriculture (3.9%) and manufacturing (6.1%) according to the Statistical Communique 2018 published by China National Statistics Bureau, Beijing. The expansion of services is a huge relief for the environment. Finally, the Chinese government signed the Paris Agreement, and the country's carbon emission is expected to peak by 2030. However,

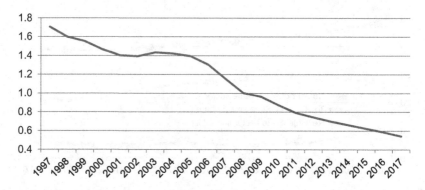

Figure 6: Energy Intensity, 1997–2017

Source: Author's own calculation by using data from *China Statistical Yearbook 2017*, China National Statistics Bureau, Beijing.

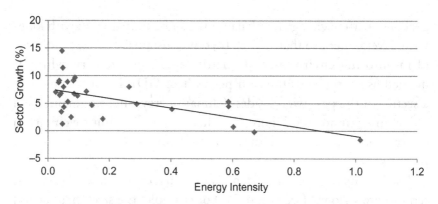

Figure 7: Sector Growth vs Energy Intensity

Source: Author's own calculation by using data from *China Statistical Yearbook 2017*, China National Statistics Bureau, Beijing.

according to some authors, China's CO_2 emission had already peaked in 2013.[9] This decline of emission may be structural and sustainable if current structural changes continue. The establishment of a new

---

[9] Dabo Guan *et al.*, "Structural Decline in China's CO_2 Emissions through Transitions in Industry and Energy Systems", *Nature Geoscience*, vol. 11, 2018, pp. 551–555, at <https://www.nature.com/articles/s41561-018-0161-1> (accessed 3 July 2018).

Ministry of Ecological Environment in March 2018 indicates the central government's commitment to address the environmental issues in the coming years.

Challenges Ahead

Regardless of the indictors used, there is evidence of structural changes in the Chinese economy. Whether the observed trends are to continue faces several challenges which may undermine the "new normal" growth of the economy in the coming decades. Though the latest statistics imply the increasing role of consumption as a growth driver nationally, there is huge disparity across the Chinese provinces (see Figure 8). With the exception of several coastal provinces and municipalities, most regions recorded a consumption share over gross regional product below 50%. Thus, investment is still the main driver for economic growth in these regions.

In 2016, among industrial firms with revenue over 20 million renminbi, SOEs accounted for 30.3% in terms of the number and 58.4% in terms of total assets (see Table 2). Thus, the state sector still plays an important role. In particular, SOEs have a market share of 99.3% in the tobacco industry, 92.0% in electricity and heat production, 81.2% in petroleum and gas production, and 58.8% in coal mining and

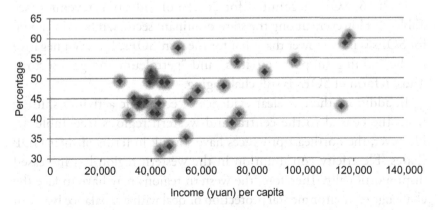

Figure 8:   Consumption over GRP, 2016

Table 2:   Distribution (%) by Ownership, 2016

Indicator	State	Private	HMTF
No. of firms	30.30	56.61	13.09
Assets	58.35	22.06	19.59
Profits	40.08	35.45	24.47
Bank loans	65.64	28.44	5.92

Note: The numbers are percentage shares by ownership and cover all industrial firms with revenues over RMB20 million. HMTF is short for "Hong Kong, Macau, Taiwan and foreign".

Source: Author's own calculation by using data from *China Statistical Yearbook 2017*, China National Statistics Bureau, Beijing.

washing according to *China Statistical Yearbook 2017* published by the China National Statistics Bureau, Beijing.

The most privatised sectors (with the market share of SOEs less than 6%) include food processing and manufacturing, paper and paper products, textile, timber and wood products, and apparel and accessories, to cite a few. It is interesting to notice that food processing and manufacturing are highly privatised. Food safety issues exposed in recent years may imply the lack of regulatory progress in these sectors.

In 2016, SOEs accounted for 20.1% of industrial revenues (see Table 3). However, among the state-dominant sectors, return to capital for SOEs is much lower than that for the non-SOEs. It is even negative in the "mining support activities" and "petroleum and gas" sectors. Thus, reform of SOEs is still challenging.

In addition, there is clear evidence of economic activities shifting from the coastal to the central and western regions (see Table 4). However, the northeast provinces have shrunk in terms of their GDP shares. Electricity consumption in the western region has increased disproportionally. Therefore, the western regions may have to face the challenge of environmental protection or deal with the balance between short-term growth and long-term sustainability.

Table 3: Selected Statistics by Ownership, 2016

Sectors	Market share (%)	Profit/Asset (%)		
	SOEs	SOEs	Private	HMTF
China	20.1	3.0	10.6	8.3
Tobacco	99.3	10.1	27.3	7.4
Electricity & heating	92.0	2.9	3.2	7.3
Mining support activities	83.2	–3.5	7.0	4.6
Petroleum & natural gas	81.2	–4.0	8.8	12.0
Water production & supply	68.3	1.1	3.7	4.1
Coal mining and washing	58.8	1.0	6.8	4.8

Note: The numbers cover all industrial firms with revenues over 20 million renminbi. "China" refers to national means. The six sectors have the highest SOE shares in turn.

Source: Author's own calculation by using data from *China Statistical Yearbook 2017*, China National Statistics Bureau, Beijing.

Table 4: Regional Shares (%)

Year	Coastal	Central	Western	Northeast
GDP				
2005	55.0	18.8	17.6	8.6
2010	52.6	19.7	19.1	8.6
2016	52.1	20.6	20.6	**6.7**
Investment				
2005	60.9	16.7	12.8	9.6
2010	46.0	26.1	15.4	12.4
2016	46.9	30.8	16.6	**5.7**
Electricity consumption				
2005	50.7	19.1	21.9	8.3
2010	49.5	19.3	24.0	7.2
2016	48.3	18.4	**27.2**	6.0

Note: The numbers cover all industrial firms with revenues over 20 million renminbi. Values in bold indicate declining shares of the Northeastern region and the increasing importance of the Western region.

Source: Author's own calculation by using data from *China Statistical Yearbook 2017*, China National Statistics Bureau, Beijing.

To sum up, changing domestic and global conditions have led to the urgency for major structural changes in the Chinese economy. This is well recognised by policymakers who adopted the term "new normal" economic growth. It is shown that modest structural shift from investment-driven to consumption-led growth is evident, with consumption growth being the main source of newly added GDP in recent years. China's service sector has replaced manufacturing to become the largest contributor to GDP though service sector GDP share is still small relative to those in the developed economies. As urbanisation accelerates, the role of the service sector is expected to expand. Furthermore, China's Gini coefficient, a popular indicator of inequality, peaked in 2008 and has since declined, which implies falling inequality. This fall in inequality is largely due to rising income of middle-income families. The rural–urban income gap has also narrowed over time. In addition, SOEs still play an important role in the economy, albeit with shrinking market share. SOEs continue to control the bulk of resources despite being less efficient than non-SOEs. However, huge regional disparity in terms of restructuring towards consumption-led growth prevails. With the exception of several coastal regions, most Chinese provinces still rely on investment as the main growth driver. Empirical evidence also demonstrates that economic activities have shifted from coastal to central and western regions, and this shift has resulted in the disproportionate increase in energy consumption in the western provinces. This may have implications for environmental protection in these relatively less-developed regions in the future.

Chapter 2

The Economic Role of the Chinese Government: Between the Centralised Political System and Decentralised Markets

CHEN Kang*

Introduction

Professor John Wong and I co-authored an article in 1995, taking stock of the changes of the economic role of the Chinese government during the reform period from the late 1970s to the early 1990s, as well as the dilemmas and problems caused by such changes.[1] Since then, nearly a quarter of a century has passed. It is meaningful for me, both professionally and personally, to revisit the issue in this commemorative volume in honour of Professor Wong.

China's economic landscape has changed profoundly since the early 1990s, but the government's involvements in the economy are still as deep and wide ranging as before. The government is responsible for delivering economic growth in the short run and implementing

*CHEN Kang is a Professor at the Lee Kuan Yew School of Public Policy, National University of Singapore.
[1] John Wong and Chen Kang, "The Evolving Role of Government in China's Transition Economy", *Asia Pacific Business Review*, vol. 1, no. 3, 1995, pp. 113–131.

industrial policies in the long run. Those objectives are achieved with the support of state-owned enterprises (SOEs) as well as state-owned banks (SOBs) and other financial institutions that are tightly controlled by the government. Furthermore, while a reasonably well-functioning goods and services market has been developed, progress has been much slower in developing factor markets where administrative interventions are much more direct and frequent. The market for labour is more advanced than the market for land, while the capital market is the least developed.

This chapter has two objectives. First, it compares the economic role of the government now to that in the early 1990s and discusses the key reasons behind those changes. Second, and more importantly, it looks into the internal logic that underpins the economic role of the Chinese government within a centralised authoritarian system that is trying to adapt to an alien decentralised market system. The efficacy of the centralised political system has been assured by a fiscal system that is characterised by the soft-budget constraint of local governments. Such a fiscal system, in turn, has been sustained by a financial system that is tightly controlled by the government. China is a unitary country with a vast territory and a huge population, and its administrative apparatus is characterised by a long chain of command within the bureaucratic hierarchy. It is therefore important to understand and appreciate that financial liberalisation is inconsistent with China's centralised political system because it will not only impose fiscal discipline on the government and weaken state capacity of the centralised authoritarian regime but also increase political risks originating from financial market volatilities. This internal logic or contradiction helps explain why financial liberalisation has constantly been delayed and postponed, even when the government states repeatedly that it wants to let the market play a decisive role in allocating resources. Meanwhile, the distortions caused by administrative intervention in capital allocation continue to propagate from the state-controlled "commanding height" to the whole economy, resulting in allocative inefficiencies and rigidities in the economy.

Comparison of the Roles of the Government

Wong and Chen summarised five key changes in the economic role of the Chinese government in the early 1990s in comparison to the pre-reform era in the late 1970s[2]: (1) price control had been significantly reduced — the prices of 90% of consumer goods and over 80% of intermediate goods were market determined by the end of 1993; (2) enterprise autonomy, which was then regarded as an important dimension of SOE reforms, had been expanded. State firms were allowed to change output quantity and variety, production technology, bonuses to workers, and to some degree output prices; (3) central planning had become largely irrelevant in the economy as production plans and material allocation plans only affected 20% of production and material distribution. Moreover, planned macroeconomic targets were not seriously implemented; (4) the government's role as a producer had been dramatically curtailed. The share of the SOEs in total industrial output fell from 78% in 1978 to 48% in 1992. The non-state sector, including township and village enterprises (TVEs), had expanded its share rapidly; (5) the government's role as a financier of investment had been greatly decreased. The percentage of SOE investment funded by the state budget had been reduced from 40% in 1978 to 13% in 1989.

Price reform in the goods and services market has continued to move in the same direction since the early 1990s. The prices of over 90% of goods and services were determined by market forces by 2015, with remaining price controls mainly found in public utilities, public transportation, telecom, financial services, education, health care and upstream heavy industrial sectors, such as steel, petroleum, natural gas and power.[3] In the labour market, wages are more or less set by market forces. In the capital market, however, interest rates are still subject to

---

[2] John Wong and Chen Kang, "The Evolving Role of Government in China's Transition Economy", pp. 113–131.

[3] Liu Shujie, "Price Reform: Where Is the Balance Point between Market and Regulation?" *Phoenix Weekly*, no. 567, 15 January 2015, at <http://www.ifengweekly.com/detil.php?id=2503>

heavy government intervention although lending rate floors and deposit rate ceilings were removed in recent years.

SOE reforms accelerated in the mid-1990s when the government introduced a program to "grasp the large, and let go of the small" which addressed the issue of ownership being more fundamental than enterprise autonomy. Under this program, large upstream SOEs are retained while smaller ones are allowed to be privatised, merged or closed down.[4] As a result, the overall value-added share of SOEs in industry fell from 55% in 1998 to 34% in 2007.[5] The reform program has improved the profit position of SOEs, which inspired the government to become bolder in setting the goals and strategies for the state sector. According to the development strategies announced by State-owned Assets Supervision and Administration Commission (SASAC) in 2006, SOEs would not only dominate the strategic sectors that are considered as vital to national security and economy but also assert strong influence and play a leading role in sectors where the state was previously expected to not intervene.[6] Furthermore, the government repeatedly states in recent years that SOEs are "the material and political foundations of Socialism with Chinese Characteristics",[7] and should be made bigger, better and stronger.[8] A series of developments has shaken the confidence of private entrepreneurs, and the phrase *guojin mintui* (the state sector is advancing while the private sector is in retreat) is increasingly used to describe the recent trend.[9] Meanwhile, SOEs

---

[4] Lowell Dittmer, "Xi Jinping's 'New Normal': quo vadis?" *Journal of Chinese Political Science*, vol. 22, 2017, pp. 429–446.

[5] Hsieh Chang-Tai and Song Zheng, "Grasp the Large, Let Go of the Small: The Transformation of the State Sector in China", *NBER Working Paper No. 21006*, 2015.

[6] See <http://www.gov.cn/ztzl/2006-12/18/content_472256.htm> (accessed 18 December 2018).

[7] See a document issued by the Chinese Communist Party (CCP) Central Committee in 2015, at <http://www.gov.cn/zhengce/2015-09/13/content_2930440.htm>

[8] President Xi Jinping made several such speeches. See for example <http://www.xinhuanet.com/politics/2016-07/04/c_1119162333.htm>

[9] Chen Kang, "Back to the Future? The Changing Role of Government in China's Economic Development", *Lee Kuan Yew School of Public Policy Research Paper No. 18–18*, 2018, at <https://ssrn.com/abstract=3263093>

continue to be less efficiently managed than non-SOEs, with a larger and increasing share of loss-making firms and lower rates of return on investments.[10]

In terms of economic planning, production plans and materials allocation plans have been abandoned completely. Paradoxically, unlike in the early 1990s when planned macroeconomic targets were not seriously carried out at the local levels, annual target rates of gross domestic product (GDP), together with other targets such as growth rates of fiscal revenue and fixed asset investment, have become key performance indicators (KPIs) that are earnestly implemented by local governments. This was certainly surprising because economic reforms were set out to abolish mandatory planned targets. Chen points out that this was the result of an important change of developmental models in 1998.[11] There are at least two China models with contrasting features and distinctive roles played by the government. In China Model I, which dominated in the period from the late 1970s to the mid-1990s, the governments mainly played an enabling role in facilitating the growth of non-state sectors and in following the demand-driven growth path to expand local tax bases under the revenue-sharing system. After 1998, China Model II began to emerge, gravitating towards the current state-led investment-driven development model which was ushered in by the central government that set "*baoba*" (guarantee 8% economic growth) as the performance target for local governments since the 1998–2002 deflationary period.

"*Baoba*" also turns China's local governments into big investors themselves because investing in large local government projects is a major avenue to achieving the GDP target. Since local governments are not allowed to run budget deficits, they fund these investment projects with proceeds generated from land sales or debts of local government financing vehicles (LGFVs) through bank loans, trust loans and wealth

---

[10] Sarah Y. TONG, "China's New Push to Reform the State Sector: Progress And Drawbacks", *China: An International Journal*, vol. 16, no. 3, 2018, pp. 35–51.
[11] Chen Kang, "Two China Models and Local Government Entrepreneurship", *China: An International Journal*, vol.14, no. 3, 2016, pp. 16–28.

management products.[12] The easy access to financial resources results in poor fiscal discipline. When local governments were under pressure to deliver economic growth, they did not hesitate to start more large-scale infrastructure projects, even in regions where infrastructure was already overinvested.[13] On the other hand, the government is still playing a dominant role as a financier because China's financial institutions (such as banks, insurance companies, trust companies, security traders, funds and fidelities) remain state-owned or under state control.[14]

It is interesting to compare the current economic role of the Chinese government with that of the early 1990s. While price decontrol continues, the overall direction of SOE reforms become uncertain. Planned targets have mostly been abandoned, but the GDP growth rate has survived to become the most seriously implemented economic target. Although the share of investments funded by the state budget continues to decrease, government investment projects are now funded by credits from SOBs and state-controlled financial institutions. The government's role as an investment financier has not decreased, albeit taking different forms. Moreover, the government itself has become a major investor.

Wong and Chen also study decentralisation because it changed the relative roles of the central and local governments.[15] Decentralisation was a key element underpinning China's bottom-up reform from the

---

[12] Chen Kang and Shin JangSup, "The Pattern of Financing Industrialization in China: Understanding Sources of Fixed Investment", *Global Economic Review*, vol. 40, no. 2, 2011, pp. 145–160.

[13] Shi Hao and Huang Shaoqing. "How Much Infrastructure Is Too Much? A New Approach And Evidence from China", *World Development*, vol. 56, 2014, pp. 272–286. Bai Chong-En, Hsieh Chang-Tai Hsieh and Song Zheng, "The Long Shadow of China's Fiscal Expansion", *NBER Working Paper No. 22801*, 2016.

[14] Liu Shaofang and Sun Haibo. *Who Controls China's Financial System? Jinrong Jianguan Yanjiuyuan* (Institute of Financial Supervision), 7 August 2018, at <http://www.gzh-shoulu.wang/article/3717871>

[15] John Wong and Chen Kang, "The Evolving Role of Government in China's Transition Economy", pp. 113–131.

late 1970s to the early 1990s. When there were few supporters of market-oriented reforms in Beijing, the reformist leader Deng Xiaoping resorted to mobilising local officials by devising an incentive-compatible mechanism based on administrative, fiscal and financial decentralisation.[16] Decentralisation enabled local government officials to benefit from market liberalisation in their domain and enticed them to support bottom-up reforms.

However, decentralisation also caused serious problems. While fiscal decentralisation gave "residual claimant" status to local governments that motivated them to support market reforms, it also resulted in a severe loss of fiscal revenue to the central government. Because local governments were in charge of tax collection and administration before the State Administration of Taxation (SAT) was set up in 1994, they could hide revenues in firms within their localities without sharing them with the centre, and funds stored in the firms could be transferred later to local governments by *ad hoc* levies.[17] As a result, the share of central revenue in total fiscal revenue continued to decline during this period.

Under financial decentralisation, local governments effectively control local banks, through their control of the careers of bank managers. Financial decentralisation helped develop the non-state sector when local governments could exert influence on bank lending to TVEs by acting as mediators, collateral providers and guarantors to partially underwrite risks.[18] Financial decentralisation also led to inefficient allocation of resources when bank credits were used to fund local extra-budgetary investment projects which contributed to local fiscal revenue. As a result, small-scale but highly inefficient producers of cigarettes,

---

[16] Chen Kang, "Back to the Future?"

[17] Christine P. W. Wong, "Central-local Relations in An Era of Fiscal Decline: The Paradox of Fiscal Decentralisation in Post-Mao China", *The China Quarterly*, vol. 128, 1991, pp. 691–715.

[18] William A. Byrd and Lin Qingsong, "China's Rural Industry: An Introduction", in *China's Rural Industry: Structure, Development, and Reform*, ed. W. A. Byrd and Lin, Q., Oxford, Oxford University Press, 1990.

alcoholic beverages, textile products and household electrical appliances proliferated all over the country.[19]

Decentralisation also led to regional protectionism and fragmentation of the domestic product market when local officials erected trade barriers between different localities. In regions well-endowed with raw materials, the local authorities had strong incentives to establish their own processing industries because they could collect more tax revenue. They used administrative means to stop locally produced raw materials from being sold and shipped to other regions, and ordered local stores to sell only locally produced processing goods.[20]

Wong and Chen conclude that in the early 1990s, the role of government at the local level had vastly expanded, while the role of government at the national level had diminished. If the reduced role of the central government could be regarded as a positive factor for China's reform process, the enhanced role of local governments had brought about serious dilemmas and problems.[21] They noted that there had been new initiatives to increase the state capacity of the central government, but were not sure if those measures could effectively stem the decline of the centre because cooperation by local governments was essential to carry out those changes.

Subsequent events proved that China's central government was effective in implementing those recentralisation measures. The system of tax sharing was first implemented in 1994 when the resistance from local governments was considerably weakened, which was then followed by two subsequent steps of further fiscal recentralisation in 2002 and 2016, respectively. These changes made the existence of local tax bureaus much less important in tax collection, and they were eventually subsumed under SAT by mid-2018 as their work scope shrank considerably.[22]

---

[19] Chen Kang, *The Chinese Economy in Transition: Micro Changes and Macro Implications*, Singapore, Singapore University Press, 1995.

[20] Chen Kang, *The Chinese Economy in Transition*.

[21] John Wong and Chen Kang, "The Evolving Role of Government in China's Transition Economy", pp. 113–131.

[22] Chen Kang, "Back to the Future?"

Moreover, financial recentralisation was introduced in the mid-1990s when policy banks were created, specialised banks were turned into state-owned commercial banks, and branches of China's central bank were reorganised into regional branches similar to the Federal Reserve System in the United States, so as to reduce the influence from provincial governments.[23] Following fiscal and financial recentralisation in the mid-1990s, a sequence of administrative recentralisation also began in 1998 when *"chuizhi guanli"* (vertical management) was introduced, and budget and personnel management of specific government agencies were shifted to the provincial or central government in an effort to ensure local conformation and compliance.[24]

In comparison, the relative roles of the central and local governments have experienced significant changes since the early 1990s, and China's central government is playing a dominant role in the economy after recentralisation efforts, reversing the decentralisation trend in the previous period.

Adapting to the Market while Maintaining State Capacity

The above discussion provides a historical account of how a centralised authoritarian system adapts to an alien decentralised market system. To CCP leaders, it is clear that market reforms are means to rejuvenate and consolidate the current regime and thus should not be introduced if they could seriously undermine the state control or fundamentally change the way the central authority runs the country. The economic role of the government is at the centre of these adaptations, adjustments and trade-off.

Some market reforms, such as decollectivisation of agriculture and building the goods and services market and the labour market, are considered beneficial, and the government was willing to accommodate

---

[23] Chen Kang and Shin JangSup, "The Pattern of Financing Industrialization in China", pp. 145–160.
[24] Chen Kang, "Back to the Future?"

these market developments. People's communes and production brigades were abolished and farmlands were leased to rural households under long-term contracts, prices of goods and services were decontrolled to facilitate market competition, and commercialisation of housing was introduced to enhance labour mobility. Those adjustments had profound implications on state–society relations because the state's institutional levers of coercion, including communes and brigades in rural areas and *danwei* (work units) in urban areas, have collapsed.[25] In an attempt to fill the void, village committees and township governments were established in the early 1980s, and CCP village branches were stipulated by the Organic Law of Village Committee in 1998 as the village's "leadership core" to ensure strong state control.[26] In recent years, "grid management" was introduced in cities — communities, street blocks or buildings are divided up into grid points, and grid administrators are held accountable for maintaining stability within the grid point.[27] Similarly, adjustments had to be made when the goods and services market was being developed. Government line ministries were abolished and loss-making SOEs were closed down in the late 1990s. However, as discussed in the previous section, several sectors have been identified as either "the lifelines of the nation's economy" or vital to national security and are kept under strong state control.[28]

Other reforms turned out to be only temporary and were reverted after they had served their intended purposes. GDP growth targets, once abolished with other planned targets, found their way back to the administrative system to become the most important KPI.

---

[25] Chen Kang, "Administrative Decentralisation and Changing State-Society Relations in China", *International Journal of Public Administration*, vol. 21, no. 9, 1998, pp. 1223–1255.

[26] Kevin J. O'Brien and Li Lianjiang. "Accommodating 'Democracy' in A One-party State: Introducing Village Elections in China", *The China Quarterly*, vol. 162, 2000, pp. 465–489.

[27] Lucy Hornby, "China Reverts to 'Grid Management' to Monitor Citizens' Lives", *Financial Times*, 5 April 2016, at <http://www.ftchinese.com/story/001066953/en?ccode =LanguageSwitch&archive>

[28] Chen Kang, "Back to the Future?"

Decentralisation was also short-lived because of the dilemmas and problems it created. Once the CCP leaders agreed to push for top-down market-oriented reform in 1992, the central government quickly recentralised to strengthen state capacity.[29]

There exist different assessments of China's state capacity. According to the *State Capability Index* compiled by Andrews and others,[30] China's state capacity in 2012 was in the middle range (neither weak nor strong) among 102 countries, but declined during the 1996–2012 period. Fukuyama thinks that the existing measures, such as Worldwide Governance Indicators that was used by Andrews *et al.* in their compilation of the index, underestimated China's state capacity, but opined that Chinese government officials have too much discretionary power and should be subject to clear rules.[31] Anecdotal evidence also points to opposite directions with regard to China's state capacity. On one hand, directives from the central leadership, such as "*baxiang guiding*" (the eight-point code of conduct), seem to be effectively followed all over the country, and the government is capable of building, at fast speed, nationwide modern infrastructure, such as highways, high-speed railways, sea ports, airports, etc. On the other hand, the phrase "*zhengling buchu zhongnanhai*" (political decrees stop at the Zhongnanhai compound) has also been frequently used to describe the situation when the central government cannot ensure compliance with its orders by lower level governments.

Given China's vast population and geographic territory, maintaining a unitary political system is no doubt a formidable task because the central authority needs to enforce rules and deliver services through a long chain of command within the bureaucratic hierarchy.

---

[29] Wang Shaoguang and Hu Angang, "Strengthening the Leading Role of the Central Government in China's Transition towards A Market Economy", report presented to the National Development Strategy Studies Group of the Chinese Academy of Sciences, Beijing, 1993.

[30] Matt Andrews, Lant Pritchett and Michael Woolcock, *Building State Capacity: Evidence, Analysis, Action*, Oxford, Oxford University Press, 2017.

[31] Francis Fukuyama, "What Is Governance? Commentary", *Governance: An International Journal of Policy*, vol. 26, no. 3, 2013, pp. 347–368.

Centralisation, which has more than 2000 years of history in China's administrative system since Qin and Han dynasties, requires local governments to carry out central directives in a timely manner, which can only be achieved when they face minimal resource constraints, fiscal or otherwise. When leaders in Beijing issue an order to local governments, they want their authority to be respected and their order to be carried out, regardless of its implications to local budgets. The Chinese leaders also firmly believe that the centralised political system has its advantages over democracies — decisions are made within a short period of time without going through lengthy debates, and priority projects are always fully funded financially and implemented on time. Policymaking and budgeting are therefore two separate and disjointed processes in China whereby leaders at higher level governments often initiate new policies, resulting in new expenditure responsibilities for lower-level governments.[32] Moreover, there is lack of a clear and detailed division of expenditure responsibilities among different levels of government under the Budget Law, and higher level governments can arbitrarily shift fiscal responsibilities to lower level governments. Clearly, the central leadership does not want to implement any type of fiscal federalism which imposes fiscal discipline on itself and reduces the efficacy of the centralised system.

Centralisation, while helping to guarantee policy coordination and consistency, has a tendency to put more and more of social life under the control of the central government, stifling local initiatives and creating rigidities in the system, thus generating more institutional costs for businesses and impeding economic development.[33] As a result, the central leaders often find themselves in dire need to use decentralisation to overcome bureaucratic gridlock and to seek innovative solutions to

---

[32] Shen Wei, "The Logic (or Illogic) of China's Local Government Debts out of Control: Law, Governance or Other Perspectives", *Hong Kong Law Journal*, vol. 44, no. 3, 2014, pp. 887–916.

[33] Chen Kang, "Who Hates Government Debt in China? Evidence from Revealed Preferences", *Lee Kuan Yew School of Public Policy Research Paper No. 18–12*, 2018, at <https://ssrn.com/ abstract=3220282>

systemic problems from local governments. Given the heterogeneous nature of China's regions and localities, local leaders have the flexibility, under decentralisation, to organise resources in different ways and sometimes even take considerable risks by going beyond the policy boundaries in order to satisfy the performance criteria set by the central government. Such behaviours, however, are often perceived by the central leaders as an indication that local governments are having too much discretionary power or in danger of developing centrifugal forces. They will then recentralise power by enforcing strict control over local leaders, ensuring their absolute conformity with the centre. China's centralised system is thus alternating constantly between decentralisation and recentralisation.[34] The decentralisation–recentralisation cycle implies that it is difficult to separate clearly the expenditure responsibilities between the central and local governments.

As discussed above, China's local governments have been given the task of generating economic growth in their domains since 1998. Over the past 20 years, a couple of generations of Chinese leaders have moved up from the rank and file within the system. The central leaders know very well, since they were in the same position previously, that the growth is generated at the local level by government investment. They also know clearly that local governments have to rely on debts to finance local investment projects. As such, they cannot completely cut off funds flowing into local government projects. As the central government's behaviour is perfectly anticipated by local leaders, more debts are incurred by local governments with implicit sanction from the centre.[35] Government debt expansion and accumulation has reached an alarming level in recent years, reaching 48 trillion yuan by the end of 2015 according to one estimation.[36] In a speech delivered at the 5th National Financial Work Conference in 2017, President Xi Jinping

---

[34] Chen Kang, "Two China Models and Local Government Entrepreneurship", pp. 16–28.

[35] Chen Kang, "Who Hates Government Debt in China?"

[36] Bai Chong-En, Hsieh Chang-Tai Hsieh and Song Zheng, "The Long Shadow of China's Fiscal Expansion".

issued a stern warning to local government officials, holding them personally accountable for their whole lifetime for debts incurred during their tenure at office. However, government debt can change in its form and appearance and be disguised under services purchased by the government, fake public–private partnerships (PPPs) with SOEs and other forms of implicit government borrowing by SOEs (including LGFVs). As long as the central government uses economic growth to justify its political legitimacy, it has to rely on local governments to deliver the result, and the issue of government debt is expected to persist.

The foregoing discussion has important fiscal implications. First, in order to maintain state capacity under the centralised political system, the central government reserves the right to dictate orders to lower level governments, and those orders have to be carried out with or without budgetary resources. It means the central government can specify a list of expenditure responsibilities for local governments, but the list is never exclusive and more items can be added as and when the centre feels necessary. Second, the decentralisation–recentralisation cycles make it difficult to implement any kind of fiscal federalism whereby the fiscal responsibilities of each level of government are legally stipulated. Finally, it is difficult to impose fiscal discipline on local governments if they are required to deliver short-term economic growth within their domain, because increasing government investment is the only way to ensure target fulfilment. All these point to soft-budget constraint of local governments.

Implications for Financial Liberalisation

Qian and Roland argue that the budget constraint of local governments will be hardened under fiscal decentralisation and intense competition between regions, but soften if there are more fiscal transfers from upper level governments and easy access to credit.[37] In fact, local government

---

[37] Qian Yingyi and Gerard Roland, "The Soft Budget Constraint in China", *Japan and the World Economy*, vol. 6, 1996, pp. 207–223.

budgets cannot remain soft if they are not accommodated and sustained by the financial system.

As soon as China moved into the government-led investment-driven growth model in 1998, the centralised financial system became incompatible and China fell into a five-year period of deflation from 1998 to 2002.[38] Bank lending to local governments resumed after 2003 to accommodate "investment hunger" of local governments under the new growth model. Local government leaders borrow money, generate GDP through government investment projects, and then are promoted or reassigned to another location and so never have to worry about debt repayment. The access to credit by local governments was further boosted in 2009 after the global financial crisis when they were allowed to borrow from financial institutions to fund investment projects, which made it extremely convenient for local governments to incur debts.[39]

The implications to financial liberalisation are clear. The central government is both unwilling and unable to relax its control over financial resources, unwilling because well-developed financial markets would impose hard budget constraints on local governments and affect the efficacy of the centralised political system, unable because financial market instabilities could lead to a political crisis if not handled properly, and the leaders do not have any confidence in controlling such risks if administrative methods are no longer available.[40] The Chinese leaders remember that the collapse of the Kuomintang government was due, to a significant extent, to financial crises including hyperinflation and a series of defunct currencies. Looking from these viewpoints, financial liberalisation is regarded as undesirable.

To be sure, there have been many attempts to partially liberalise the financial system. However, the partial approach is ill-suited to financial

---

[38] Chen Kang, "Two China Models and Local Government Entrepreneurship", pp. 16–28.

[39] Bai Chong-En, Hsieh Chang-Tai Hsieh and Song Zheng, "The Long Shadow of China's Fiscal Expansion".

[40] Chen Kang, "Who Hates Government Debt in China?"

system reforms because they create regulatory rents through distortions in relative prices of financial products, which induce rent-seeking behaviours and financial instabilities as capital can flow at a high speed with low costs.[41] The instabilities invite strong regulation which results in more distortions. A wholesale reform, on the other hand, is even more unlikely because any timing will always be off. There is no impetus for reform when the financial system appears to be healthy, and there is no courage to seek reform either when the financial system is facing a crisis.

China's financial system worked well in the early years when the government controlled key financial resources and used them to boost production of consumer goods in the 1980s and early 1990s, and to increase infrastructure investment in the late 1990s and early 2000s. However, it is getting more difficult to make right investment decisions now as China's economic development advances into a new stage. The CCP leadership seems to understand that government investment is getting less efficient, and that the key to the success of supply-side structural changes is to let the market play a decisive role in allocating resources. However, financial liberalisation has constantly been delayed and postponed. Maintaining state capacity under the centralised political system and developing an efficient financial market became two conflicting goals which signify the limit to which the decentralised decision-making can be reluctantly allowed and accepted.

Concluding Remarks

This chapter reviews the evolving role of government in China's 40 years of reform process and finds that the Chinese government does not always adjust its economic role to accommodate market reforms. In the case of capital market development, the government has taken a firm stance that it is only willing to accept limited changes to the existing financial system. Financial liberalisation is inconsistent with

---

[41] He Jia, "How innovation and regulation aggravate instability in China's financial system", 3 November 2018, at <http://www.sohu.com/a/273008994_465500>

China's centralised political system because financial market volatilities can lead to uncontrollable political risks and a well-functioning capital market can impose hard budget constraints on local governments, both of which will weaken state capacity. Financial liberalisation is also unpopular among central leaders because its introduction may create unacceptable political risks.

This does not mean that developing an efficient capital market in China is absolutely impossible as the analysis in this chapter actually provides a list of key reform measures towards this aim. For example, it is important to harden the budget constraint of local governments so as to reduce the dependence on government-controlled financial system. The recent decision to subject all government budgets to performance management is certainly a step in the right direction,[42] but removing GDP growth targets from local governments' KPIs can have a far greater achievement in hardening the soft budget constraint. Also, government leaders need to respect the budgeting process and allow their policy initiatives to be carried out after the related expenditure provisions are included in the next budget cycle. However, these changes are by no means easy within China's existing political culture.

---

[42] For the recent CCP decision, see <http://www.xinhuanet.com/fortune/2018-09/25/c_1123481260.htm> (accessed 18 December 2018).

Chapter 3

China's Fiscal Reforms: Towards High-Quality Economic Growth

LIN Shuanglin*

Introduction

The Chinese economy has grown at an astonishing rate for four decades since the economic reform and opening up started in 1978. Per capita GDP has increased from 385 yuan in 1978 to 59,660 yuan or $91,670 in 2017.[1] Based on the constant retail price, the Chinese economy grew at an annual growth rate of 8.2%.[2] However, the economy has been facing serious challenges recently. Income inequality has increased to a high level, environmental pollution has aggravated, local government debt has reached an unsustainable level and the economic growth has been slowing down. This chapter provides an analysis of the problems faced by the Chinese economy and discusses how to reform the fiscal system to achieve high-quality economic growth.

Many factors have contributed to China's economic growth, including the dismantling of the People's communes and distributing

---

* LIN Shuanglin is a Professor and Director at the China Centre for Public Finance, National School of Development, Peking University and Noddle Distinguished Professor at the Department of Economics, University of Nebraska.
[1] Calculated based on the exchange rate on 31 December 2017, $1 = 6.5063 yuan.
[2] See National Bureau of Statistics of China (1984, 2016).

farmland to farmers to produce whatever agricultural products they want, allowing private enterprises to exist and grow, forcing state-owned enterprises (SOEs) to pursue profits and compete with other enterprises, attracting foreign investment and massively exporting goods to other countries.[3] The government's growth-promoting fiscal reforms and fiscal policies have also played an important role in China's economic growth.[4] Over the years, the central government has established a consumption tax-oriented tax system, spent a large pro-portion of its expenditure on economic construction, adopted expan-sionary fiscal policies and finance infrastructures by issuing government debt, and allowed local governments to raise revenue through land sales and by borrowing from banks and disbursed the revenue freely. All these fiscal measures have greatly stimulated China's economic growth.

Quality of growth is an important issue, and many factors affect the quality of economic growth. Barro mentioned the factors that affect the quality of economic growth — for example, income distribution and environmental quality, life expectancy and fertility — and aspects of political institutions — such as electoral rights, maintenance of the rule of law and the extent of official corruption as well as the crime rate measured by murder rates.[5] It is easy to add more factors as determi-nants of the quality of growth, such as health, education, leisure as well as the increase of wealth. Here are some examples. If, as economy grows, the number of children wearing glasses declines, then the

[3] Lin Shuanglin, "Export Expansion and Economic Growth: Evidence from Chinese Provinces", *Pacific Economic Review*, vol. 4, no. 1, 1999, pp. 65–77; Lin Shuanglin, "Resource Allocation and Economic Growth in China", *Economic Inquiry*, vol. 38, no. 3, 2000, pp. 515–526.

[4] Lin Shuanglin, "Fiscal Policy and China's Economic Growth", in *The Rise of the BRICS in the Global Political Economy: Changing Paradigms*, ed. Vai Io Lo and Mary Hiscock, Edward Elgar Publishing Ltd., 2013.

[5] Robert J. Barro, "Quantity and Quality of Economic Growth", in *Economic Growth: Sources, Trends, and Cycles*, ed. Norman Loayza and Raimundo Soto, Santiago, Chile, Central Bank of Chile, 2002.

quality of growth is improved; if, as economy grows, the number of children wearing glasses increases, then the quality of growth may not have deteriorated. If, as the economy grows, the average years of education increased at the same pace, then the growth is high-quality growth; otherwise, the quality of growth is not high. If, as the economy grows, people's leisure time increases, then the quality of growth is high; if, as the economy grows, people work longer hours, then the quality of growth is not high. Moreover, intergenerational distribution of wealth should be an important factor to measure the quality of growth. There are two serious concerns of intergenerational redistributions along with fast economic growth: resource deletion and government debt. If the growth is based on excessively exploring some of the scarce resources, such as oil, gas and mineral deposits, then the future generations will have less resources, and so the quality of growth should not be considered high. Also, if the high growth is based on high government borrowing and a large accumulation of government debt, then the quality of growth is not high. Currently, growth is measured by the growth of GDP. In fact, GDP growth does not imply the growth of wealth, which includes tangible and intangible assets and natural resources. If a producer pollutes the water and air or excessively uses natural resources, then it may only increase the GDP but not wealth of the nation. High-quality growth should increase the wealth of the nation.

Wang, Wang and Wang addressed the alarming environmental consequences of China's growth patterns within an overall quality growth framework and provided a comprehensive overview of China's success in economic growth and the challenges it faces.[6] Fiscal policy is one of the most powerful instruments that governments can use to redistribute income within and across generations and to correct externalities, and therefore, to improve the quality of economic growth. López, Vinod and Wang also studied the effect of fiscal policies on the

---

[6] Wang Xiaolin, Wang Limin and Wang Yan, *The Quality of Growth and Poverty Reduction in China*, Springer, 2014.

quality of growth.[7] They found empirically that government spending on public goods was strongly associated with faster economic growth, greater poverty reduction and higher environmental quality. In addition, they found that tax policies (e.g. taxation of natural resource rents and shifting some of the tax burden from indirect taxes to direct taxes) also affect the quality of economic growth.

As the Chinese economy grows, severe problems have emerged, raising doubt about the quality of economic growth. First, income inequality has increased. The Gini coefficient increased from 0.288 in 1978 to 0.465 in 2016. The ratio of rural income to urban income decreased from 54.87% in 1983 to 36.78% in 2016. Second, pollution becomes a severe problem, such as air pollution, water pollution, soil pollution and solid waste pollution. Food and drug safety has also become a serious issue, with food, particularly meat and fruits, being polluted by over-standard pesticide and chemical remains, and drugs, including vaccines, being unqualified. Third, resource depletion has also become a serious problem with excessive exploitation of natural resources, such as water, oil, gas and mineral deposits. Also, substantial waste of resources in infrastructure development is common and the quality of some infrastructures is rather low. Fourth, government debt has been increasing and has reached a substantial level, leaving future generations with a large burden of debt. To solve these problems, further fiscal reforms are urgently needed.

This chapter analyses the growth-promoting fiscal reforms and fiscal policies and rapid economic growth, discusses the challenges faced by the fiscal system, and provides suggestions for further fiscal reforms to achieve high-quality economic growth. The section "Fiscal Reforms and Fiscal Policies in the Past Four Decades" discusses the fiscal reforms and fiscal policies since the start of economic reforms. The next section shows the rapid economic growth seen over the past 40 decades. The section "Challenges Facing the Fiscal System" analyses the problems faced by the Chinese economy and China's public finance, followed by

---

[7] Ramón E. López, Vinod Thomas and Wang Yan, "The Effect of Fiscal Policies on the Quality of Growth", The World Bank, Washington, DC, 2010.

one which provides policy suggestions on fiscal reforms for high-quality economic growth. The final section concludes this chapter.

Fiscal Reforms and Fiscal Policies in the Past Four Decades

After many years of economic stagnation, economic growth became the priority of the government in 1978. This section discusses growth-oriented tax reforms, fiscal decentralisation and the expansionary fiscal policies in the last four decades.

Earlier tax reforms: Fiscal decentralisation (1979–1993)

A major feature of the fiscal system under centrally planned economic system is centralisation of all revenues and centralisation of all expenditures. That is, the central government collected fiscal revenues from SOEs and through local governments, and covered all expenditures of local governments and SOEs. The inefficient centrally planned economic system resulted in economic catastrophes in China. China started fiscal reforms and fiscal decentralisation at the end of the 1970s.

In 1979, the government allowed the SOEs to keep part of their profit in order to expand production and to issue bonuses and awards to workers. In *1983–1984*, the government launched a reform called "substituting taxes for profit (*li gai shui*)", permitting SOEs to pay income taxes, instead of submitting profits to the government. In 1986, a Contract Responsibility System (CRS) was established, under which SOEs were contracted to pay a given level of income tax and adjustment tax. In *1989*, to increase government fiscal revenue, the government launched a fiscal reform called *profit sharing (li shui fenliu)*, under which SOEs submit a portion of their profits to the government after paying corporate income taxes. All these tax reforms had failed to increase the share of total government budgetary revenue in GDP, which declined from 31% in 1978 to only 12.3% in 1993, down to only 22% in 1993.

Tax-sharing system: Fiscal recentralisation within the budget

In 1994, China established a tax-sharing system. Taxes are divided into three categories: central government taxes, local government taxes, and central and local shared taxes. The income tax rate for all enterprises was unified to 33% (joint ventures preserve their preferential tax rates); value-added tax (VAT) was extended to all manufactory industries, with 25% being given to local governments and 75% being given to the central government. Consumption tax was introduced, which is an additional tax after the VAT on some special products, such as alcoholic products, tobacco products, automobiles, etc.

After the 1994 tax reforms, consumption taxes became dominant. Figure 1 shows the composition of taxes in China. It can be seen that consumption-type taxes, including valued-added tax, consumption tax, education fees, VAT and consumption tax on imports, and urban construction and maintenance tax, accounted for more than 40% of

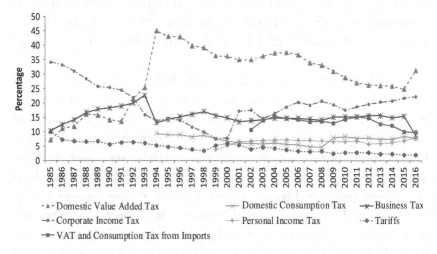

Figure 1: Share of Major Taxes in Total Tax Revenue (%)

Source: Data for 1985–2015 are from National Bureau of Statistics, at http://data.stats.gov.cn/easyquery.htm?cn=C01. Data for 2016 are from Ministry of Finance, at http://gks.mof.gov.cn/zhengfuxinxi/tongjishuju/201701/t20170123_2526014.html (accessed 19 March 2017).

the total tax revenue in 2016. Figure 1 shows the composition of government tax revenue in China. The total consumption-type tax can be obtained by adding up VAT, domestic consumption tax, VAT and consumption tax for imports, urban maintenance and construction tax, and additional fees for education.[8] It is well known that consumption tax is in favour of savings, investment and growth, but not income redistribution.[9]

In the United States, income tax dominates the tax system. In 2015, personal income tax accounted for 44.4% of total Federal government tax revenue, with social insurance contributing to 34.4% of total tax revenue, corporate income tax 13.2% and excise tax being only 2.9%.[10]

In 2001, stamp tax from stock transactions was allocated to the central government gradually from 50% to 97% in 2002 and 100% in 2016. All other stamp taxes still belong to local governments. In 2002, the share of the central government in individual income tax and corporate income tax of local SOEs increased from 0% to 50% in 2002 and 60% in 2003.

Tax reduction

In 2005, the government abolished the agricultural tax (tax on food production and animal husbandry). In 2008, the government merged the corporate tax rates for domestic firms and foreign firms at a uniform rate of 25%, with the corporate tax rate being 15% for firms in the

---

[8] The tax base of the urban maintenance and construction tax, and additional fees for education is the VAT.

[9] Laurence S. Seidman, "Boost Saving With a Personal Consumption Tax", *Challenge*, vol. 32, no. 6, 1989, pp. 44–50; Robert Hall and A. Rabushka, "The Flat Tax: A Simple, Progressive Consumption Tax", in *Frontiers of Tax Reform*, ed. Boskin M., Stanford, Hoover Institution Press, 1996, pp. 27–53.

[10] Bureau of Economic Analysis, US, at <https://www.bea.gov/iTable/iTable.cfm?reqid=9 &step=3&isuri=1&910=X&911=0&903=86&904=1999&905=1000&906=Q#reqid=9 &step=3&isuri=1&904=1999&903=86&906=q&905=1000&910=x&911=0> (accessed 8 May 2018).

high- and new technology industries. In 2009, investment was excluded from the VAT base and VAT changed from the production type to consumption type.

On 1 May 2016, the government announced the replacement of business tax with VAT. VAT was originally collected from manufacturing industries by the central and local governments. Business tax was collected almost entirely by local governments from service industries, such as transportation, telecommunication and financial services. Business tax was one of the major taxes in China for a long time.

Fiscal freedom to local governments

Although the central government got a large share of budgetary revenue, local governments got a large amount of revenue outside the budget. In the second half of 1980s, 1990s and early 2000s, the central government adopted a self-collection and self-utilisation policy. That is, a local government had the freedom to dispose the revenue they collected. The revenue is called the extra-budgetary revenue. This policy gave the local government a great incentive to collect revenues, and local governments began to collect various fees which were a major part of extra-budgetary revenue. In 1992, the extra-budgetary revenue was higher than the budgetary revenue! At the end of 1990s, complaints of fee collection from enterprises and general public became extremely high, and so the government began to eliminate fees or replace fees with taxes. Extra-budgetary revenue declined dramatically and was eliminated in 2011.

After the Asian Financial Crisis 1997, the central government adopted an expansionary fiscal policy by issuing government debt. Meanwhile, local governments began to set up urban development companies to borrow money from policy and commercial banks for infrastructure development. In the beginning, the borrowing was very limited, and after the global financial crisis in 2008 it became very large. Local governments borrowed money and invested the money in projects they preferred. In the early 2000s, the central government began to abolish the old housing allocation system for SOEs and government employees, and encouraged people to buy residential houses. As industrialisation and urbanisation proceeds, the demand for urban houses increases. Local governments control land — the key factor for housing construction. They own all the urban land and can expropriate rural farmland. Thus, local governments began to sell urban land to developers at extremely high prices to raise revenue, and bought farmlands at low prices and sold them at high prices to make profits. They have obtained a huge amount of revenue from land sales, and they can dispose the revenue at their will. Thus, over the years, the local governments have great fiscal freedom outside the general budget, and the off-budget revenue has been extremely large.

Table 1 shows the extra-budgetary revenue from 1982 to 2010. It can be seen that extra-budgetary revenue accounted for 92.22% of total general budgetary revenue and 14.51% of GDP in 1990, 102.98% of total general budgetary revenue and 14.89% of GDP in 1991, and 110.67% of total general budgetary revenue and 14.32% of GDP in 1992. After excluding the extra-budgetary revenue of SOEs, the extra-budgetary revenue was still large, accounting for 32.94% of total general budgetary revenue and 4.05% of GDP in 1993, 35.69% of total general budgetary revenue and 3.86% of GDP in 1994, 38.55% of total general budgetary revenue and 3.96% of GDP in 1995, and 52.56% of total general budgetary revenue and 5.47% of GDP in 1996.

In addition, local governments have freedom to dispose government funds, most of which have been from local government land sales. Table 2 shows government funds from 2010 to 2016. It can be seen that revenue from funds accounted for 84.57% of total local government budgetary revenue and 8.55% of GDP in 2010, 47.67% of total local government budgetary revenue and 5.85% of GDP in 2015, and 49.95% of total local government budgetary revenue and 5.86% of GDP in 2016. Of the total government fund, the revenue from land sales accounted for 82.11% of total local government fund and 7.02% of GDP in 2010, 77.82% of total local government fund and 4.55%

Table 1: China's Extra-budgetary Revenue (1982–2010)

Year	Total	Extra-budgetary Revenues (billion yuan)						Share in GDP (%)	Share in Budgetary Revenue (%)
		Administrative and Institutional Units	Local Govts	SOEs and Supervisory Ministries	Fundraising of Township Govts	Government Funds	Others		
1982	80.27	10.12	4.53	65.63				15.08	66.22
1985	153.00	23.32	4.41	125.27				16.97	76.32
1990	270.86	57.70	6.06	207.11				14.51	92.22
1991	324.33	69.70	6.88	247.75				14.89	102.98
1992	385.49	88.55	9.09	287.86				14.32	110.67
1993	143.25	131.78	11.47					4.05	32.94
1994	186.25	172.25	14.00					3.86	35.69
1995	240.65	223.49	17.17					3.96	38.55
1996	389.33	339.58	22.47		27.29			5.47	52.56
1997	282.60	241.43	11.59		29.58			3.58	32.67
1998	308.23	198.19		5.47	33.73	47.84	23	3.65	31.21

1999	338.52	235.43	5.01	35.89	39.65	22.54	3.77	29.58
2000	382.64	265.45	5.92	40.33	38.35	32.58	3.86	28.57
2001	430.00	309.00	6.00	41.00	38	36	3.92	26.24
2002	447.90	323.80	7.20	27.2	37.6	52.1	3.72	23.69
2003	456.68	333.57	5.23	29.31	28.71	59.85	3.36	21.03
2004	469.92	320.84	6.41	21.31	35.13	86.23	2.94	17.80
2005	554.42	385.82	4.78	19.29	35.93	108.59	3.00	17.52
2006	640.79	421.68	4.49	22.13	37.65	154.84	2.96	16.53
2007	682.03	468.11	4.02	18.03		191.89	2.57	13.29
2008	661.73	483.58	4.71	22.07		151.36	2.11	10.79
2009	641.47	459.81	8.41	22.06		151.19	1.88	9.36
2010	579.44	369.18	5.81	25.72		178.73	1.44	6.97

Note: The scope of extra budgetary revenue and expenditure was adjusted between 1993–1995 and 1996, not comparable with previous years. Since 1997, the extra-budgetary revenue and expenditure has not included those funds (fees) which have been brought into budgetary management, not consistent with the previous year.

Sources: Ministry of Finance of China (2000, 2005, 2007–2009, 2012).

Table 2: China's Government Funds from 2010 to 2016 (10 billion yuan, %)

Year	GDP	Budgetary Revenue of Local Government	Revenue from Funds of Local Government	Fees for the Sale of State-Owned Land	Revenue of State-Owned Land Use	Fees for the Sale of State Owned Land/GDP	Fees for the Sales of State-Owned Land/Budgetary Revenue of Local Government	Fees for the Sale of State-Owned Land/Revenue from Funds of Local Government
2010	4015.13	406.10	343.42	281.98	10.25	7.02	69.44	82.11
2011	4728.82	525.47	391.79	311.4	10.94	6.59	59.26	79.48
2012	5189.42	610.77	353.96	266.52	8.97	5.14	43.64	75.30
2013	5880.19	690.11	494.50	390.73	12.60	6.64	56.62	79.02
2014	6361.39	758.77	513.61	403.86	14.14	6.35	53.23	78.63
2015	6767.08	829.83	395.59	307.84	10.25	4.55	37.10	77.82
2016	7435.86	872.39	435.75	356.40	11.90	4.79	40.85	81.79

Source: Ministry of Finance of China, *Finance Yearbook of China*, Beijing: China Fiscal Press, 2011–2016.

of GDP in 2015, and 81.79% of total local government fund and 4.79% of GDP in 2016. Local governments can utilise this funds following their inclinations.

In addition, local governments have run a huge amount of debt, which is mainly from bank borrowing. Local governments used the money borrowed mainly for urban infrastructure development. The National Audit Office provided data on local government debt and the growth rate of local government debt. Based on this information, the local government deficit can be figured out. Table 3 shows the share of local government deficit as percentage of GDP. Local government deficits accounted for 1.62% of GDP in 2000, 2.48% in 2005, 9.03% in 2009, 2.96% in 2010 and 2.36% in 2016.

With extra-budgetary revenue, government funds and bank borrowing, the revenue off the general budget is enormous. For example, in 2010, the local government fund was 3,434.2 billion yuan and local government borrowing was 1,700 billion yuan, but the local government revenue was only 4,061 billion yuan.[11] Local government funds and local government borrowing together accounted for 126% of the local government budgetary revenue! Thus, China's local governments had great fiscal freedom for many years. This fiscal freedom stimulated China's economic growth.

Expansionary fiscal policy

From 1979, the government started to borrow from domestic and international markets, but until 1993 the magnitude was small. After 1994, government domestic borrowing started to increase rapidly and foreign borrowing started to slow down. In 1997, the Asian Financial Crisis occurred and China began to adopt an expansionary fiscal policy in 1998. In 2008, China adopted an expansionary fiscal policy again because of the global financial crisis. It can be found that the total government fiscal deficit accounted for 1.17% of GDP in 1996, 4.11%

---

[11] Local government borrowing is calculated based on the data given by National Audit Office of the People's Republic of China (2011).

in 2000, 11.265% in 2009, 4.6% in 2010 and 6.15% in 2016![12] It is well known that the limit for the ratio of government budget deficit to GDP set by the European Union for its members is 3%. Thus, in the past 20 decades, the Chinese government adopted very aggressive expansionary fiscal policies.

Rapid Economic Growth

With reforms and opening up, the Chinese economy has grown rapidly. Table 3 shows China's total GDP and per capita GDP, as well

Table 3:   China's Per Capita GDP and Total GDP

Year	Per Capita GDP (yuan)	Per Capita GDP Index with GDP of 1978 being 100	Total GDP (billion yuan)	Total GDP Index with GDP of 1978 being 100
1978	385	100	367.87	100
2008	24,121	1236.3	31,951.50	1712.8
2009	26,222	1345.8	34,908.10	1873.8
2010	30,876	1481.8	41,303.00	2073.1
2011	36,403	1615.4	48,930.10	2270.8
2012	40,007	1733.8	54,036.70	2449.2
2013	43,852	1859.1	59,524.40	2639.2
2014	47,203	1984.7	64,397.40	2831.8
2015	49,351	2110.9	67,670.80	3027.2
2016	53,980	2240.2	74,412.70	3229.7
2017	59,660		82,712.20	

Source: National Bureau of Statistics of China, at <http://data.stats.gov.cn/easyquery. htm?cn=C01> (accessed 19 May 2018).

[12] The ratio of central government deficits to GDP is calculated based on the data from the National Bureau of Statistics of the People's Republic of China, at <http://data.stats.gov. cn/ks.htm?cn=C01>. The statistics of the local government's deficits/GDP are calculated based on the data from the National Audit Office of the People's Republic of China, *Auditing Report on Local Government Debt*, 27 June 2011 and the Wind Database.

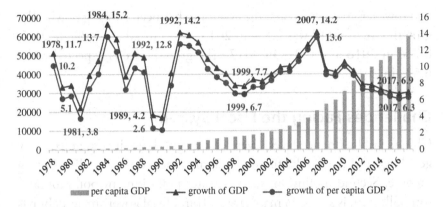

Figure 2: Per Capita GDP, Growth Rate of GDP and Growth Rate of Per Capita GDP (1978–2017)

Source: National Bureau of Statistics of China, at <http://data.stats.gov.cn/easyquery. htm?cn=C01> (accessed 19 May 2018).

as the index of total and per capita GDP. It can be seen that China's per capita GDP at the constant price increased by 22.4 times from 1978 to 2016, and total GDP at the constant price increased by 32.3 times.

The growth rate of GDP based on the 1978 constant retail price was 7.69% (1978–1994) and reached 10.6% (1994–2016). Figure 2 shows per capita GDP, the growth rate of GDP and the growth rate of per capita GDP based on official statistics. It can be seen that the growth rate of GDP was accelerated to 10.7% in 2005, 12.1% in 2006 and 14.2% in 2007. Per capita GDP increased from 1,663 yuan in 1990 to 59,660 in 2016. China has become an upper-middle income country.

Rapid economic growth was a result of economic reforms and opening up to the world. The economy has changed from a centrally planned economy to a market-oriented economy. In rural areas, People's communes were dismantled and land was rented to farmers on a 30-year contract and rented again with another contract for 30 years. Rural labour was allowed to migrate to cities. Private enterprises were allowed to emerge and expand. Foreign trade and foreign investment increased dramatically. In addition, as mentioned earlier, the central government gives local governments considerable fiscal freedom.

However, in recent years, the economy has been slowing down. The growth rate of GDP was 7.7% in 2013, 7.4% in 2014, 6.9% in 2015, 6.7% in 2016 and 6.9% in 2017. The growth rate is expected to be 6.5% in 2018.

Challenges Facing the Fiscal System

China's public finance faces severe challenges. First, income inequality gets large and the public finance system is ineffective in redistributing income. Second, pollution, such as water pollution, air pollution and soil pollution, is severe in many areas. Third, local government debt has increased to a high level. Fourth, resource depletion has become a serious problem, with oil and natural gas deposits decreasing and fresh water in the northern part of China becoming scarcer. Fifth, the economy has been slowing down, and the growth rate may further decline if the trade war with the United States continues.

Income inequality

China's income inequality increased since the early 1980s. Figure 3 shows China's Gini coefficients from 1981 to 2016. It can be seen that the Gini coefficient was 0.249 in 1982, 0.49 in 2001 and 0.465 in 2016. The Gini coefficient increased year by year, but has been slowly declining in recent years. The change in Gini coefficient seems consistent with the Kuznets Curve, i.e. income inequality increases as income increases in the beginning of economic development, reaches the highest level and then starts to decline. However, it is too early to claim that the Gini coefficient will not increase further in the future, since the decline may be caused by the slowdown of the economic growth recently.

The Gini coefficients for 1981–1994 and 2000–2001 are from Martin Ravallion and Chen Shaohua, "China's (uneven) Progress against Poverty", *Journal of Development Economics*, vol. 82, 2007, pp. 1–42. Ravallion and Shaohua calculated them using the income data from the NBS urban and rural household surveys and the 2002 Gini coefficient is from Bjorn Gustafsson, Li Shi, Terry Sicular and Yue Ximing, "Income Inequality and Spatial Differences in China,

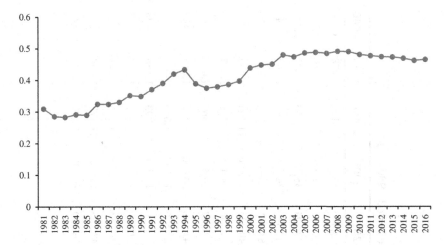

Figure 3:   China's GINI Coefficient (1981–2016)

Source: Data for 2003–2016 is from National Bureau of China, at http://www.stats.gov. cn/ztjc/zdtjgz/yblh/zysj/201710/t20171010_1540710.html. Data for 1995–1999 is from National Bureau of China, at http://www.stats.gov.cn/tjzs/tjsj/tjcb/zggqgl/200210/ P020130912449774383370.htm.

1988, 1995, and 2002", in *Inequality and Public Policy in China,* ed. Björn A. Gustafsson, Li Shi and Terry Sicular, Cambridge University Press, 2008, pp. 35–60. Also, see Li Shi, "Recent Changes in Income Inequality in China", *World Social Science Report 2016: Challenging Inequalities: Pathways to a Just World,* UNESCO Publishing, 2016, pp. 84–88.

Meanwhile, the disparity of per capita income across provinces is large. Table 4 shows per capita GDP of each province from 1980 to 2016. In 2016, per capita GDP was 118,198 yuan in Beijing, 116,562 yuan in Shanghai, 115,053 yuan in Tianjin and 96,887 yuan in Jiangsu, but it was only 33,326 yuan in Guizhou, 31,093 yuan in Yunnan and 27,643 yuan in Gansu. Per capita GDP in Beijing was 4.3 times as large as that in Gansu.

Table 5 shows per capita GDP as percentage of per capita GDP in Beijing from 1980 to 2016. It can be seen that per capita GDP was only 23.39% that of Beijing for Gansu, 26.31% for Yunnan, 28.13%

Table 4: Per Capita GDP of China's Provinces during the Period 1980–2016

Province	2016	2015	2014	2013	2012	2011	2010	2005	2000	1990	1980
Beijing	118,198	106,497	99,995	94,648	87,475	81,658	73,856	45,444	24,122	4,878	1,584
Shanghai	116,562	103,796	97,370	90,993	85,373	82,560	76,074	51,474	29,671	5,910	2,738
Tianjin	115,053	107,960	105,231	100,105	93,173	85,213	72,994	35,783	17,353	3,621	1,392
Jiangsu	96,887	87,995	81,874	75,354	68,347	62,290	52,840	24,560	11,765	2,103	541
Zhejiang	84,916	77,644	73,002	68,805	63,374	59,249	51,711	27,703	13,416	2,122	470
Fujian	74,707	67,966	63,472	58,145	52,763	47,377	40,025	18,646	11,194	1,763	348
Guangdong	74,016	67,503	63,469	58,833	54,095	50,807	44,736	24,435	12,736	2,537	480
Inner Mongolia	72,064	71,101	71,046	67,836	63,886	57,974	47,347	16,331	6,502	1,478	361
Shandong	68,733	64,168	60,879	56,885	51,768	47,335	41,106	20,096	9,326	1,815	402
Chongqing	58,502	52,321	47,850	43,223	38,914	34,500	27,596	10,982	5,616	—	
Hubei	55,665	50,654	47,145	42,826	38,572	34,197	27,906	11,431	6,293	1,556	428
Jilin	53,868	51,086	50,160	47,428	43,415	38,460	31,599	13,348	7,351	1,746	445
Shanxi	51,015	47,626	46,929	43,117	38,564	33,464	27,133	9,899	4,968	1,241	334
Liaoning	50,791	65,354	65,201	61,996	56,649	50,760	42,355	18,983	11,177	2,698	811
Ningxia	47,194	43,805	41,834	39,613	36,394	33,043	26,860	10,239	5,376	1,393	433

Hunan	46,382	42,754	40,271	36,943	33,480	29,880	24,719	10,426	5,425	1,288	365
Hainan	44,347	40,818	38,924	35,663	32,377	28,898	23831	10,871	6,798	1,589	354
Qinghai	43,531	41,252	39,671	36,875	33,181	29,522	24,115	10,045	5,138	1,558	473
Hebei	43,062	40,255	39,984	38,909	36,584	33,969	28,668	14,782	7,592	1,465	427
Henan	42,575	39,123	37,072	34,211	31,499	28,661	24,446	11,346	5,450	1,091	317
Xinjiang	40,564	40,036	40,648	37,553	33,796	30,087	25,034	13,108	7,372	1,799	410
Heilongjiang	40,432	39,462	39,226	37,697	35,711	32,819	27,076	14,434	8,294	2,028	694
Jiangxi	40,400	36,724	34,674	31,930	28,800	26,150	21,253	9,440	4,851	1,134	342
Sichuan	40,003	36,775	35,128	32,617	29,608	26,133	21,182	9,060	4,956	1,134	321
Anhui	39,561	35,997	34,425	32,001	28,792	25,659	20,888	8,670	4,779	1,182	291
Guangxi	38,027	35,190	33,090	30,741	27,952	25,326	20,219	8,788	4,652	1,066	278
Shanxi	35,532	34,919	35,070	34,984	33,628	31,357	26,283	12,495	5,722	1,528	442
Tibet	35,184	31,999	29,252	26,326	22,936	20,077	17,027	9,114	4,572	1,276	471
Guizhou	33,246	29,847	26,437	23,151	19,710	16,413	13,119	5,052	2,759	810	219
Yunnan	31,093	28,806	27,264	25,322	22,195	19,265	15,752	7,835	4,769	1,224	267
Gansu	27,643	26,165	26,433	24,539	21,978	19,595	16,113	7,477	4,129	1,099	388

Source: National Bureau of Statistics, at <http://data.stats.gov.cn/easyquery.htm?cn=E0103> (accessed 19 May 2018).

Table 5: Per Capita GDP as Percentage of Per Capita GDP in Beijing (1980–2016)

Province	2016	2015	2014	2013	2012	2011	2010	2005	2000	1990	1980
Beijing	118198	106497	99995	94648	87475	81658	73856	45444	24122	4878	1584
Shanghai	98.62	97.46	97.37	96.14	97.6	101.1	103	113.27	123	121.16	172.85
Tianjin	97.34	101.37	105.24	105.77	106.51	104.35	98.83	78.74	71.94	74.23	87.88
Jiangsu	81.97	82.63	81.88	79.61	78.13	76.28	71.54	54.04	48.77	43.11	34.15
Zhejiang	71.84	72.91	73.01	72.7	72.45	72.56	70.02	60.96	55.62	43.50	29.67
Fujian	63.2	63.82	63.48	61.43	60.32	58.02	54.19	41.03	46.41	36.14	21.97
Guangdong	62.62	63.38	63.47	62.16	61.84	62.22	60.57	53.77	52.8	52.01	30.30
Inner Mongolia	60.97	66.76	71.05	71.67	73.03	71	64.11	35.94	26.95	30.30	22.79
Shandong	58.15	60.25	60.88	60.1	59.18	57.97	55.66	44.22	38.66	37.21	25.38
Chongqing	49.49	49.13	47.85	45.67	44.49	42.25	37.36	24.17	23.28	—	—
Hubei	47.09	47.56	47.15	45.25	44.09	41.88	37.78	25.15	26.09	31.90	27.02
Jilin	45.57	47.97	50.16	50.11	49.63	47.1	42.78	29.37	30.47	35.79	28.09
Shanxi	43.16	44.72	46.93	45.56	44.09	40.98	36.74	21.78	20.6	25.44	21.09
Liaoning	42.97	61.37	65.2	65.5	64.76	62.16	57.35	41.77	46.34	55.31	51.20
Ningxia	39.93	41.13	41.84	41.85	41.61	40.47	36.37	22.53	22.29	28.56	27.34

Province											
Hunan	39.24	40.15	40.27	39.03	38.27	36.59	33.47	22.94	22.49	26.40	23.04
Hainan	37.52	38.33	38.93	37.68	37.01	35.39	32.27	23.92	28.18	32.57	22.35
Qinghai	36.83	38.74	39.67	38.96	37.93	36.15	32.65	22.1	21.3	31.94	29.86
Hebei	36.43	37.8	39.99	41.11	41.82	41.6	38.82	32.53	31.47	30.03	26.96
Henan	36.02	36.74	37.07	36.15	36.01	35.1	33.1	24.97	22.59	22.37	20.01
Xinjiang	34.32	37.59	40.65	39.68	38.64	36.85	33.9	28.84	30.56	36.88	25.88
Heilongjiang	34.21	37.05	39.23	39.83	40.82	40.19	36.66	31.76	34.38	41.57	43.81
Jiangxi	34.18	34.48	34.68	33.74	32.92	32.02	28.78	20.77	20.11	23.25	21.59
Sichuan	33.84	34.53	35.13	34.46	33.85	32	28.68	19.94	20.55	23.25	20.27
Anhui	33.47	33.8	34.43	33.81	32.91	31.42	28.28	19.08	19.81	24.23	18.37
Guangxi	32.17	33.04	33.09	32.48	31.95	31.01	27.38	19.34	19.29	21.85	17.55
Shaanxi	30.06	32.79	35.07	36.96	38.44	38.4	35.59	27.5	23.72	31.32	27.90
Tibet	29.77	30.05	29.25	27.81	26.22	24.59	23.05	20.06	18.95	26.16	29.73
Guizhou	28.13	28.03	26.44	24.46	22.53	20.1	17.76	11.12	11.44	16.61	13.83
Yunnan	26.31	27.05	27.27	26.75	25.37	23.59	21.33	17.24	19.77	25.09	16.86
Gansu	23.39	24.57	26.43	25.93	25.12	24	21.82	16.45	17.12	22.53	24.49

Source: National Bureau of Statistics, at <http://data.stats.gov.cn/easyquery.htm?cn=E0103> (accessed 19 May 2018).

for Guizhou and 29.77% for Tibet in 2016. The per capita GDP as s percentage of per capita GDP in Beijing in all provinces or regions increased from 1980 to 2016, except Shanghai, Gansu, Tibet, Heilongjiang and Liaoning, indicating that per capita GDP is converging among provinces. However, for 20 out of 30 provinces (or regions), the gap between per capita with Beijing enlarged since 2013.

The income gap between the rural households and urban households is substantial. Table 6 shows per capita disposable income of urban and rural households from 1978 to 2016. Per capita disposable average annual income for urban households was 33,616 yuan in 2016, while it was only 12,363 yuan for rural households. The average urban per capita income was 2.7 times as high as the rural average per capita income! Figure 4 shows the ratio of rural households' per capita income to urban households' per capita income.

Moreover, from 1978 to 2016, the income gap between rural and urban residents has increased. Per capita disposable annual income of rural households as a percentage of per capita disposable annual income of urban households was 38.91% in 1978, 54.87% in 1983, 45.44% in 1990, 35.88% in 2000, 30.97% in 2010 and 36.78% in 2016.

Large income inequality may be detrimental to economic growth and human development, and may cause social instability. It is usually believed that inequality is a price worth paying for economic growth. Theoretically, if the inequality is low, an increase in inequality may stimulate economic growth; but if the inequality is too large, a decrease in inequality may increase economic growth. Fei, Ranis and Kuo showed that in Taiwan from 1952 to 1971 the economy experienced rapid growth, and meanwhile the Gini coefficient was extremely low.[13] Thus, high growth rate and low income inequality are possible. Aghion, Caroli and Garcia-Penalosa showed that when capital markets are imperfect, there is not necessarily a trade-off between equity and efficiency, i.e. there may exist a negative impact of inequality and a positive

---

[13] John C. H. Fei, Gustav Ranis and Shirley W. Y. Kuo, *Growth with Equity: The Taiwan Case*, New York, Oxford University Press, for World Bank, 1979.

Table 6:   Per Capita Disposable Income of Urban and Rural Households (1978–2016)

Year	Per Capita Disposable Annual Income of Urban Households	Per Capita Disposable Annual Income of Rural Households	Rural/ Urban	Year	Per Capita Disposable Annual Income of Urban Households	Per Capita Disposable Annual Income of Rural Households	Rural/ Urban
2016	33616.25	12363.41	36.78	1996	4838.9	1926.1	39.80
2015	31194.83	11421.71	36.61	1995	4283	1577.7	36.84
2014	28843.85	10488.88	36.36	1994	3496.2	1221	34.92
2013	26467	9429.59	35.63	1993	2577.4	921.6	35.76
2012	24564.7	7916.6	32.23	1992	2026.6	784	38.69
2011	21809.8	6977.3	31.99	1991	1700.6	708.6	41.67
2010	19109.4	5919	30.97	1990	1510.2	686.3	45.44
2009	17174.7	5153.2	30.00	1989	1373.9	601.5	43.78
2008	15780.8	4760.6	30.17	1988	1180.2	544.9	46.17
2007	13785.8	4140.4	30.03	1987	1002.1	462.6	46.16
2006	11759.5	3587	30.50	1986	900.9	423.8	47.04
2005	10493	3254.9	31.02	1985	739.1	397.6	53.80
2004	9421.6	2936.4	31.17	1984	652.1	355.3	54.49
2003	8472.2	2622.2	30.95	1983	564.6	309.8	54.87
2002	7702.8	2475.6	32.14	1982	535.3	270.1	50.46
2001	6859.6	2366.4	34.50	1981	500.4	223.4	44.64
2000	6280	2253.4	35.88	1980	477.6	191.3	40.05
1999	5854	2210.3	37.76	1979	405	160.2	39.56
1998	5425.1	2162	39.85	1978	343.4	133.6	38.91
1997	5160.3	2090.1	40.50				

Note: The statistical calibres and statistical methods of the data after 2013 are different from those before 2013.

Source: National Bureau of Statistics, at <http://data.stats.gov.cn/easyquery.htm?cn=C01> (accessed 19 May 2018).

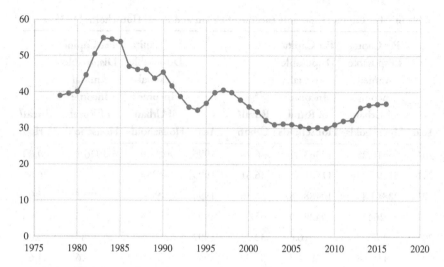

Figure 4: The Ratio of Rural to Urban Households' Per Capita Disposable Income

Source: National Bureau of Statistics, at <http://data.stats.gov.cn/easyquery.htm?cn=C01> (accessed 19 May 2018).

effect of redistribution upon growth.[14] Research by OECD has shown that when income inequality rises, economic growth falls, partially because poorer members of society are less able to invest in their education.[15] Thus, when inequality is high, reducing inequality can make our societies fairer and our economies stronger.

Environmental degeneration

Air pollution is serious. PM 2.5 in some cities reach 1000. On 14 December 2012, the United States Environmental Protection Agency set National Ambient Air Quality Standard for fine particles (PM 2.5) to 12.0 micrograms per cubic meter ($\mu g/m^3$). The World Health Organisation (WHO) set a standard for PM 2.5 to be 10 $\mu g/m^3$ on average annually.

[14] Philippe Aghion, Eve Caroli and Cecilia Garcia-Penalosa, "Inequality and Economic Growth: The Perspective of the New Growth Theories", *Journal of Economic Literature*, vol. 37, no. 4, 1999, pp. 1615–1660.

[15] OECD, *Focus on Inequality and Growth*, December 2014.

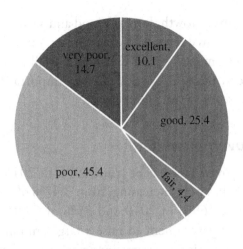

Figure 5:   The Ground Water Quality in China

Source: Ministry of Environmental Protection of China, *Report on the State of the Environment in China*, 2016.

Based on the *2016 Report on the State of the Environment in China*, in 338 cities above prefecture level across the country, 84 cities reached the air quality standard, accounting for 25% whereas 254 cities failed to reach the standard, accounting for 75%. In 338 cities, the days with PM 2.5 causing heavy pollution or worse accounted for 80.3%.[16] Pollution was concentrated in Xinjiang, Hebei, Shanxi, Shandong, Henan, Beijing and Shaanxi. A skyscraper-sized air purifier was built in Xi'an to clear the air. Industries polluting the environment create GDP; however, they also produce air purifiers to create more GDP. The quality of growth is clearly low.

Water quality is low in China. It can be seen from Figure 5 that the proportion of poor and very poor ground water quality totalled 60.1%, and the proportion of excellent ground water was 10.1%. There is also serious soil pollution, noise pollution and solid waste pollution. The degradation of the environment is detrimental to

---

[16] See Ministry of Environmental Protection of China, *Report on the State of the Environment in China*, 2016.

sustainable economic growth. López, Vinod and Wang found that taxation of natural resource rents is another important area requiring the attention of policymakers.[17] For example, by failing to tax rents on natural resources, many countries miss an important source of tax revenue that causes economic inefficiency.

High local government debt

Table 7 shows government debt from 1996 to 2016. China's local government debt has been increasing, from 3.37% of GDP in 1996 to 7.95% in 2000, 26.69% in 2010 and 35% of GDP in 2016. Debt finance allows the government to raise a large amount of funds in a short period of time without increasing taxes or fees. The debt finance is good if the return from the debt-financed projects is larger than the cost of the debt, and the debt finance is bad if the return from the debt-financed projects is smaller than the cost of the debt. Based on the law of diminishing marginal productivity, if the debt is too large, implying government spending is too large, then the marginal return will be small and the benefit from debt may be smaller than the cost of the debt. Also, since debt must be repaid in the future, debt finance may benefit the current generations and hurt the future generations.

Government debt is uneven across provinces. Figure 6 shows government debt–GDP ratio in each province. Including debt that need to be repaid by local governments, debt guaranteed by local governments and debt needing assistance for repayment by local governments, the debt–GDP ratio in some provinces is higher than 100%. For example, in 2016 the debt–GDP ratio was 106.69% in Guizhou, 83.9% in Qinghai, 58.24% in Sichuan, 57.93% in Gansu, 56.97% in Liaoning and 53.57% in Hainan.

High local government debt threatens the financial system and the sustainability of local government finance. Recently, some local governments have already encounter the problem of repaying the debt. A large

---

[17] Ramón E. López, Vinod Thomas and Wang Yan, "The Effect of Fiscal Policies on the Quality of Growth".

Table 7:   China's Local Government Debt (1996–2016)

Year	Total Local Debt (billion yuan)	Growth Rate (%)	GDP (billion yuan)	Debt–GDP Ratio
1996	239.931		711.766	3.37
1997	299.482	24.82	789.73	3.79
1998	443.832	48.20	844.023	5.26
1999	591.717	33.32	896.771	6.60
2000	788.877	33.32	992.146	7.95
2001	1051.73	33.32	1096.552	9.59
2002	1402.167	33.32	1203.327	11.65
2003	1771.217	26.32	1358.228	13.04
2004	2237.402	26.32	1598.783	13.99
2005	2826.286	26.32	1849.374	15.28
2006	3570.164	26.32	2163.144	16.50
2007	4509.831	26.32	2658.103	16.97
2008	5568.74	23.48	3140.454	17.73
2009	9016.903	61.92	3409.028	26.45
2010	10717.49	18.86	4015.128	26.69
2011	12410.74	15.80	48930.06	25.36
2012	15640.43	26.02	54036.74	28.94
2013	17766.71	13.59	59524.44	29.85
2014	22075.22	24.25	64397.4	34.28
2015	23453.37	6.24	68905.21	34.04
2016	26231.39	11.84	74412.72	35.25

Source: The figures in this table were calculated based on the National Audit Office of the People's Republic of China, *Auditing Report on Local Government Debt*, 27 June 2011. The remaining debt data are from the Wind Database. GDP data is from the National Bureau of Statistics, *Statistical Yearbook of China*, 2017.

proportion of local government debt is the loan from banks. For example, by the end of June in 2010, the local governments were responsible for repaying 47% of the debt and guaranteed to repay 33% of the debt, and 61% of the debt that local governments were responsible for repaying with assistance was the loans from commercial and

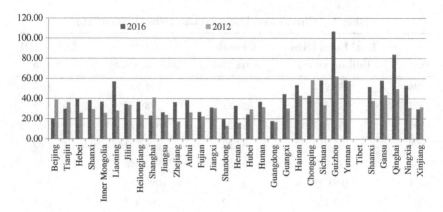

Figure 6: Debt–GDP Ratio in Each Province

Source: Wind Database.

policy banks.[18] Banks now worry that local governments will be unable to repay the debt. Some lenders recently only received the interest payment of the loan from the local governments but not the principle. High local government debt threatens the stability of the banking system.

The central government has also had debt. The debt–GDP ratio was only 1% in 1980, but increased to 5.38% in 1995, 12.98% in 2000 and 19.05% in 1997, and was 16% in 2016. In addition, central government branches and the railroad corporation have also incurred debt, which is about 5% of GDP. Meanwhile, the social security account has explicit debt. Over the years, local governments have used the funds from individual or personal accounts to finance the deficits in the pay-as-you-go social pooling accounts, resulting in individual account debts.[19] Adding all these debts, China's total government debt is close to 60% of GDP.

---

[18] See National Audit Office of the People's Republic of China, *Auditing Report on Local Government Debt*, 27 June 2011.

[19] See Li Chengjian and Lin Shuanglin, "Resource Allocation and Economic Growth in China", *Economic Inquiry*, vol. 38, no. 3, 2000, pp. 515–526.

Low-quality projects and products and waste resources

The quality of the infrastructures, such as roads, bridges, buildings and pipelines, is questionable. Many constructions (e.g. buildings, equipment, facilities, etc.) become obsolete quickly due to low quality and lack of maintenance. For example, on 13 August 2007, a bridge in Fenghuang county of Hunan province collapsed even before completion, causing the death of 64 people. In June 2017, a small bridge in Shanxi province collapsed only two hours after it was completed. These collapsed constructions added to GDP but reduced the wealth of the nation. Also, the quality of drugs and food products made in China is worrisome. In 2008, kidney disease broke out due to a baby formula contaminated by melamine, resulting in the death of six babies and illness of many more. The producer, Sanlu Group, claimed the contaminant came from milk suppliers. In July 2018, hundreds of thousands of vaccines provided for Chinese children were found to be faulty by China's Food and Drug Administration.

The growth patterns lead to overexploitation of natural resources, and natural resource depletion is a serious problem in China. China's economic growth has relied on massive use and irreversible damage of natural resources. Overfishing has caused the large reduction of fish stock in rivers and seas near China. China's consumption of gasoline has been increasing. It was estimated that proven reserves of crude oil per capita is only 18.1 barrels, much less than the world average of 227 barrels.[20] Rivers in the southern part are polluted, while rivers in the northern part have dried out. Renewable internal freshwater resources per capita have been declining and was down to 2,062 m³ in China in 2014, lower than the world average of 5,921 m³.[21] Economic growth based on massive use of natural resources is not high-quality growth.

---

[20] See CIA World Factbook, at http://world.bymap.org/OilReserves.html (accessed 17 January 2017).
[21] World Bank, at <https://data.worldbank.org/indicator/ER.H2O.INTR.PC?year_high_desc=true> (accessed 8 May 2018).

Fiscal Reforms for High-Quality Growth

Fiscal policies can play an important role in improving the quality of economic growth. The government can reform the tax system to make the income distribution more equal and reform the expenditure structure to provide more public goods to benefit the poor. The government can also collect more environmental taxes and natural resource taxes to prevent environment degradation and natural resource depletion. In addition, the government can cut its budget deficits to leave the future generations with a smaller burden of debt.

Tax reforms

There is much room for tax reforms in China. First, introduce personal housing property tax as soon as possible. A study on tax and economic growth by the OECD showed that taxes on immovable property are the least harmful for economic growth while corporate income taxes are the most harmful type of tax.[22] The value of personal housing property in China accounted for 212% of GDP in 2014, higher than that of the United States.[23] The introduction of personal housing property tax can allow the local governments to not only raise a substantial amount of revenue for education and for repaying local government debt, but also collect more taxes from the wealthy people with a large amount of housing property and thus reduce income inequality.

Second, reform personal income tax by establishing a comprehensive income tax system. Currently, various incomes, such as wage income, rental income, royalty, etc., are taxed independently. Also, wage income is collected without considering the number of dependents the wage earner has. China should establish a comprehensive

---

[22] OECD, "Tax Policy Reform and Economic Growth", *OECD Tax Policy Studies No. 20*, OECD Publishing, 2010.

[23] See Wind (a Chinese database). In 2014, the value of personal housing property was $22.224 trillion (136,520 billion yuan) in China and it was $23.035 trillion in the United States.

income tax system, with all incomes combined and with the number of dependents considered. In addition, every year the tax brackets should be adjusted according to the inflation rate.

Third, collect environmental taxes to improve the environment. China started collecting environment tax on 1 January 2018 based on the environmental protection law passed in 2016, replacing the fee system. China has collected "pollutant discharge fee" since 1979. However, some local governments exploited loopholes and exempted enterprises that should pay the fee. Polluters pay taxes for noise, air and water pollutants, and solid waste. The tax is a local tax; the central authorities will set upper limits and allow local governments to determine the rates on their own. The law targets enterprises and public institutions that discharge listed pollutants directly into the environment.[24] Currently, some local governments reduce and exempt taxes for enterprises that should pay the fee to attract business investment. The central government should enforce the environmental tax law and prevent cross-border pollution.

Fourth, collect personal vehicle pollution tax to reduce air pollution. There are too many personal vehicles in big cities, emitting waste gas into the air. The government should increase the cost of owning vehicles to reduce the number of vehicles. Meanwhile, the government should develop better public transportation, such as buses and subways, to reduce the urban traffic. Singapore sets an excellent example for taxing personal vehicles, developing public transportation and reducing urban traffic congestion. China should learn from Singapore in this aspect. At the moment, some Chinese local governments, such as Beijing, control the number of vehicles by letting buyers draw lots. This is definitely an inefficient way of resource allocation.

Fifth, collect more resource taxes to preserve natural resources. The government has launched resource tax reforms and adjusted the tax rates, from specific tax to *ad valorem* taxes.

---

[24] See <http://www.chinadaily.com.cn/a/201801/02/WS5a4aeccba31008cf16da4988. html> (accessed 08 May 2018).

Reallocating government expenditure

Government can improve the quality of growth, i.e. reducing inequality and pollution, through its proper spending. López, Vinod and Wang confirmed that government spending in public goods is associated with higher and better growth.[25]

First, increase public education expenditure. An increase in public education expenditure can stimulate human capital accumulation for the low income groups and reduce income inequality. The Chinese government should implement 12-year compulsory education, as the United States and other countries did, half a century ago. At the moment, public education expenditure accounts for about 4% of GDP, lower than the world average which is about 5%. Also, the Chinese government should allocate a large proportion of education expenditure on higher education, and it should allocate a large proportion on secondary education as many industrialised countries do.

Second, spend more on public infrastructure. Public infrastructures are not only crucial to the production of goods and services, but also can improve the quality of people's everyday life. The government should spend on public transportations, public parks, public health, public sanitation, etc. Public infrastructure benefits the poor people more than the rich. Thus, more expenditure on public infrastructure can reduce income inequality and can improve the environment.

Third, transfer more to the poor. To reduce income inequality, the government may provide poverty relief to poor families with more subsidies, such as food stamps and scholarships for education, and cover a larger portion of the medical insurance fees and medical expenses for the poor families. The rural old is the poorest and most disadvantageous group in China now. They did not have freedom to migrate to cities when young and were forced to stay in rural areas engaging in heavy manual labour, living a miserable life. They do not have much savings if any, and they do not have assets since land is not privately owned. Now their children are moving to urban areas, struggling to integrate with the urban life. They can no longer rely on their

---

[25] Ramón E. López, Vinod Thomas and Wang Yan, "The Effect of Fiscal Policies on the Quality of Growth".

children for security in their old age. Many of them actually work to death. The social security benefit gap between retired urban workers and the rural old is too large. The government should provide more social security benefit to the rural old.

Curtailing local government debt

The government should make more efforts to reduce the local government debt. In China, since local government officials are appointed by the central government, they make fiscal decisions without consulting the local public. Thus, the central government has a certain responsibility for the local government debt. A hard limit should be set for local government debt, i.e. the ratio of local government debt to GDP cannot exceed a given level, say 35%. For provinces with high debt–GDP ratios, a part of the new tax revenue should be used to repay the debt. Meanwhile, the government should continue to carry out the debt-to-equity swap program. In addition to establishing personal housing property tax for local governments, the central government may allocate more tax revenue from the shared tax, such as the VAT. The central government may also undertake more spending responsibilities, including social security, health care, education and poverty relief.

Stimulating economic growth by cutting corporate income tax

Economic growth can increase output and make the pie larger. Usually, it is harder to make the pie larger than to distribute the pie fairly. Economic growth can make the reduction of poverty possible. Also, as GDP grows, the debt–GDP ratio will decrease. Thus, it is possible to grow out of debt. The most urgent fiscal policy for stimulating economic growth is the reduction of corporate income tax.

Studies have shown the optimal capital income tax should be zero.[26] An OECD study based on the data from OECD countries showed that

---

[26] See Christopher Chamely, "Optimal Taxation of Capital Income in General Equilibrium with Infinite lives", *Econometrica*, vol. 54, no. 3, 1986, pp. 607–622; Robert E. Lucas,

corporate income tax is most detrimental to economic growth. In the past four decades, most industrialised countries have reduced their corporate income tax. For example, in 2016, the share of corporate income tax in total tax revenue increased by 8.62% in the United States and 8.45% in the United Kingdom.[27] However, China's corporate income tax increased significantly. The share of corporate income tax in total tax revenue has increased from 7.9% in 2000 to 22% in 2016.[28] In the United States, marginal corporate income tax rate for the highest corporate income has recently been reduced from 35% to 21%.

The Chinese government has announced many measures of tax reduction this year. Most of the tax reductions in China are discretionary or conditional, and there is no general tax reduction, for instance, a cut of corporate income tax rate as the United States. Thus, the tax cut cannot benefit all enterprises and is, of course, ineffective. Ironically, as the government advocates tax cut, the total tax revenue increased significantly. Data show that from January to April of 2018, the national general public budget revenue was 690.9 billion yuan, which increased by 12.9%. Among them, tax revenue was 608.98 billion yuan, which increased by 16.5%; non-tax revenue was 812.1 billion yuan, with a year-on-year decrease of 8.8%. Specifically, from January to April 2018, the revenue from corporate income tax increased by 13%, VAT 18.4%, consumption tax 24%, personal income tax 20.8%, VAT and consumption tax on imports 15.8%, and tariffs 6.2%. Meanwhile, the growth rate of GDP in the first half of 2018 was 6.8%.[29] Clearly, the increase in taxes were disproportional to the increase in GDP.

"Supply-side Economics: An Analytical Review", *Oxford Economic Papers,* vol. 42, no. 2, 1990, pp. 293–316.

[27] See OECD, Tax on Corporate Profits (indicator), at <https://data.oecd.org/tax/tax-on-corporate-profits.htm#indicator-chart> (accessed 25 August 2018).

[28] See National Bureau of Statistics of China, at <http://data.stats.gov.cn/easyquery.htm?cn=C01> (accessed 18 March 2017).

[29] See Ministry of Finance of China, at <http://gks.mof.gov.cn/zhengfuxinxi/tongjishuju/201805/t20180514_2894051.html> (accessed 08 May 2018).

Cutting corporate income tax is imperative for economic growth. Currently, the standard corporate income tax rate is 25%; however, for high-tech industries, the corporate income tax rate is 15%. There is still room for cutting the tax rate. Also in the United States and other industrialized countries, the corporate tax base is small due to a large number of deductions. In China, there are limited deductions. China has increased deductions for corporate income tax following industrialised countries. With a smaller burden of corporate income tax, business investments will increase and the economy will continue to grow.

Conclusion

China's rapid economic growth in the past four decades largely relied on pro-growth tax reforms, fiscal decentralisation and expansionary fiscal policies. As per capita income grows in China, income inequality, pollution, resource depletion and local government debt have increased dramatically, raising questions on the quality of economic growth. Further fiscal reforms are needed for high-quality growth. First, establishing new taxes such as personal housing property tax and establishing a comprehensive income tax system are necessary to reduce the income inequality as well as collecting more environmental taxes and taxes on natural resources to prevent environmental degradation and natural resource depletion. Second, increase the government expenditure on public consumption goods, increase the government expenditure for 12-year compulsory education, increase transfers to the poor to reduce poverty and improve income distribution. Third, set a hard limit for the local government debt to contain it, so that the future generations are left with less debt burden. Fourth, cut corporate income tax to stimulate economic growth. Economic growth will eventually enable the government to go out of debt and to redistribute the increased wealth among different income groups.

Chapter 4

Capital Account Liberalisation in China

Sarah CHAN*

Introduction

RMB convertibility for capital account transactions has been a long-term goal of the Chinese government and is regarded as an important target of overall economic reform. In 1993, a plan to liberalise the capital account by 2000 was announced but was disrupted by the Asian financial crisis. The process of liberalising the capital account resumed over the next few years, but progress on capital account convertibility has proceeded slowly and in discrete stages.

While China achieved full current account convertibility in late 1996, capital account liberalisation has been carefully sequenced, gradual and heavily managed by the authorities. In particular, China has calibrated the pace of capital flows in order to manage the volatility associated with the opening of the capital account. For instance, the authorities manage or control inward and outward portfolio flows through quotas. Schemes like the Qualified Foreign Institutional Investors (QFII) and Renminbi Qualified Foreign Institutional

* Sarah CHAN is a Research Fellow at the East Asian Institute, National University of Singapore.

Investors (RQFII) are subject to lock-in periods and ceilings. Similarly, the Qualified Domestic Institutional Investors (QDII) investing overseas are subject to investment quotas. All cross-border issuance of securities and foreign borrowing require approvals.

Compared with the more volatile portfolio flows, the authorities have liberalised longer term and more stable flows like Foreign Direct Investment (FDI) given their preference for such type of capital to facilitate economic development. Further, to maintain some control over the outflow of capital, policymakers have traditionally granted more freedom to official and institutional investors (such as China's state-owned enterprises) to undertake capital account transactions, compared to other types of investors such as non-financial corporations.

China's cautious approach to capital account liberalisation stems from the fact that convertibility for capital account transactions can be a double-edged sword for developing economies. Liberalising the capital account improves capital allocation efficiency and helps foster financial development, which in turn stimulate economic growth. However, an open capital account can precipitate capital in(out)flows that can be destabilising to the economy. Empirical studies and country experiences have shown that premature liberalisation of the capital account could adversely affect economic development. In Chile and Thailand, for instance, the opening of capital accounts had led to exchange rate and banking crises. These two cases suggest that certain preconditions — a stable macroeconomic environment, a sound banking system and developed financial markets — are perhaps necessary before a country makes its currency convertible for capital account transactions.

Liberalisation with "Chinese Characteristics"

China has gradually opened up its capital account, but there remain considerable restrictions on capital flows. According to the International Monetary Fund (IMF) Annual Report on Exchange Arrangements and Exchange Restrictions, as of 2016, China had restrictions of some sort

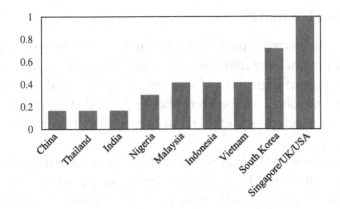

Figure 1:   Chinn-Ito Financial Openness Index
Source: http://web.pdx.edu/~ito/Chinn-Ito_website.htm.

in 14 out of 15 categories of capital transactions. The only ones China does not restrict are inflows and outflows of commercial credit.[1]

The Chinn-Ito index, a measure of capital account openness of 181 countries in the world with a scale of 0 (completely closed capital account) to 1 (completely open capital account), shows that China's capital account (with an index of only 0.165) was quite closed in 2015, the latest update available at the time of writing. In fact, it appears that China's capital account is even more closed than Nigeria and remains more closed than other economies (like Vietnam) at a similar level of development (Figure 1).[2]

In China, the different types of private capital flows — direct, portfolio, investment and other — have been liberalised at different rates, reflecting the authorities' measured and sequenced approach in managing the capital account.

---

[1] Latest online data available, IMF AREAER, 2016, at https://www.imf.org/en/Publications/Annual-Report-on-Exchange-Arrangements-and-Exchange-Restrictions/Issues/2017/01/25/Annual-Report-on-Exchange-Arrangements-and-Exchange-Restrictions-2016-43741.
[2] Similarly, China has a low level of integration with the global financial system (as measured by the sum of its external assets and liabilities as a share of GDP) given its per capita income.

(i) Direct investment

FDI has dominated capital inflows to China, in part due to such flows being subject to fewer restrictions than other forms of capital flows. The expectations of high rates of investment (given rapid productivity growth) and China's accession to the World Trade Organisation have led to an acceleration of FDI inflows in the aftermath of 2001 (Figure 2).

Chinese outward direct investment has been considerably smaller than FDI in China (Figure 2), amounting on average to only 1% of GDP over the past decade or so. However, it has been increasing in recent years, largely reflecting outward investment by Chinese firms to expand overseas to acquire natural resources and seek new markets. In the last three years or so, net FDI flows have become more balanced; FDI inflows were historically larger, but these have gradually slowed due to a rise in labour costs in mainland China. In addition, concerns about a weaker RMB coupled with a slower rate of return on investment (as a result of overinvestment and industrial overcapacity) in China have also led to the repatriation of FDI profits.

At the same time, outward FDI has also picked up but moderated in 2017 (refer to Figure 2) as the authorities tightened surveillance of outbound FDI deals given the "irrational" or speculative investments by Chinese companies in sectors outside their core areas of business. Concerns about domestic financial stability risks were heightened, given that some private Chinese companies had financed overseas acquisitions using debt. Investment in sectors such as real estate, entertainment and tourism was formally restricted, while outward FDI in sectors tied to China's strategic goals was encouraged (such as natural resources, advanced manufacturing and investment related to the Belt and Road Initiative).

(ii) Banking-related flows

While historically smaller than FDI, banking-related flows have become an increasingly important component of China's capital account in recent years. This has particularly been the case since the

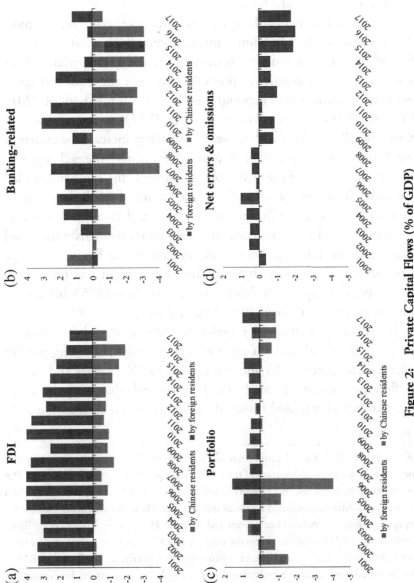

Figure 2: Private Capital Flows (% of GDP)

authorities took steps to internationalise the RMB from around 2010.[3] Banking-related flows comprise mainly loans, currency and deposits, as well as trade credit and advances.

Figure 2 shows that banking-related flows have accounted for most of the recent variation in China's private capital flows. Compared with FDI which can have long investment horizons, banking-related flows tend to be more responsive to prevailing market conditions and sentiment, such as changes in expectations about the future path of RMB. The start of the People's Bank of China's (PBOC) rate cut cycle in November 2014, along with moves to ostensibly increase the exchange rate flexibility in August 2015 with the adjustment of the exchange rate regime (i.e. reform of the RMB central parity fixing mechanism), led to sizeable banking-related outflows. As a result of RMB depreciation expectations, many Chinese entities repaid foreign currency-denominated debt (i.e. reduced their foreign currency liabilities) and increased forex (FX) deposits in order to reduce their foreign exchange exposure. Such corporate balance sheet adjustment was one of the drivers behind capital outflows (approximately US$655 billion) in the seven quarters between 2014Q3 and 2016Q1.

The volatility of the foreign exchange and equity markets tempered the pace of capital account reforms significantly. Following market volatility in August 2015 and the decline in FX reserves and capital outflows, the PBOC decided to tighten controls that were already in place as well as imposed some additional controls, such as the 20%

---

[3] Before 2010, RMB-related activities in the offshore market were quite limited, often contributing to a marked deviation of the CNH exchange rate from that of the CNY. The two exchange rates became more closely linked after a series of developments in late 2010 boosted the RMB-denominated financial transactions. These developments include the approval granted to financial institutions and banks in Hong Kong (HK) to open RMB accounts and for HK banks to access the onshore interbank market, activation of a swap line between the PBOC and the HK Monetary Authority, and a flurry of RMB-denominated bond issuance activities. Eswar Prasad, "China's efforts to expand the international use of the Renminbi", report prepared for the US–China Economic and Security Review Commission, February 2016, at <https://www.brookings.edu/wp-content/uploads/2016/07/RMBReportFinal.pdf> (accessed 8 August 2018).

unremunerated reserve requirement. Tighter restrictions were also placed on overseas cash withdrawals, along with greater scrutiny over foreign currency purchases and cross-border RMB transfers.[4] In 2017, as expectations for RMB depreciation moderated and capital outflows abated, the government abolished the rule to reserve a 20% deposit on forward sales of foreign exchange that was initially established in 2015 to curb outflows and stabilise the yuan.

(iii) Portfolio flows

To date, portfolio flows have been a much smaller component of China's capital account than direct investment and banking-related flows, reflecting various controls on both debt and equity flows.[5] In particular, portfolio investors must use various schemes that are all subject to quotas. The QFII program, for instance, allows authorised foreign institutions to invest in China's onshore capital markets, subject to an allocated quota. This scheme was broadened in 2011 when authorities launched a related scheme that allows licensed foreign institutions to invest in mainland China using offshore RMB funds. Outward portfolio investment — for foreign securities purchased by residents — is channelled through QDII, subject to institution-specific ceilings.

Between 2014 and 2016 when RMB depreciation expectations were pronounced, the pace of China's capital account liberalisation slowed as the government stopped issuing new quotas for schemes that allow Chinese residents to purchase overseas debt and equity. In contrast, schemes that allow foreigners to invest in China were relaxed and the quota for individual institutions to invest under the QFII program was

---

[4] The PBOC required stricter monitoring of foreign exchange transfers and prohibited companies from repaying loans borrowed overseas in advance of the contractual due date. Further, there were tighter transaction limits on overseas withdrawals using UnionPay cards and purchases of savings-like insurance products abroad.

[5] IMF data on international investment position suggest that China's openness to portfolio investment is still low. Portfolio investment inflows (liabilities) and outflows (assets) were both below 5% of GDP in 2017, indicating extensive restrictions on such transactions.

loosened in February 2016 and the minimum investment period was reduced from one year to three months.[6]

(iv) Others/net errors and omissions

A large channel of capital outflows captured within the "residual component" is manifested in the "net errors and omission" (NEO), which by definition, is a residual term that arises when the total of the officially recorded entries in the current account and that in the capital and financial accounts do not match up. Theoretically, this should be zero on average, but in China's case, it has been growing more negative in recent years (Figure 2), reflecting capital outflows due to changing expectations in the value of the RMB exchange rate against the US dollar.

Controlled Capital Account Liberalisation

There seems to be greater scope for future reforms to focus on further opening up portfolio investment, which is the most restricted component of the capital account. If the authorities considerably ease restrictions on portfolio flows, the amount of capital that would enter and leave China could be huge.

On the inbound side, easier access to onshore Chinese assets will bring portfolio inflows although the current lack of depth and liquidity in RMB assets will continue to act as a constraint. The inclusion of Chinese-listed A shares in MSCI's Emerging Markets Index in June 2018 is expected to lead to modest capital inflows even though it is a symbolic step in China's capital account opening. In the near term, capital inflows are likely to be relatively less than outflows due to concerns about transparency and regulatory interference and restrictive capital controls.

---

[6] Reserve Bank of Australia, "Trends in China's Capital Account", *RBA Bulletin*, 1 June 2018.

As China's capital controls have traditionally focused more on preventing outflows than inflows, the relaxation of controls will likely initially lead to more net outflows, as domestic residents seek to diversify their assets offshore. Previous studies[7] estimated that if China's capital account were to be fully opened, gross portfolio outflows from China could be as high as 15–25% of Chinese GDP over five years in the event of China's liberalisation of the capital account. He *et al.* (2012)[8] found similar results, estimating that net capital outflows would occur following capital account liberalisation in China.

Large capital flows would imply closer links between Chinese and global financial markets. However, as pointed out by the former PBOC Governor Zhou Xiaochuan, China's goal is not a fully open capital account with the ability to freely convert the renminbi into other currencies and invest abroad. "The capital account convertibility China is seeking to achieve is not based on the traditional concept of being full or freely convertible … China will adopt a concept of managed convertibility."[9]

The pilot Shanghai Free-Trade Zone (SFTZ), for instance, highlights that the experiment zones for onshore RMB convertibility and capital account liberalisation in no way suggest a *laissez-faire* approach to liberalising the capital account but rather a 'managed' approach to capital account convertibility. Established in 2013, the SFTZ was intended as a sort of stress test to see how Chinese financial enterprises would function in a market with freely convertible currencies and

---

[7] Bayoumi T and F Ohnsorge, "Do inflows or outflows dominate? Global Implications of Capital Account Liberalisation in China", *IMF Working Paper No. WP/13/189*, 2013.

[8] He Dong, Lillian Cheung, Zhang Wenlang and Tommy Wu, "How Would Capital Account Liberalization Affect China's Capital Flows and the Renminbi Real Exchange Rates?", *China and the World Economy*, vol. 20, no. 6, 2012, pp. 29–54.

[9] PBOC Governor Zhou Xiaochuan made the point at a meeting of the International Monetary and Financial Committee in April 2015. According to Zhou, even after achieving Renminbi convertibility, China will continue to manage capital account transactions including the use of macroprudential measures to limit risks arising from cross-border capital flows.

liberalised interest rates. The SFTZ initially generated a lot of excitement as it was perceived as a step towards deeper structural change. However, the promises of external liberalisation via the SFTZ — notably the liberalisation of capital outflows for institutional investors and the liberalisation of intrafirm, cross-border corporate financing — have not come to fruition.[10] PBOC's mandate to protect financial exchange rate stability puts it in a conflicting position to support external liberalisation — it did not help when PBOC officials were particularly concerned with managing the downward pressure on the RMB amid capital outflows in 2015. Subsequently in early 2016, the central government downgraded its policy priority of RMB convertibility.

The stock connect schemes (Shanghai–Hong Kong (HK) Stock Connect and Shenzhen–Hong Kong Stock Connect) are also an alternative approach to control the process of capital account liberalisation by allowing cross-border equity investment by a broad range of investors. Key characteristics common to both the schemes are the ban on arbitrage activity,[11] their closed-loop design and the exclusive use of offshore RMB liquidity for funding the trading under the schemes.[12] For instance, the regulatory requirement that all foreign exchange trades for settling the Stock Connect trades must be done in HK using only its offshore RMB funds clearly shows that Beijing still wants to keep the onshore market segregated from the offshore (HK) market in order to shield the onshore stock market from volatility, using only offshore RMB liquidity to support such schemes.[13] Such a closed-loop

---

[10] Domenico Lombardi and Anton Malkin, "Domestic Politics and External Financial Liberalisation in China: The Capacity and Fragility of External Market Pressure", *Journal of Contemporary China*, vol. 26, no. 108, June 2017.

[11] No price arbitrage is allowed for the interlisted stocks between HK and China's stock exchanges. The sales proceeds must return to their home market bank accounts and not be used for other purposes, such as purchasing other asset classes or goods and services, in the destination market.

[12] Chi Lo, *Demystifying China's Mega Trends: The Driving Forces That Will Shake Up China and the World*, UK, Emerald Publishing, 2017.

[13] *Ibid.*

mechanism does not really allow free capital flows in and out of the country, and essentially, it only extends the boundary of capital controls over the mainland Chinese capital to HK.[14]

Substantial obstacles will impede significant further capital account liberalisation. In many academic studies, several researchers have explored the preconditions for "safe" capital account liberalisation and have concluded that they are not yet fulfilled in China. The preconditions for successful capital account liberalisation are generally a stable macroeconomic environment, a sound banking system and developed financial markets (including a sufficiently large debt market).[15] Interest rate liberalisation and exchange rate flexibility are also prerequisites for capital account convertibility.[16]

There is general consensus that China faces significant challenges in moving towards a substantially more liberalised capital account. First is the state of the domestic banking system. When a country's banking system is perceived as weak, opening the capital account can accelerate capital outflows as depositors shift funds to other banks perceived to be relatively safe. If sufficiently large, these outflows, in turn, can lead to a sharp decline in the value of the domestic currency and create currency mismatches. Firms and individuals with foreign currency-denominated

---

[14] Chinese investors who buy HK shares must sell the shares back in the HK market. Similarly, HK and international investors who buy Chinese shares in Shanghai and Shenzhen must sell the shares back in the respective Chinese stock exchanges. Such schemes are only baby steps towards liberalizing the China's capital account due to its closed-loop design.

[15] Barry Eichengreen, Rachita Gullapalli and Ugo Panizza, "Capital Account Liberalization, Financial Development and Industry Growth: A Synthetic View", at https://pdfs. semanticscholar.org/5663/60f3410b02726a7962c1011760fa7b9af376.pdf (accessed 3 August 2018).

[16] Refer to studies by Nicholas Lardy and Patrick Douglass, "Capital Account Liberalization and the Role of the Renminbi", Working Paper 11–6, Washington, DC, Peterson Institute for International Economics, 2011. Eswar S Prasad, Qing Wang and Thomas Rumbaugh, *Putting the Cart before the Horse? Capital Account Liberalization and Exchange Rate Flexibility in China*, IMF Policy Discussion Paper No. 05/1, 2005, at https://www.imf. org/en/Publications/IMF-Policy-Discussion-Papers/Issues/2016/12/31/Putting-the-Cart-Before-the-Horse-Capital-Account-Liberalization-and-Exchange-Rate-17967 (accessed 16 August 2018).

debts will likely experience a sharp increase in the burden of servicing their loans, potentially leading to a financial crisis.

In a distorted domestic financial system with interest rate regulations and credit controls that lack sufficient supervision, opening of the capital account will lead to capital flight. It is essential to gradually reduce and finally eliminate financial repression prior to liberalising the capital account, otherwise depositors, particularly households, may shift their funds out of the domestic banking system, potentially creating a liquidity crisis for the banking system.[17] In the long run, interest rate liberalisation is therefore essential to the strengthening of China's banking system.[18] As long as banks operate in a highly cosseted interest rate environment, competition in the banking system will remain limited and banks will have insufficient ability and incentive to price risk appropriately and operate on a commercial basis.[19]

Second is the underdevelopment of China's financial system. Local debt markets are lacking in depth and liquidity, and this makes it difficult for the country to ease restrictions on capital flows since it will not be easy for the economy to absorb large capital inflows without creating asset bubbles. While China has a significant market for government bonds, the local market in corporate debt is not well developed. The magnitude of funds raised through the corporate debt market is small, especially when measured against the funding provided

---

[17] Nicholas Lardy and Patrick Douglass, "Capital Account Liberalization and the Role of the Renminbi", *Working Paper 11–6*, Washington, DC, Peterson Institute for International Economics, February 2011.

[18] Interest rates have yet to be genuinely liberalised, despite the scrapping of all the lending and deposit interest rate ceilings and floors by 2015. Some senior Chinese officials believe that China is not ready for the free-market interest rate because the soft budget constraints that local governments and SOEs are still enjoying have made market interest rates irrelevant. Retaining the benchmark lending rates mutes the effects of interest rate liberalisation and is representative of the hidden interest rate controls. Chi Lo, "The 'Debt Bomb' and Deleveraging Dilemma", in *Demystifying China's Mega Trends: The Driving Forces That Will Shake Up China and the World*.

[19] Nicholas Lardy and Patrick Douglass, "Capital Account Liberalization and the Role of the Renminbi".

to the corporate sector through the banking system. Moreover, issuance is dominated by a handful of large state-owned institutions, notably China Railway and major banks.

Greater exchange rate flexibility is also an essential precondition to moving toward further liberalisation of the capital account. Along with the authorities' efforts to internationalise the RMB now that the currency has been included in the IMF SDR basket, China will have to move to greater exchange rate flexibility if it were to maintain an independent monetary policy, given the constraints posed by the Impossible Trinity.[20]

Implications for Further Liberalisation

Capital account liberalisation can provide numerous benefits for an economy in terms of greater financial integration, more efficiency in the use of capital and diversification of its assets. But there are also risks associated with the transition to a more open capital account. China's gradual and controlled approach to liberalising capital flows has reflected its attempt to balance these considerations.

Efforts to liberalise the capital account (refer to Appendix) are likely to be carefully calibrated and aimed at mitigating excessive fluctuations in the RMB exchange rate, especially as China continues to grapple with financial vulnerabilities such as risks in its domestic financial system. Domestic factors could influence the momentum in financial liberalisation and capital market opening. The high level of corporate debt (163% of GDP), for instance, adds uncertainties to the outlook of China's financial sector and heightened macrofinancial risk. Currently, China is pushing forward with deleveraging efforts to tackle its mounting corporate debt and tightening regulations on banks' shadow banking activities. If the deleveraging process proceeds smoothly, financial liberalisation could accelerate. However, if deleveraging turns disorderly and leads to a situation of severe credit crunch that

---

[20] Sarah Chan, "Policy Challenges in Maintaining Renminbi Stability in China", *Asian Survey*, vol. 57, no. 2, March/April 2017.

results in rising loan defaults that in turn affect banks' balance sheets, the authorities may likely slow down the process of financial and capital market liberalisation.

China has lately signalled its intent to accelerate financial market opening for foreign participation. At the Boao Forum in April 2018, some measures were announced that include removing the long standing 20% limit on foreign participation in Chinese banks by a single entity (and 25% if joint entities) with immediate effect. In addition, foreign investors will have majority ownership (up to 51%) in securities, fund management and futures companies (vs 49% previously), with investment caps removed in three years. Further, foreign insurance companies do not need to have a representative office in China for two consecutive years prior to establishing a fully owned institution. Although these measures may have been announced to diffuse the tension with the United States in the current China–US trade tussle, they came at a time when China faces less capital outflows and currency depreciation pressures compared to the 2014–2016 period. These show the government's

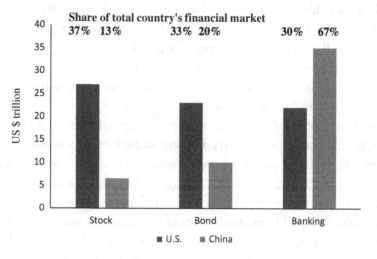

Figure 3: Financial Market Comparison between China and the United States, 2016

Source: Citibank.

managed and calibrated approach to liberalise the capital account in accordance with China's economic and financial situation.

Understandably, liberalising the capital account will inevitably make the task of macroeconomic management more challenging. Full RMB internationalisation entails capital market opening which may exert pressure on the domestic financial system if financial markets are not well developed. Capital markets will need to deepen alongside the supervisory and financial sector regulatory framework to safeguard financial stability. China's financial market remains relatively undeveloped compared to developed economies like the United States (Figure 3), but there remains scope for further financial market deepening.

The process of capital account liberalisation will bring tremendous policy challenges as the "Impossible Trinity" that comes with capital account convertibility will push China to confront the dilemma between monetary autonomy and exchange rate control. The exchange rate should be relatively flexible to allow the use of an independent monetary policy to manage the economy. However, freeing up the exchange rate could result in increased volatility of the currency, which can be detrimental to the economy. The pace at which China pushes ahead with financial reform will have implications for its own economy and financial system, and inevitably on rest of the world.

Appendix: Gradual Opening Up of China's Capital Markets

Year	Program	Recent Developments
2002	QFII	Opening up China's A-share market to foreign investors for the first time. As of end May 2018, 287 overseas institutions had received quotas amounting to a total of US$100 billion under the program.
2011	RQFII	RMB version of QFII officially announced, allowing onshore securities to be traded. Till end 2017, there have been 18 countries or regions that received the RQFII quota, with the total amount of 1.74 trillion renminbi, 76.6 billion renminbi increasing from the year 2016.

(Continued)

Appendix: (*Continued*)

Year	Program	Recent Developments
	QFII/RQFII	To further simplify management, facilitate operations and further expand opening up, the Central Bank of China and SAFE recently released a new round of foreign exchange management reforms on 12 June 2018.
		The reform measures are mainly concentrated on three aspects:
		1. First, the 20% cap of QFII monthly fund remittance is lifted;
		2. Second, the QFII and RQFII principal lock-in period requirements are removed so that QFII and RQFII can remit the principal according to the investment;
		3. Third, the authorities allow QFII and RQFII investors to hedge their exchange rate risks to its domestic investment.
		The new policies regarding QFII and RQFII have eased the main concerns of foreign investors in participating in these programs. Meanwhile, allowing QFII and RQFII to conduct FX hedging in China's domestic market can also help expand the onshore FX market. The move is seen as a critical step in the opening up of China's capital market and helping promote RMB internationalisation, as well as the development of both Shanghai as a global financial centre, and HK as an offshore RMB hub and destination for mainland investors.
2014	Shanghai–HK Stock Connect	Launched in late 2014 to allow two-way equity flows between China and HK.
2015	China Interbank Bond Market ("CIBM") Direct Access scheme	China opened its interbank bond market and onshore foreign exchange market to foreign institutional investors such as central banks, sovereign wealth funds and selected global financial organisations such as the IMF and the World Bank. Opening the interbank bond market to foreign institutional investors is a further step towards developing the bond market and broadening participation in capital markets. China–HK Mutual Recognition of Funds scheme was also launched in July 2015. In September 2015, China scrapped quotas for Chinese firms to raise funds in overseas bond and loan markets.

(*Continued*)

Appendix: (*Continued*)

Year	Program	Recent Developments
2016	Shenzhen–HK Stock Connect	Under such schemes, investors in each market are able to trade shares in the other market using their local brokers and clearing houses.
2017	Inclusion of A-shares into MSCI's Emerging Markets Index	In June 2018, more than 230 A-shares were included in the emerging markets index.
2018	QDLP, QDIE	The Qualified Domestic Limited Partnership (QDLP) program was launched in Shanghai in 2012 and the Qualified Domestic Investment Enterprise (QDIE) program in Shenzhen in 2014 to actively support domestic firms to conduct various types of outbound investments, including investments in offshore securities, hedge funds, private equity funds, real estate funds and other types of investments. The QDLP scheme was unofficially suspended when China tightened capital controls amid turmoil in its stock and currency markets since late 2015. Since early 2018, the SAFE has steadily advanced the QDLP and QDIE programs on a pilot basis in Shanghai and Shenzhen, respectively. Under these programs, the investors in these two cities are allowed to make overseas investments with a quota of US$5 billion each.

Source: BBVA Research.

Chapter 5

Implementing Competition Policy in China

QIAN Jiwei*

Introduction

In July 2018, the United States telecommunication firm Qualcomm dropped a US$44 billion bid for NXP Semiconductors, a Netherland-based company. One major reason why Qualcomm dropped the deal was that the merger failed to receive the approval from China's competition policy authority, State Administration for Market Regulation (SAMR),[1] while it had been approved by seven other jurisdictions including the United States, Japan and the European Union.

Competition policy is an indispensable part of a regulatory framework to address market imperfections and ensure effective and fair market competition. Currently, more than 100 countries have adopted the competition law.

Based on economic size, China is now one of the major jurisdictions for competition law in the world. Since the 1980s, the government has recognised the negative effects of monopolistic behaviour and promulgated a series of laws and regulations to address the problem.

---

* QIAN Jiwei is a Senior Research Fellow at the East Asian Institute, National University of Singapore.
[1] See <https://www.reuters.com/article/us-nxp-semicondtrs-m-a-qualcomm/china-keeps-qualcomm-guessing-on-nxp-fate-as-bid-enters-final-hours-idUSKBN1KF193> (accessed 26 September 2018).

These include the Anti-Unfair Competition Law (AUCL) and price law, among others.

The Anti-Monopoly Law (AML), the core of competition policy, has been introduced since 2008 in China to correct market imperfections and protect consumers' interests. The AML draws elements from both the United States and the European Union competition laws though it is more closely associated with the European Union model.[2] It may also be reflective of the political and economic conditions in China.[3] In the AML, monopolistic behaviours including collusive agreement, vertical restrictions, abuse of market dominance and administrative monopoly have been defined, and sanctions for corresponding behaviours specified.

Between the release of the AML in 2008 and 2018, the enforcement of AML came under three major government agencies. The National Development and Reform Commission (NDRC) takes charge of collusive agreements involving pricing decisions and price-related abuse of a dominant position. It is also responsible for all price-related issues and the enforcer of the price law.

The State Administration for Industry and Commerce (SAIC) oversaw non-price-related abuse of a dominant position and collusive agreements involving non-price coordination. The Ministry of Commerce (MOFCOM) administered merger control provisions and has long been responsible for the policy domain of foreign businesses.

The AML enforcement has significant achievements. It was reported that 163 cases of market collusive agreements and 54 cases of abusing market dominance have been adjudicated between 2008 and 2018.[4] The amount of fine on firms violating AML in these ten years has

---

[2] US–China Business Council, *Competition policy and enforcement in China*, 2014.

[3] H. Stephen Harris *et al.*, *Anti-monopoly Law and Practice in China*, Oxford University Press, 2011.

[4] See <http://politics.people.com.cn/n1/2018/0802/c1001-30191667.html> (accessed 29 September 2018).

reached 11 billion renminbi.[5] In the same period, 183 cases of administrative monopoly and 2,283 merger review have been adjudicated.[6]

However, there were a few concerns in AML enforcement. First, staff capacity of these government agencies in enforcing AML was low. There had also been a shortage of expertise in the government agencies responsible for enforcing AML.

Second, there is a conflict of interest in the implementation of industrial policy and competition policy. Promoting domestic and State-Owned Enterprises (SOEs) as one of the objectives of industrial policy in China is in conflict with the competition policy. It is observed that the AML enforcement toward SOEs is not very effective.[7]

Third, another concern is that there is a lack of transparency in the process of the AML enforcement. In particular, there are no explanations provided from MOFCOM as to why those M&A cases (i.e. over 2,000 cases) have been approved.

Fourth, fragmentation in enforcing the AML may lead to coordination problems. For example, as some cases are related to both price and non-price issues, coordination problems among the three government enforcement agencies may arise.

To address the above issues, three major policies have been initiated by the government. First, complementary to the AML, in June 2016, the Chinese government initiated an *ex ante* administrative procedure (公平竞争审查制度). All government departments need to comply with the fair competition requirements for proposed regulations and policies.[8]

---

[5] See <http://politics.people.com.cn/n1/2018/0802/c1001-30191667.html> (accessed 29 September 2018).

[6] See <http://politics.people.com.cn/n1/2018/0802/c1001-30191667.html> (accessed 29 September 2018).

[7] See B. J. Naughton, *The Chinese Economy: Adaptation and Growth*, MIT Press, 2018, p. 387. Also, W. Ng, *The Political Economy of Competition Law in China*, Cambridge University Press, 2018, pp. 8–9.

[8] See <http://www.xinhuanet.com/legal/2018-01/05/c_129783744.htm> (accessed 3 November 2018).

Second, since March 2018, SAMR has been established as the single government agency responsible for enforcing the AML.[9] Bureaus under NDRC, MOFCOM and SAIC responsible for enforcing AML have been merged into SAMR to enhance the capacity.

Third, in October 2018, the principle "Competitive Neutrality" (竞争中立), which is promoted by OECD to address how to manage the SOEs, was highlighted by the Governor of People's Bank of China, Yi Gang, in a speech at an international conference. According to a recent official report, the principle of "Competitive Neutrality" will be used by SAMR based on the AML, and SOEs are expected to be treated equally with enterprises in other ownerships.[10]

However, there are some remaining issues in enforcing competition law. First, how to enforce the "competitive neutrality" is still an issue. Second, the division of labour between the central- and local-level enforcers is another concern. Third, how to enforce AML for the cases of administrative monopoly is still a problem. Fourth, the compliance of domestic firms in competition law when they invest in other countries is another concern. Fifth, how to enforce the competition law in the age of the internet economy is a new challenge.

Monopoly as Market Imperfection in China

Monopoly has given rise to the soaring prices of consumer products.[11] Firms largely profit by creating and strengthening a monopolistic position in the market. Monopoly can take advantage of market

---

[9] See <http://www.gov.cn/zhengce/2018-08/02/content_5311172.htm> (accessed 29 September 2018).

[10] See <http://www.chinanews.com/wap/detail/zw/gn/2018/11-06/8669434.shtml> (accessed 12 November 2018).

[11] Price setting in the context of natural monopoly could be a different case. For example, in some industries such as public utility, a single firm can serve an entire market at a lower cost than multiple firms could.

power[12] and reduce the competitiveness of the market by its anti-competitive actions such as collusive agreements, anti-competitive mergers and exclusionary tactics.

Monopoly results not only in higher prices but also in less choices for consumers, lower output, and slower innovation and economic growth.[13] In the short term, monopolies survive due to high prices and not efficiency. In the long term, monopolies have no incentive to innovate and improve. Social welfare is also compromised. Market mechanisms cannot regulate monopoly. Government regulation is necessary to keep the market competitive and efficient.

In China, two major effects of monopoly can be felt. First, it jacks up consumer prices. For example, in the pharmaceutical sector, the prices of imported drugs with expired patents in China can be as high as 5–10 times that of generic drugs produced and sold in India.[14]

Monopoly is also associated with less innovation and slower economic growth. A recent research shows that in China, productivity of a sector with a more intensive competition is more likely to improve productivity.[15]

An issue which is unique to China is the abuse of administrative power, which impacts negatively on consumers' welfare and China's economic growth to create or increase market power[16] (i.e. administrative monopoly). Administrative monopoly takes the form of regional

---

[12] Market power refers to the case of the producer pricing above the marginal cost. See Tirole, *The Theory of Industrial Organization*, MIT Press, 1988, p. 284.

[13] M. Motta, *Competition Policy: Theory and Practice*, Cambridge University Press, 2004. See also D. A. Crane, *Rationales for Antitrust: The Oxford Handbook of International Antitrust Economics*, 2014, pp. 3–16.

[14] See <http://sc.people.com.cn/n2/2018/0704/c345167-31775063.html> (accessed 12 November 2018).

[15] Aghion, Philippe, Jing Cai, Mathias Dewatripont, Luosha Du, Ann Harrison and Patrick Legros, "Industrial Policy and Competition", *American Economic Journal: Macroeconomics*, vol. 7, no. 4, 2015, pp. 1–32.

[16] J. J. Laffont, *Regulation and Development*, Cambridge University Press, 2005, p. 37.

monopoly (local protectionism),[17] sector monopoly (i.e. restriction of market access to certain sector) and compulsory trading.[18]

Regional monopoly restricts market access of external goods and services. In many cases, it is the local governments that create entry barriers which will segmentalise the market. Local protectionism is a major obstacle for an integrated national market in China.[19]

Sector monopoly refers to the case in which "industrial sector administrations abuse their powers by eliminating or restricting competition".[20] Compulsory trading occurs when "consumers are forced to purchase goods or services that are provided by designated operators".[21]

Development of Competition Policy in China

Competition policy refers to the "government policy to preserve or promote competition among market players and to promote other government policies and processes that enable a competitive environment to develop".[22] Competition law is the major policy instrument for

---

[17] C. Xu, "The Fundamental Institutions of China's Reforms and Development", *Journal of Economic Literature*, vol. 49, no. 4, 2011, pp. 1076–1151. Also, see C. E. Bai, Y. Du, Z. Tao and S. Y. Tong, "Local Protectionism and Regional Specialization: Evidence from China's Industries", *Journal of International Economics*, vol. 63, no. 2, 2004, pp. 397–417. Also, see a recent study by C. X. Long and J. Wang, "Judicial Local Protectionism in China: An Empirical Study of IP Cases", *International Review of Law and Economics*, vol. 42, 2015, pp. 48–55.

[18] C. Wu and Z. Liu, "A Tiger without Teeth? Regulation of Administrative Monopoly under China's Anti-Monopoly Law", *Review of Industrial Organization*, vol. 41, no. 1–2, 2012, pp. 133–155. Also, see W. Ng, *The Political Economy of Competition Law in China*, p. 91.

[19] Alwyn Young, "The Razor's Edge: Distortions and Incremental Reform in the People's Republic of China", *Quarterly Journal of Economics*, vol. 115, no. 4, 2000, pp. 1091–1135.

[20] C. Wu and Z. Liu, "A Tiger without Teeth? Regulation of Administrative Monopoly under China's Anti-Monopoly Law", pp. 133–155.

[21] *Ibid.*

[22] UNCTAD, "The Relationship between Competition and Industrial Policies in Promoting Economic Development", 2009.

implementing the competition policy,[23] and more than 100 countries have adopted it.[24]

According to Motta (2004), the competition policy[25] is to protect consumers' welfare and smaller firms from abuses of the dominance of monopoly and promote market integration. Economic analysis to assess the impacts of monopoly on consumers' welfare level is thus necessary.

Table 1 shows the development of competition law in China. The first competition law in China was released in 1980 by the State Council,[26] eliminating regional and ministerial blockade.

Table 1: Development of Competition Laws in China

Competition Laws	Year	Main Emphases	Institution Enacting the Law
A regulation about promoting socialism competition[27]	1980	Addressing regional and ministerial blockade	State Council
AUCL[28]	1993	Prohibiting administrative monopoly, below cost sales, tying and bid rigging	National People's Congress
Price law[29]	1997	Prohibiting collusion for price fixing	National People's Congress

Source: Compiled by the author.

---

[23] Ibid.

[24] A. Heimler and K. Mehta, "Monopolization in Developing Countries", in The Oxford Handbook of International Antitrust Economics, ed. R. D. Blair and D. D. Sokol, vol. 2, Oxford University Press, 2014.

[25] M. Motta, Competition Policy: Theory and Practice.

[26] Guowuyuan Guanyu Kaizhan He Baohu Shehui Zhuui Jingzheng de Zanxing Guiding, <http://finance.sina.com.cn/g/20050418/12411526820.shtml> (accessed 15 November 2018).

[27] See <http://finance.sina.com.cn/g/20050418/12411526820.shtml> (accessed 15 November 2018).

[28] See <http://www.gov.cn/banshi/2005-08/31/content_68766.htm> (accessed 15 November 2018).

[29] See <http://www.gov.cn/banshi/2005-09/12/content_69757.htm> (accessed 15 November 2018).

In 1982, 1990 and 2001, several regulations were released by the central government to address local protectionism.[30] AUCL has been enacted since 1993 to prohibit administrative monopoly, below-cost sales, tying and bid rigging. In 1997, a price law was released, prohibiting "unfair price activities" including collusion in price fixing.

However, in these laws and regulations, anti-monopoly was not the major focus, nor did not incorporate international best practices for anti-monopoly. To fully address the concern for anti-monopoly, a more systematic competition law, AML, has been enacted since 2008. Reportedly, the EU competition law and best practices from other major countries including those of the United States were referenced during the drafting process of the AML.

A systematic competition law, AML, has been enacted since 2008. Reportedly, competition laws in European Union, Germany and best practices from other major countries, including those of the United States, were referenced during the drafting process of the AML.[31]

Table 2 shows major sanctions of the AML. Chapter 2 of the AML prohibits a range of horizontal and vertical anti-competitive agreements on price fixing, output restriction, and market sharing and restrictions on products or technology developments.[32]

Article 14 of the AML prohibits two types of vertical agreements: fixing resale prices and setting minimum resale prices. Fines of between 1% and 10% of firms' turnover in the preceding financial year will be imposed.

The AML prohibits firms from abusing their dominant position to eliminate or restrict competition such as unfair pricing, below-cost sales, refusals to deal, exclusive[33] or designated dealings, tying or

---

[30] C. A. Holz, "No Razor's Edge: Reexamining Alwyn Young's Evidence for Increasing Interprovincial Trade Barriers in China", *The Review of Economics and Statistics*, vol. 91, no. 3, 2009, pp. 599–616.

[31] W. Ng, *The Political Economy of Competition Law in China*, p. 4.

[32] See <http://www.gov.cn/flfg/2007-08/30/content_732591.htm> (accessed 12 November 2018).

[33] Exclusive behaviour is defined as practices that a firm might undertake to deny a rival access to a market. See D. Bernheim and Randall Heeb, "A Framework for the Economic

Table 2: Sanctions For Monopoly Conduct in AML

Types of Behaviours	Definition	Market Imperfection	Sanction in AML
Collusive agreement	Collusion among firms to set price, output or market segmentation	Higher price/lower output	Penalty between 1% and 10% of firms' turnover in the preceding financial year
"Horizontal" merger	Merger between direct competitors	Market concentration	Prohibited if it is restricting competition
"Vertical" agreement/ integration	Agreement between parties located at different stages of the production and distribution chain	Higher price/market concentration	Penalty between 1% and 10% of firms' turnover in the preceding financial year
Abuse of market domination	Using the dominant position to eliminate or restrict competition	Restriction on market entry/unfair price	Penalty between 1% and 10% of firms' turnover in the preceding financial year
Administrative monopoly	Market power is created by the abuse of administrative power	Higher price/ restriction on market entry to region/sector	Prohibited

Source: Compiled by the author.

imposing other unreasonable transactional terms and discriminatory dealing. Fines of between 1% and 10% of firms' turnover in the preceding financial year can be imposed.

Under Article 20 of the AML, the concept of "concentrations of undertakings" includes mergers, acquisitions of control of other undertakings through purchasing shares or assets, and contract or other means.

Analysis of Exclusionary Conduct", in *Handbook on International Antitrust Economics*, ed. Roger D Blair and D Daniel Sokol, Oxford University Press, 2015.

Under the AML, a concentration of undertakings may be prohibited if it has or is likely to have the effect of eliminating or restricting competition, unless the parties can prove that it will lead to improvements in competition that significantly outweigh its adverse effects on competition, or that the concentration is otherwise in public interest.

Article 8 of the AML generally prohibits the abuse of administrative powers by public authorities to eliminate or restrict competition (i.e. "administrative monopoly").

AML Enforcement

The AML can take the form of public enforcement or private litigation. The structure of the public enforcer is two-tiered (Figure 1). The first tier of the public enforcer is the Anti-Monopoly Commission under the State council. Between 2008 and 2018, the second tier of the public enforcer refers to three anti-monopoly enforcement government departments: NDRC, SAIC and MOFCOM.

The Anti-Monopoly Commission reports directly to the State Council and is responsible for promulgating guidelines and coordinating the work of three anti-monopoly enforcement authorities. The Anti-Monopoly Commission consists of representatives from more than a dozen ministries. When the Anti-Monopoly Commission of

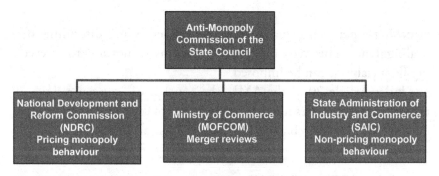

Figure 1: Structure of Anti-Monopoly Agencies (2008–2018)

Source: Compiled by the author.

the State Council was established in 2008, then Vice Premier Wang Qishan was appointed as the Director.

The daily operation of the Commission had been assigned to MOFCOM, and the Commission may consult with external experts including economists in anti-monopoly enforcement.[34]

The Price Supervision and Anti-Monopoly Bureau of the NDRC oversees the provisions in collusive agreements that involve pricing decisions and price-related abuse of a dominant position, while the Anti-Monopoly and Unfair Competition Enforcement Bureau of the SAIC is the supervisory body for non-price-related abuse of a dominant position and collusive agreements involving non-price coordination; MOFCOM is charged with merger control provisions.

The NDRC deals with price fixing and monopoly pricing, while SAIC handles non-price-related abusive use of administrative power to eliminate or restrict competition.[35]

M&A reviews fall under two categories: one based on global turnover and the other on total turnover in China. For the former, transactions must exceed RMB10 billion in the previous fiscal year and each of at least two of the parties should have a turnover exceeding RMB400 million in China in the previous fiscal year. For the latter, the figures should be RMB2 billion and RMB400 million, respectively.

A merger can be approved either conditionally, or unconditionally or prohibited. Two cases have been rejected by MOFCOM since 2009 (i.e. A. P. Møller–Mærsk A/S and MSC Mediterranean Shipping Company and CMA CGM S. A. in 2014, and The Coca-Cola Company and Huiyuan Juice in 2009). The conditions imposed by MOFCOM include divestiture of assets, information firewalls and mandatory licensing (Table 3).

The enforcement involves both central and local enforcers. Both the NDRC and SAIC have local branches that they could delegate

---

[34] See <http://circ.gov.cn/web/site0/tab129/info81837.htm> (accessed 12 November 2018).

[35] C. Wu and Z. Liu, "A Tiger without Teeth? Regulation of Administrative Monopoly under China's Anti-Monopoly Law", pp. 133–155.

Table 3: Two Rejected Cases for M&A Reviews

Case	Year	Sector	Country	Reason of Rejection	Evidences
A. P. Møller–Mærsk A/S, MSC Mediterranean Shipping Company and CMA CGM S. A.	2014	Shipping	Denmark and France	Significantly increased the degree of market concentration and barriers to entry	Market share was reported before and after merger market concentration index was reported
The Coca-Cola Company and Huiyuan Juice	2009	Soft drink	USA and China	Significantly increased the degree of market concentration	No quantitative evidences

Source: Compiled by the author.

authority to different levels of the local governments: local Development and Reform Commission and local Administration for Industry and Commerce.

All three government agencies have passed a number of regulations to complement the implementation of the AML since 2009, significantly improving enforcement since 2013.

The AML also allows a company to opt for litigation against monopolistic behaviours of other companies and government agencies; this has triggered an increase in the number of private litigations since 2008 (Table 4).

The number of litigations has been increased dramatically. In 2008 and 2009, only 10 anti-monopoly cases were accepted by courts in total. In 2017, the figure was 114.

Achievements and Issues of Recent Developments of Competition Policy

Based on the economic size, China is now one of the major jurisdictions for competition law in the world, along with those of the United

Table 4:   Anti-Monopoly: Private Litigation in China

Year	First-Instance Cases Accepted by Courts	First-Instance Cases Adjudicated by Courts
2008–2009	10	6
2010	33	23
2011	18	24
2012	55	49
2013	72	69
2014	86	79
2015	156	116
2016	156	178
2017	114	76
Total	700	620

Source: US–China Business Council, *Competition policy and enforcement in China 2014* and *Chinese IPR Newspaper*, August 24, 2018.

States and the European Union. MOFCOM has reviewed a number of M&A cases among major multinational companies including Bev–Anheuser Busch (2009), Western Digital–Hitachi (2012), Google–Motorola (2012), Marubeni–Gavilon (2013) and Thermo Fisher–Life Technologies (2014).[36]

Competition policy enforcement saw a decline in consumer prices of some sectors. Examples are the fees for automobile aftersales for brands such as Audi and Mercedes-Benz.[37] Price for over 10,000 products of Mercedes-Benz dipped by 15% on average after investigation in 2014.[38] Milk powder brand Wyeth reduced the retail price by 11% on average after the NDRC investigation in 2013.[39]

---

[36] US–China Business Council, *Competition Policy and Enforcement in China.*

[37] See <http://news.163.com/15/0813/13/B0TD7F9B00014AED.html> (accessed 12 November 2018).

[38] See <http://www.time-weekly.com/html/20140807/25956_1.html> (accessed 12 November 2018).

[39] See <http://shipin.people.com.cn/n/2013/0808/c85914-22485692.html> (accessed 12 November 2018).

Competition policy enforcement also witnessed an increase in the use of economic analyses, which are consistent with international best practices,[40] in the enforcement and implementation of the AML. More rigorous economic analyses have been applied in the merger review. For example, in the two rejected M&A cases, MOFCOM applied the rule of reasons to evaluate the impact on market structure by using price change forecast and market concentration (Table 4).

For the merger of Coca-Cola–Huiyuan in 2009, the final report from MOFCOM lacked quantitative evidences. In contrast, for the case of MSC Mediterranean Shipping Company and CMA CGM S. A., MOFCOM reported market shares for all involved parties and calculated the market concentration index (HHI) before and after the merger. MOFCOM finally concluded that the merger between MSC Mediterranean Shipping Company and CMA CGM S A will change the market structure significantly and market competitiveness will be reduced.

Since 2008, there has been a marked increase in the number of cases for M&A review (Table 5). Between 2008 and 2017, 2,036 cases and 1,999 cases were approved unconditionally. Only 35 cases were approved with condition.

By September 2018, SAIC had announced 70 anti-monopoly cases, and 58 cases had been closed.[41] Most of the cases were related to collusion and abuse of market dominance.

There were some famous cases in AML enforcement.[42] For example, in February 2015, a penalty of RMB6 billion, or about 8% of the United States telecommunication firm Qualcomm's 2013 China

---

[40] W. E. Kovacic and C. Shapiro, "Antitrust policy: A Century of Economic and Legal Thinking", *The Journal of Economic Perspectives*, 2000, pp. 43–60.

[41] See <http://home.saic.gov.cn/fldyfbzdjz/jzzfgg/index.html> and <http://m.thepaper.cn/wifiKey_detail.jsp?contid=2424911&from=wifiKey> (accessed 12 November 2018).

[42] In September 2018, 10 most important cases of competition law enforcement in China were announced by the Chinese government. See <http://www.xinhuanet.com/legal/2018-09/06/c_1123391162.htm> (accessed 14 November 2018).

Table 5: M&A Reviews in China (2008–2017)

Year	Total Reviewed	Approved		Rejected
		Unconditionally	Conditionally	
2008	20	19	1	0
2009	71	66	4	1
2010	110	109	1	0
2011	168	164	4	0
2012	164	158	6	0
2013	207	203	4	0
2014	245	240	4	1
2015	312	310	2	0
2016	395	393	2	0
2017	344	337	7	0
Total	2,036	1,999	35	2

Source: *China Commerce Yearbook*, various years.

revenue, was imposed by NDRC for abusing market dominance.[43] It is the heaviest fine imposed under China's AML after its enactment in 2008. Another prominent case is related to the Swiss company Tetra Pak, the world's largest manufacturer of liquid food packaging. In 2016, Tetra Pak was fined USD$96 million for abusing the market dominance by SAIC.[44]

While achievements have been made after the introduction of the AML in 2008, there are several issues in the AML enforcement in the first 10 years of implementation (i.e. 2008–2018). First, staff capacity of these government agencies in enforcing AML was low. After AML

---

[43] See <http://finance.sina.com.cn/chanjing/gsnews/20150317/040421735797.shtml> (accessed 15 November 2018).
[44] See <https://www.competitionpolicyinternational.com/china-tetra-pak-fined-96-million-for-antitrust/> (accessed 13 November 2018).

was enacted, there were about 40 people in SAIC and 35 people in MOFCOM for anti-trust enforcement.[45]

In the early 2010s, at NDRC, there were 150 people on AML enforcement including both central- and local-level officials.[46] In the United States, there are more than 1,100 employees in the Federal Trade Commission, one of the two major agencies working on anti-trust enforcement.

The competition policy enforcement is not very effective with the constraints of human resource. For example, China was the last jurisdiction to approve Google's acquisition of Motorola, which was cleared only on the last day of the review period in China.[47] Similarly for Dell's US$60 billion buyout of EMC in 2016.

Second is the conflict between industrial policy and competition policy. China has launched industrial policies to promote economic growth since the 1980s. While an effective industrial policy requires competitive markets, promoting domestic and SOEs as one of the objectives of industrial policy in China is in conflict with the competition policy.

Since the 2000s, the Chinese government has strengthened its support of big SOEs (dubbed "national champions") through subsidies, protectionism and procurement policies in strategic industries, including automobile and telecommunication.[48] These measures counter the objectives of the competition policy.

The conflict is also evident within the NDRC. NDRC is the major agency for both industrial policymaking and enforcing the competition policy. Under its care, the Industry Coordination Bureau (产业协调司)

---

[45] A. H. Zhang, "Bureaucratic Politics and China's Anti-Monopoly Law", *Cornell International Law Journal*, vol. 47, 2014, p. 671.

[46] A. H. Zhang, "Bureaucratic Politics and China's Anti-Monopoly Law", p. 671.

[47] See <http://www.bloomberg.com/bw/articles/2012-03-21/why-china-is-holding-up-the-google-motorola-deal> and <http://www.theguardian.com/technology/2012/may/21/china-google-approval-motorola-mobility> (accessed 12 November 2018).

[48] T. A. Hemphill and G. O. White, "China's National Champions: The Evolution of a National Industrial Policy — Or a New Era of Economic Protectionism?", *Thunderbird International Business Review*, vol. 55, no. 2, 2013, pp. 193–212.

is tasked with industrial policymaking, while the Price Supervision and Anti-Monopoly Bureau (价格监督检查与反垄断局) is charged with the enforcement of anti-monopoly policies.

In this context, it is observed that the AML enforcement is not effective toward SOEs. Two rejected cases of merger review are transactions related to foreign-owned companies. Also, 35 out of 35 conditionally approved cases of merger review between 2008 and 2017 are related to foreign-owned companies.[49]

Third, another concern is that there is lack of transparency in the process of the AML enforcement. In particular, there are no explanations provided from MOFCOM for all approved M&A cases (i.e. over 2,000 cases). How the decisions have been made by the AML regulators is not very transparent.

Fourth, the coordination among different government departments in enforcing AML may not be effective. For example, price-related cases come under the NDRC and non-price-related cases fall under the jurisdiction of the SAIC. As some cases concern both price and non-price issues, coordination problems among the three government enforcement agencies may arise.

Recent Initiatives in Competition Policy

In recent years, there are several important government initiatives to address concerns. First, in June 2016, the Chinese government initiated an *ex ante* administrative procedure (公平竞争审查制度) to provide a complementary mechanism for the AML.

Based on this procedure, all government departments have to confirm *ex ante* that they have complied with the fair competition requirements defined by AML for proposed regulations and policies related to market entry, domestic trade, industrial development, procurement, project bidding, etc.[50]

---

[49] See <http://opinion.caixin.com/2018-05-03/101242646.html> (accessed 12 November 2018).
[50] See <http://www.xinhuanet.com/legal/2018-01/05/c_129783744.htm> (accessed 3 November 2018).

In October 2017, a detailed guideline for this review process was released by the State Council. It was required that all government departments including central ministries, provincial-level governments as well as other government departments draft action plans to set the details in implementing this review process.

Second, since March 2018, SAMR has been established as the single government agency responsible for enforcing the AML.[51] Bureaus under NDRC, MOFCOM and SAIC responsible for enforcing the AML have been merged into SAMR to enhance the capacity.

With the consolidation of these government departments, the duty of the SAMR focuses on the competition policy enforcement. Also, it is expected that the effectiveness of coordination among different government departments in the enforcement process can be improved.

The Anti-Monopoly Commission of the State Council also now operates under SAMR. In 2018, Wang Yong, the State Councillor was appointed as the Director of the commission.[52]

Third, in October 2018, the principle "Competitive Neutrality" (竞争中立), which is promoted by OECD to address how to manage the SOEs, was highlighted by the Governor of People's Bank of China, Yi Gang, in a speech at an international conference. The principle of "Competitive Neutrality" will be used by SAMR based on the AML and SOEs are expected to be treated equally with enterprises in other ownerships.[53]

However, there are some remaining issues. First, how to implement the principle of "Competitive Neutrality" over SOEs is a concern. Many centrally controlled SOEs (*Yangqi*) usually have vice-ministerial

---

[51] See <http://www.gov.cn/zhengce/2018-08/02/content_5311172.htm> (accessed 29 September 2018).

[52] See <http://www.gov.cn/zhengce/content/2018-07/19/content_5307747.htm> (accessed 12 November 2018).

[53] See <http://www.chinanews.com/wap/detail/zw/gn/2018/11-06/8669434.shtml> (accessed 12 November 2018).

rank even ministerial rank (e.g. China Railway). It is conceivable that there will be difficulties for the competition policy authority to implement the AML in these centrally controlled SOEs.

Second, the division of labour between central and local enforcers could be another issue to be addressed. In principle, the local enforcer has better information/knowledge about the local business environment.

However, currently, in many cases, the local-level regulator can start to investigate an anti-monopoly case only after getting authorization from the central-level regulator (个案授权).[54] This arrangement may not be very effective in enforcing the local-level anti-monopoly cases.

Third is administrative monopoly. Currently, government agencies for enforcing the AML can only suggest the existence of violation, but very rarely was the law enforced. The enforcement capacity for administrative monopoly is doubted given that other government agencies such as the local government are also guilty of administrative monopoly.[55]

Fourth, while it is reported that competition policy enforcement may be biased towards SOEs, SOEs may still need to improve their awareness and compliance for the competition law in other countries when they invest overseas. The amount of money in Chinese acquisitions overseas has increased from US$43.4 billion in 2012 to US$119.6 billion in 2017 (Figure 2).[56] M&A accounts for about 80% of China's outward FDI. However, many M&A proposals could be subject to competition law in the European Union, United States or other OECD countries.[57] Increasing the awareness and promoting the compliance of competition law in other jurisdictions is another concern.

---

[54] See <http://home.saic.gov.cn/fldyfbzdjz/zcfg/xzgz/200910/t20091013_233540.html> (accessed 12 November 2018).

[55] "Xifa Panjue Shouci Dui Xingzhen Longduan Shuobu", *Legal Daily*, 16 February 2015.

[56] Data from Ministry of Commerce, at <http://fec.mofcom.gov.cn/article/tjsj/> (accessed 15 November 2018).

[57] A. H. Zhang, "The Antitrust Paradox of China Inc.", *New York University Journal of International Law and Politics*, vol. 50, 2017, p. 159.

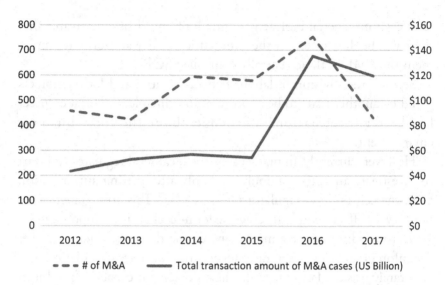

Figure 2: Number of Overseas M&A Transactions and Total Amount of Outward FDI of China

Source: Ministry of Commerce.

Fifth, in general, it is a new challenge to enforce the competition law towards platforms on the internet. Recently, some research has raised the issue that anti-competitive behaviour may not be only justified by the changes of the consumer welfare.[58] With big internet platforms, such as Amazon, Google or Facebook, consumer prices are likely to be lower and consumer welfare could be higher. However, some internet platforms may have structural power to affect a significant share of the economy with a large amount of data. In the Chinese context, the challenge is also very relevant. In particular, the policymaker may need to consider how to address the balance between innovation and anti-competition in the future enforcement of competition law.

---

[58] L. M. Khan, "Amazon's Antitrust Paradox", *Yale Law Journal*, vol. 126, 2016, p. 710.

Part 2

Education, Innovation and New Trend in Development

Chapter 6

Science, Technology and Innovation in China: Progress, Problems and Prospects

CAO Cong*

There are differing, and even conflicting, views on China's role in the global stage of science, technology and innovation (S&TI). On one hand, as this chapter demonstrates, various indicators show that China's S&TI capability has been rising significantly and China will be highly likely to become a world leader in S&TI soon. On the other hand, most recently, ZTE Corporation, China's second largest telecommunications equipment maker, not only saw its market value plummeting some $43 billion but also had to cease its operation because it was cut off from the key components such as semiconductors that it used to source from the United States for its violation of the American export control regime. It points to serious foreign technological dependence and vulnerability of not only ZTE but also probably China's high-tech industry as a whole. Therefore, amid the ongoing trade disputes between China and the United States, it seems to be the right time to take a comprehensive look at where China stands in terms of its S&TI.

*CAO Cong is the Professor in Innovation Studies at the Faculty of Business, University of Nottingham, Ningbo, China.

In what follows, I will first survey what China has achieved in making its innovation system more responsive to domestic and international challenges. We also need to discuss what has been behind the phenomenal progresses, and examine the problems that may derail China's efforts to become an innovation-oriented nation and a global leader in science and technology (S&T) while speculating where China will go in the next couple of decades. The analyses are based on not only statistical data collected from various Chinese sources but also insights obtained from talking to policymakers, scientists, researchers and policy analysts in China as well as observations on the ground over a period of several decades.

Notable Progress

In a span of four decades, China has evolved from a peripheral player to become the world's most robust and dynamic economy. Along with its rapid economic progress, and the many improvements in the quality of life for a large proportion of the Chinese population, a variety of indicators suggest that China's S&TI capabilities are also on a sharply rising trajectory. Since the 1990s, spending on S&T and research and development (R&D) in China has been increasing at a rate faster than that of overall economic growth. In 2017, China reported that it spent 1.75 trillion renminbi ($259 billion), or 2.12% of its increasing gross domestic product (GDP), on R&D.[1] This represents the highest number among countries at a similar economic development level, and was higher than that of European Union's average while still much lower than that of the United States, whose respective figures were estimated at $510 billion and 2.74% of GDP in 2016.[2]

---

[1] National Bureau of Statistics of China, "Statistical Communiqué of the People's Republic of China on National Economic and Social Development in 2017" (in Chinese), 28 February 2018, at <http://www.stats.gov.cn/tjsj/zxfb/201802/t20180228_1585631.html> (accessed 31 August 2018).

[2] Richard Van Noorden, "China Tops Europe in R&D Intensity", *Nature*, vol. 505, 9 January 2014, pp. 144–145; National Science Foundation, National Center for Science and Engineering Statistics, *National Patterns of R&D Resources: 2015–2016 Data Update*,

In the recent decade, there has been a steady rise in the contributions of Chinese scientists to international publications. Measured by the number of papers published in journals indexed by *Science Citation Index (SCI)*, a bibliometric database compiled by Clarivate Analytics, a company formed after Onex Corp and Baring Private Equity Asia acquired the intellectual property and science assets, including *SCI*, from Thomason Reuters, in 2016, China ranked second in the world, accounting for some 20% of the world's total. In 1997, China only contributed 0.2% of the world's hottest papers, or papers cited among the top one-tenth of one percent; but in 2016, that statistic rose to 20%.[3] In 2007, China overtook the United States as the number one contributor to papers catalogued by the *Engineering Index (EI)*.

International collaboration contributes significantly to the rise of *SCI* publications. Measured by the number of *SCI* papers, the share of China's internationally collaborative papers increased from 22.1% in 2010 to 25.8% in 2016, with the total number of such papers also on the rise. During this period, China's leading collaborating partners included the United States, United Kingdom, Australia, Canada, Japan and Germany.[4] Data are unavailable to measure the role of Chinese diaspora in international collaboration, but their impacts should have been significant given their size in the international scientific community.[5] Chinese and foreign scientists have mostly worked on

NSF 18–309, Alexandria, VA: United States National Science Foundation, May 2018 (revised June 2018).

[3] Yang Wei, "Papers Supported by the National Natural Science Foundation of China Accounted for One-Ninth of the Papers Published Globally" (in Chinese), at <http://www.nsfc.gov.cn/publish/portal0/tab434/info69785.htm> (accessed 31 August 2018).

[4] He Tianwei, "International Scientific Collaboration of China with the G7 countries", *Scientometrics*, vol. 80, no. 3, 2009, pp. 571–582; Zhou Ping and Wolfgang Glänzel, "In-depth Analysis on China's International Cooperation in Science", *Scientometrics*, vol. 82, no. 3, 2010, pp. 597–612; David Tyfield, Zhu Yongguan and Cao Jinghua, "The Importance of the 'International Collaboration Dividend': The case of China", *Science and Public Policy*, vol. 36, no. 9, November 2009, pp. 723–735.

[5] For an earlier study on the subject, see Jin Bihui, Ronald Rousseau, Richard P. Suttmeier and Cao Cong, "The Role of Ethnic Ties in International Collaboration: The Overseas Chinese Phenomenon", in *Proceedings of the ISSI 2007 (11th International Conference of*

disciplines of basic research, such as biology, chemistry, physics, materials science and geosciences, along with clinical science in recent years.

Chinese inventors also have filed more patent applications in recent years.[6] In particular, China has witnessed a continuous growth in patent applications with the Patent Cooperation Treaty (PCT), an international patent law treaty. In 2017, the number of PCT applications filed by Chinese inventors reached 48,882, ranking the country second in the world for the first time, after the United States (56,624), but taking over Japan (48,208). Huawei Technologies, China's largest telecommunications equipment maker, and ZTE, the company that almost collapsed, ranked first and second with 4,024 and 2,965 PCT patent applications filed, respectively, in 2017.[7]

China's talent pool is the world's largest. In 2016, China had 5.83 million R&D personnel, or 3.88 million person-year in terms of full-time equivalent (FTE), more than any country in the world.[8] Meanwhile, the human resources pipeline is full as a result of the expansion of higher education that started in the late 1990s. Chinese institutions of higher education are now turning out an increasing

---

the *International Society for Scientometrics and Informetrics)*, ed. Daniel Torres-Salinas and Henk F. Moed, Madrid, Spain, Centre for Scientific Information and Documentation of the Spanish Research Council, 2007, pp. 427–436.

[6] See, for example, Fang Jing, He Hui, and Li Nan, "China's Rising IQ (Innovation Quotient) and Growth: Firm-Level Evidence", *IMF Working Paper*, WP/16/249, Washington, DC, International Monetary Fund, December 2016, at <https://www.imf.org/external/pubs/ft/wp/2016/wp16249.pdf> (accessed 31 August 2018).

[7] World Intellectual Property Organisation (WIPO), "China Drives International Patent Applications to Record Heights; Demand Rising for Trademark and Industrial Design Protection", Geneva, 21 March 2018, at <http://www.wipo.int/pressroom/en/articles/2018/article_0002.html> (accessed 31 August 2018).

[8] Ministry of Science and Technology and National Bureau of Statistics (comp.), *2017 China Science and Technology Statistical Yearbook*, Beijing, China Statistics Press, 2018; Table 1-1: R&D Personal (2016) and Table 1-2: Full-time Equivalent of R&D Personnel. These figures differ significantly from the ones analysed in National Science Board, *Science and Engineering Indicators 2018*, Alexandria, VA, National Science Foundation, 2018; Figure O–4: Estimated number of researchers, selected region or country: 2000–2015.

number of well-prepared graduates in S&T.[9] In 2007, China graduated some 194,000 students with master's and doctoral degrees, on top of 4.48 million undergraduates. In 2016, the number of undergraduate graduates reached 7.04 million, and postgraduates 564,000, with 55,011 at the doctoral level, slightly more than 55,006 from the United States. China is unequivocally the largest country and one of the most important countries in the world in higher education.

Foreign capital as well as technology, know-how and equipment have poured into China. Initially, such investment geared towards labour-intensive manufacturing in toys, clothing, sneakers and other products. But gradually, China got integrated into the global value chain, becoming an indispensable manufacturing centre of high-tech products from PCs and smartphones to semiconductors. While MNCs contribute a significant amount of China's high-tech exports, China undertakes manufacturing owing to its quick response time, nimbleness, the advantages of having a pool of highly skilled engineers and scientists, a sophisticated infrastructure, a cluster of related high-tech industries that benefit each other, R&D capability, engineering and supply chain management, marketing and strategy.

More recently, many of the world's technologically most innovative companies have decided to move beyond using China as a manufacturing centre to establishing adaptive and, now, more innovative R&D centres to develop new products and services for global markets as well as the Chinese domestic market. As the number of foreign corporate R&D centres now operating in China reaches 1,800, quite a number of them have gone through the stages of cost-driven and market-driven and are now in the stage of knowledge-driven, that is, they become important nodes in corporate global innovation networks.

China has also invested a significant amount of money into constructing modern and world-class facilities. For example, Deng Xiaoping, then China's paramount leader, attended the groundbreaking and opening ceremonies of the Beijing Electron–Positron

---

[9] Denis Fred Simon and Cao Cong, *China's Emerging Technological Edge: Accessing the Role of High-End Talent*, New York, Cambridge University Press, 2009, pp. 110–165.

Collider (BEPC), a high-energy facility, in 1984 and 1988, respectively, signifying China's determination to "occupy a seat in the world's high-tech arena", as Deng called for at BEPC's opening. At that time, China's economic situation might not have justified such an investment, but the facility has become an important site for international collaboration. The BEPC went through a major upgrade between 2004 and 2009. As one of the most advanced double-ring colliders in the world, the modified BEPCII continues to lead in its class. Using Beijing Spectrometer III, a large-scale universal magnetic spectrometer, Chinese and foreign scientists have achieved many world-class research results. Also, the Beijing Synchrotron Radiation Facility has provided an arena for conducting powerful experiments in basic research and applied basic research in condensed matter physics, chemistry, life sciences, earth sciences, environmental science, medicine, metrology and optics.

As its economy has gained strength, China has — in the recent decade — constructed the Jiangmen Underground Neutrino Observatory, the Five-hundred-meter Aperture Spherical radio Telescope (FAST), Controlled Nuclear Fusion Facility, etc. The presence of three clusters of large S&T facilities in Shanghai Zhangjiang, Anhui Hefei and Beijing Huairou will also help turn these cities into the nation's comprehensive science centres.

Last but not least, China has also become a technologically sophisticated society. Measured by such statistics as number of leading high-tech companies, including those emerging "unicorns", venture capital investment, high-tech trades, internet and especially mobile internet users, volume of e-commerce, etc., China seems to rival Silicon Valley and the world's other high-tech zones.

The Role of S&TI Policies

China's exponential rise in S&TI terms can be attributed to the reform and open-door policy, especially the reform of the S&T system; the leadership's vision on the role of S&TI in the country's economic development and modernisation; the government's commitment in

S&TI, evidenced in its increasing appropriation to S&T and R&D; and the emergence of a very large talent pool whose quality has been improving. Also underlying the impressive performance taking place in the Chinese S&TI scene is the role of the state by way of S&TI policies.[10]

In particular, in the mid-1980s, the S&T system was among the first to be reformed, aiming to solve the problem of the separation between research and the economy. Later on, the concept of innovation was introduced to China, elevating the view that innovation is more than S&T and R&D and that a holistic approach is necessary, encouraging the parts played by intermediaries, such as legal service, taxation, accounting, venture investment, consulting and others. Thus, the system of national innovation started to take shape.

Against such a backdrop, the leadership has formulated a series of policies, from "rejuvenating the nation with science, technology, and education" (*kejiao xingguo*) in the mid-1990s and "empowering the nation with talent" (*rencai qiangguo*) at the turn of the 21st century to placing emphasis on the importance of patents and technical standards. Accumulation of all these led to the formulation of the Medium- to Long-Term Plan for the Development of Science and Technology (2006–2020) (MLP) in early 2006. The MLP set ambitious national priorities and formalised the leadership's commitment to allocate substantial financial and human resources to turn China into an innovation-oriented nation by 2020 and a world leader in S&T by 2050. In addition, the plan specifically defined enhancing indigenous innovation (*zizhu chuangxin*) capability, leapfrogging in key scientific disciplines and utilising S&TI to support and lead future economic growth as its major objectives.[11]

---

[10] Liu Feng-chao, Denis Fred Simon, Sun Yu-tao and Cao Cong, "China's Innovation Policies: Evolution, Institutional Structure, and Trajectory", *Research Policy*, vol. 40, no. 7, 2011, pp. 917–931.

[11] Cao Cong, Richard P. Suttmeier and Denis Fred Simon, "China's 15-Year Science and Technology Plan", *Physics Today*, vol. 59, no. 12, 2006, pp. 38–43.

Alongside these policies/strategies/initiatives/plans are the various national S&T programs that have been launched over the last three or so decades. In March 1986, amid the global high-tech revolution, four senior scientists at the Chinese Academy of Sciences (CAS) who had been involved in China's strategic weapons program wrote to Deng Xiaoping suggesting following the world's high-tech trends and developing China's high technology. Deng immediately endorsed the proposal, and a State High-Tech Research and Development Program was soon started. Mostly known as the 863 Program to commemorate the fact that the program was initiated in March 1986, it was administered by the Ministry of Science and Technology (MOST) with an initial allocation of RMB10 billion (US$1.2 billion) over a period of 15 years and a significant emphasis on seven fields — biotechnology, space technology, information, lasers, automation, energy and new materials. Given the situation of the Chinese economy, the amount invested was huge.

Although the 863 Program also included basic research components underpinning high technologies, focus was placed on achieving technological advantages. Therefore, a program to predominantly target basic science and mission-oriented fundamental research was initiated in 1989 to make up the gap in research. The so-called Climbing Program intended to attract China's brightest scientists to work on 30 critical research projects, such as high-temperature superconductivity, nonlinear science, important chemical problems in life processes, brain function and its cellular and molecular basis, and so on.

This program evolved into a State Basic Research and Development Program, or the 973 Program, to commemorate the initiation of the program in March 1997, which would showcase China's endeavours in pursuing excellence in basic research. Also under the administration of the MOST, the program received an initial investment of some 2.5 billion renminbi (US$300 million) over five years (1998–2002) to support projects at an average level of 30 million renminbi (US$3.6 million). The projects to be supported were in six broad areas relevant to the nation's economic and social development — population and health, information, agriculture, resources and the environment, energy and new materials. Projects were also required to meet one of three criteria: first, they attempted to solve major problems associated with China's social, economic, and scientific and technological development; second, they were related to major basic research problems with inter-disciplinary and comprehensive significance; and third, they could take advantage of China's strength and special characteristics, such as natural, geographic and human resources, and help China "occupy a seat" at the frontier of international research, to echo Deng Xiaoping's remarks at the opening ceremony of the BEPC in 1988.

In the aftermath of the MLP, the Chinese government has come up with several critical programs advancing the indigenous innovation rhetoric. For example, the Strategic Emerging Industries (SEI) Program prioritised seven critical high-tech industries from new advanced infor-mation technology, automated machine tools and robotics and new materials, to biopharma and advanced medical products. Most recently, the Made in China 2025 Program is perceived to be significantly simi-lar to and consistent with the MLP, highlighting similar priority sec-tors. The policymakers also called on utilising indigenous or China-based patents, inventions and ideas, rather than those imported from abroad, to be skilfully adapted. In particular, it is expected that China will increase the use of domestic components in production to 40% by the year 2020 and as high as 70% by 2025.[12] The policy has drawn reactions from the United States, which wants to curtail China's state-sponsored approach towards high-tech development.

Most of the national S&T programs, mentioned here as well as many others, have disappeared as the most recent round of reform of the S&T system has attempted to integrate all of them into five streams. These streams include basic research, major national S&T programs, key national R&D programs, special funds to guide technological

---

[12] Scott Kennedy, "Critical Questions: Made in China 2025", Center for Strategic and International Studies, Washington, DC, 1 June 2015, at <https://www.csis.org/analysis/made-china-2025> (accessed 31 August 2018).

innovation and special funds for programs for developing human resources and infrastructure.[13]

Meanwhile, there have been other ministerial, institutional and organisational programs aiming at fulfilling their respective missions. For example, in 1993, the Ministry of Education (MOE) launched a program to position some 100 of China's universities as world-class academic institutions by the early 21st century. To that end, the ministry identified and supported 107 leading universities and approximately 600 scientific disciplines at these universities. In May 1998, in his speech on the occasion of the centennial anniversary of the founding of Peking University, the then General Secretary of the Central Committee of the Chinese Communist Party (CCP) and President of the People's Republic of China Jiang Zemin reaffirmed the goal of building world-class universities in China. The 985 Program, so named to commemorate Jiang's May 1998 speech, chose Peking, Tsinghua, Zhejiang, Nanjing, Fudan and Shanghai Jiao Tong universities; the University of Science and Technology of China; Xi'an Jiao Tong University and the Harbin Institute of Technology as the flagship universities of the 985 Program, which also included 29 other universities. A significant amount of public funds has been invested in the improvement of the infrastructure at Chinese universities, especially leading ones, and setting up "key" national laboratories open to both domestic scientists and

---

[13] These five streams are basic research supported through the National Natural Science Foundation of China (NSFC); the mega-engineering programs under the MLP and programs administered by different government agencies; the 863 Program, the 973 Program, State Key Technologies R&D Program (the *zhicheng* Program), the mega-science programs under the MLP, other programs administered by the MOST, national S&T programs of public goods run at 13 government agencies, as well as special industrial development R&D programs administered by the National Development and Reform Commission (NDRC) and the Ministry of Industry and Information Technology (MOIIT); programs of technological innovation at the NDRC, MOIIT, MOST and the Ministries of Finance and Commerce; and programs for national laboratories under various names administered by the MOST, the Ministry of Education (MOE) and the NDRC. But with the new development — under which the NSFC is being merged into the MOST — it remains to be seen whether these streams will be reorganised.

those from abroad has become common practice.[14] Now, the MOE is introducing another program, Developing World's First-Class Universities and First-Class Disciplines, or Double First-Class Program also known as World Class University 2.0 Program, continuing its push, whereby some Chinese universities or disciplines could be at the international frontier of excellence in research and teaching education.[15]

The CAS has also experienced some significant changes to its organisations, priorities and operation. At the height of the S&T system reform in the mid-1980s, the academy implemented a "one academy, two systems" policy by concentrating most of its efforts on research that directly benefits the Chinese economy and spinning off enterprises themselves to meet the needs of the market while keeping a small staff for basic research. Such a move indicated a substantial departure from the academy's tradition of being a purely academic institution. Starting from 1998, the CAS launched a Knowledge Innovation Program, aiming to build it into the nation's knowledge innovation centre in the natural sciences and high technology, and a base for world-class state-of-the-art scientific research, fostering first-rate scientific talent and for the development of high-tech industries.[16] And most recently, under another program, Pioneering Action Initiative, the CAS has new orientations towards major national demands, the international frontier of science and the major battleground for the national economy.[17]

[14] Simon and Cao, *China's Emerging Technological Edge*; Wang Qing Hui, Wang Qi and Liu Nian Cai, "Building World-Class Universities in China: Shanghai Jiao Tong University", in *The Road to Academic Excellence: The Making of World-Class Research Universities*, ed. Philip G. Altbach and Jamil Salmi, Washington, DC, World Bank, 2011, pp. 33–62.

[15] Wang Qi, "Programmed to Fulfill Global Ambitions", *Nature*, vol. 545, 25 May 2017, p. S53.

[16] Richard P. Suttmeier, Cao Cong and Denis Fred Simon, "'Knowledge Innovation' and the Chinese Academy of Sciences", *Science*, vol. 312, 7 April 2006, pp. 58–59; Richard P. Suttmeier, Cao Cong and Denis Fred Simon, "China's Innovation Challenge and the Remaking of the Chinese Academy of Sciences", *Innovations: Technology, Governance, Globalization*, vol. 1, no. 3, 2006, pp. 78–97.

[17] Cao Cong and Richard P. Suttmeier, "Challenges of S&T System Reform in China", *Science*, vol. 335, 10 March 2017, pp. 1019–1021.

Meanwhile, in the 1990s, to strengthen the research and the economy, the government initiated the plan to turn some R&D institutes under the then industrial ministries into corporations, some of which have later been listed on the domestic and international stock markets. Non-SOEs also have come of age in developing high and new technologies. High-tech parks have proliferated to commercialise high-tech research and transfer technology from institutions of learning. Returnees have brought back their overseas experience to not only help the transformation of scientific research and higher education but also engage in start-up and entrepreneurial activities.

Unresolved Problems and the Prospects

With notable progress attracting the attention of observers around the world, and many more achievements being expected from new reform measures/policies and new programs in the coming years, a balanced perspective on the prospects for Chinese S&TI requires an examination of some of the challenges that China faces in realising its ambition.

The improving role of enterprises in innovation

While overall statistics show that enterprises now account for three-quarters of China's R&D expenditure, or the level seen in the OECD countries, enterprises have been constrained financially or allocated less financial resources to carry out innovative R&D activities. According to a survey of China's scaled enterprises in 2014, the latest with detailed, micro-level information, Chinese firms on average spent merely 0.8% of their sales on R&D. Only 12.6% of the surveyed enterprises had set up S&T institutes. Only 8.6% of the R&D personnel at enterprises possessed a postgraduate degree.[18] Companies such as Huawei, ZTE and BYD, a battery-maker turned hybrid and electric vehicle

---

[18] China Academy of Science and Technology for Economic Development and School of Economics, Central University of Finance and Economics, *Chinese Enterprise Innovation Capability: An Evaluation Report 2016*, Beijing, Scientific and Technical Documentation Press, 2016.

manufacturer in which Warren Buffet's Berkshire Hathaway took a stake in 2009, which do spend heavily on R&D are the outliers, not the norm. For example, Huawei consistently spends some 10% of its sales on R&D and 40% of its employees have higher education. In 2017, as mentioned, Huawei, alone submitted 4,024 of the China's 48,882 PCT applications. These few firms seem to have developed a more sophisticated approach to technological learning, knowledge acquisition and intellectual property right (IPR) management.

Chinese enterprises also have developed interest in engaging domestic institutions of learning for R&D efforts. The reform in the S&T system since the mid-1980s has to some extent activated the enthusiasm of researchers at these institutions in supplying technology, and now, enterprises on the demand side are willing to acquire technology from domestic sources. For example, in recent years, some 60% of the extramural R&D expenditure at Chinese enterprises was spent on acquiring technology from or collaborating with domestic universities and R&D institutes, and enterprises spent more money acquiring domestic than foreign technologies.[19] That is to say, the deeply rooted problems of the separation of innovation and the economy and of the organisational rigidity between enterprises and institutions of learning have begun to be eased.

Nonetheless, the dependency of Chinese enterprises upon key foreign technology and equipment still exists. Even ZTE, the company that filed the second largest number of PCT patent applications in 2017, almost went bankrupt when the American government prohibited it from sourcing key comments from American companies. The case points to the vulnerability of China's high-tech industry and raises concerns about the importance of developing indigenous innovation capability. Recent innovations in the internet-related businesses have mainly benefited from business model innovation by adapting business successes elsewhere to the Chinese situation. The high-speed train,

---

[19] China Academy of Science and Technology for Economic Development and School of Economics, Central University of Finance and Economics, *Chinese Enterprise Innovation Capability*.

mobile payment, e-commerce and shared bikes, or the so-called "Four New Inventions", are mainly applications based on the improvement of existing inventions.

Is money wasted?

It remains a question whether the increasing sums of money provided by the Chinese government — central and increasingly local — have been well spent. It is no secret that a significant portion of the research carried out in China, even those supported by the national S&T programs at China's leading institutions of learning, is derivative of what has been done elsewhere, thus surely wasting increasing but still limited resources. This explains why Chinese scientists have not yielded significant breakthroughs commensurate with rising expenditure in R&D. While China has witnessed both quantitative and qualitative improvements in the publications by its scientists, there has also been concern whether *SCI* publications should be the yardstick of Chinese science.

Misconduct in research, such as plagiarism, falsification and fabrication, seems to be more common recently. In 2015, scientific publisher BioMed Central withdrew 43 papers over the "fabrication" of peer reviews, and the authors of these papers are all Chinese.[20] Two years later, in 2017, the Springer Nature Publishing Company withdrew 107 papers published in the journal *Tumor Biology* between 2012 and 2016 as the investigation found that their Chinese authors faked peer review by supplying the journal's editors with made-up contact information of third-party reviewers.[21] These cases involved Chinese scientists from leading academic institutions such as Peking University, Shanghai Jiao Tong University, Fudan University and China Medical University. While these retractions only represent a small amount of the papers

---

[20] Mara Hvistendahl, "China Pursues Fraudsters in Science Publishing", *Science*, 20 November 2015, at <http://www.sciencemag.org/news/2015/11/china-pursues-fraudsters-science-publishing> (accessed 31 August 2018).

[21] David Cyronoski, "China Cracks down on Fake Peer Reviews", *Nature*, vol. 546, 22 June 2017, p. 464.

that Chinese scientists publish in international journals annually, they have generated very negative images for Chinese science as a whole. An overemphasis of *SCI* publication in researchers' performance evaluation and in the decision on their salary, funding applications and promotions may have resulted in such and other cases, which have not only wasted a not-so-small-part of funds but also eroded the morale of the research community.

More serious cases of misuse of funds and cheating have surfaced from time to time. For example, in 2006, Chen Jin at Shanghai Jiao Tong University was found to have secured hundreds of millions worth of funds from various government agencies, including the MOST, the then Ministry of Information Industry and the NDRC, for research on semiconductors; it was discovered, unfortunately, that he was using a purchased chip as his innovation. Chen Jin was fired by the university, had his various honours removed and returned a portion of the research money, but Chen himself never was prosecuted for his cheating and it is said that he is still active. Many members of the Chinese research community have believed that the Chen Jin case is just the tip of the iceberg in research misconduct.[22] A decade or so later, in the name of indigenous innovation, Redcore, a Chinese start-up, was found making a false claim that its browser is "the world's only purely China-own browser to break the U.S. monopoly"; but it turns out to be just based on Google's Chrome software.[23]

Concerns over intellectual property protection

We should give China credit as the country over the years has improved its IP regime. For example, China promulgated its Patent Law in 1984, and amended it several times — in 1992, 2000 and 2008 — to harmonise with the international norms, and it was amended again recently. In fact, a decentralised China has made IPR protection difficult, if not

---

[22] David Barboza, "In a Scientist's Fall, China Feels Robbed of Glory", *The New York Times*, 15 May 2006.

[23] Sherry Ju Fei, "Chinese Start-up Apologises over Chrome Similarities", *Financial Times*, 17 August 2018.

impossible, and China's weakness in this aspect has been a major concern for numerous foreign companies, which have also alleged Chinese companies as engaging in activities of forced technology transfer and IP theft.

Entering the 21st century, two of the three key initiatives — patents and technical standards — put forward by China's scientific leadership are IPR-related (the other is about the development of talent). This is not only because the leadership realises that China needs to be more responsive to the operating standards of the current international IPR regime. Just as important, to be a serious player in global innovation, China has to generate its own IPR. In other words, China itself will not become innovative unless it takes the issue of IPR protection more seriously. Indeed, as discussed in this chapter, China has achieved progress in this particular aspect.

Lingering talent challenge

China still faces a serious talent challenge as it seeks to sustain domestic economic growth and promote technological advance despite possessing an impressive S&T talent pool and having a full talent pipeline. In 2009, my collaborator Denis Simon and I suggested that a slew of factors had ensued collectively China's talent challenge in the early 21st century. The after-effects of the Cultural Revolution still lingered; during the 10 years between 1966 and 1976, higher education was disrupted and professionals were prosecuted and deprived of the right to carry out their work, leading to a dearth of well-educated specialists in all areas. The "brain drain" of talents abroad after China opened its door in the late 1970s had constrained the domestic access to the best and brightest minds. The qualitative improvement of the talent pool had been sacrificed amid the quantitative expansion of higher education since the late 1990s. And China was fast approaching an "aging society," which would have significant implications for the supply and utilisation of the talent.[24]

---

[24] Simon and Cao, *China's Emerging Technological Edge*, pp. 22–56.

Some 10 years have passed, and it may be the time to revisit such propositions. The "Cultural Revolution" challenge is mostly gone. Most of the so-called "worker–peasant–soldier" college students have retired, with few who remain active having made up their educational deficiency through advanced education at home and/or abroad. The generation of scientists and professionals receiving higher education in the reform and opening-up era is more than coming of age.

The "brain drain" challenge still exists, although the situation is not as severe as it was 10 years ago. This is attributed to various programs that have been launched by the central and local governments and different institutions to tackle the problem. Consequently, China has witnessed the return of a growing number of ethnic Chinese scientists, engineers, entrepreneurs and other professionals with foreign experience. The availability of opportunities also has attracted foreign experts to China. While the majority of Chinese PhDs still hope to travel abroad, most plan to return to pursue professional careers in their homeland. However, among returnees are not only academically competent and experienced "sea turtles" (*haigui*) who are welcome but also "seaweed" (*haidai*) who struggle professionally given their education at undergraduate and master's levels. In recent years, students have gone overseas at a younger age, even at the high-school level. As mentioned, American universities have had more students at undergraduate programs than at postgraduate programs. The prospect of members of this group to become "sea treasures" (*haibei*) — those who are generally better prepared for global success — is uncertain as domestic and international environments could orient and reorient their career planning and mobility.

China is still facing the "quality/skill/demand mismatch" challenge given the structural issues that have led to the problems. There are geographical mismatches and mismatches between supply and demand, between knowledge acquired through education and skills required by jobs, and between the types of positions to be filled and the availability of talent to fill the positions.

The "ageing society" challenge is getting more serious. The number of students sitting for domestic higher education examinations (*gaokao*) has been declining, which indicates that the ageing effect may have kicked in earlier than expected. The government's recent loosening on the one-child policy is probably too late as "it takes 10 years to grow a tree but one hundred years to educate/nurture a person." It will be difficult and take time to reverse the trend of China's becoming an ageing society, whose implications for China's talent issue and ambition to become an innovation-oriented nation remain to be seen.

The talent shortage could have a negative impact in the near-to-medium term. China's pace of economic growth, especially in terms of the development of new, technology-intensive sectors, might be jeopardised. Having realised the urgency of the talent issue, the Chinese leadership has initiated various programs that attract, retain and nurture talents, especially those at the high end.

In December 2008, in order to further address the "brain drain" issue and also take advantage of the global financial crisis that cost some professionals, including scientists and researchers, their jobs, the Central Leading Group for Coordinating Talent Work launched an Attracting Overseas High-End Talent Program, also known as the Thousand Talent Program, pledging to attract some 2,000 expatriate Chinese scholars to their homeland within 5–10 years. The program initially targeted full professors at well-known foreign institutions of learning, experienced corporate executives and entrepreneurs with core technologies under 55 years old for leapfrogging China's scientific research, high-tech entrepreneurship and economic development. In return for their permanent return and services, the central government offers a resettlement subsidy of RMB1 million tax free and a significant amount of fund for research or entrepreneurship, while local governments and employers match with research fund, housing benefit and a salary close to their overseas level.

Some prominent academics who have been attracted back to China include Wang Xiaodong, the first United States-bound mainland Chinese student in the open-door era to become a member of the United States National Academy of Sciences (NAS) and a Howard Hughes Medical Institute (HHMI) investigator at the University of Texas Southwestern Medical Centre; Shi Yigong, a chair professor and also a Howard HHMI investigator at Princeton University; and most recently, Xie Xiaoliang, the first mainland Chinese in the open-door era to hold a tenured full professorship at Harvard University who is also a fellow of the American Academy of Arts and Sciences and a member of the NAS, as well as many others from the world's leading institutions of learning.[25] However, quite a significant number of awardees have been unable or unwilling to return to China permanently because of various reasons, which is against the initial goal of the program.[26] Therefore, the government had to add a component for those who commit a couple of months of part-time work for three years and has not made the list of Thousand Talent Program awardees public.

Under these circumstances, in December 2010, the Central Leading Group for Coordinating Talent Work approved adding a component for emerging young scholars — the Young Thousand Talent Program — within the Thousand Talent Program. Administered by the NSFC, the program set to attract some 400 promising young talents from overseas annually between 2011 and 2015 and turn them into innovative leaders in academia or high-tech entrepreneurship with moral character, outstanding professional ability and comprehensive quality.

However, several sources point to a dubious overall quality of the returnees. For example, returnees with doctorates and with bachelor's degrees account for 10% each, with the rest spending one or two years abroad for a master's degree.[27] Of some 470,000 returnees seeking certification for their foreign educational credentials between 2008 and

---

[25] Sharon LaFraniere, "Fighting Trend, China Is Luring Scientists Home", *The New York Times*, 7 January 2010, p. A1.

[26] Wang Huiyao, "China's New Talent Strategy: Impact on China's Development and Its Global Exchange", *SAIS Review*, vol. 31, no. 2, Summer–Fall 2011, pp. 49–64; Denis Fred Simon and Cao Cong, "Human Resources: National Talent Safari", *China Economic Quarterly*, vol. 15, no. 2, June 2011, pp. 15–19; David Zweig and Wang Huiyao, "Can China Bring Back the Best? The Communist Party Organizes China's Search for Talent", *The China Quarterly*, no. 215, September 2013, pp. 590–615.

[27] "Experts: The Quality of Returnee Students Is Not High, Nearly Half of the Income Less Than RMB6000" (in Chinese), at <http://rencai.gov.cn/Index/detail/14220> (accessed 31 August 2018).

2014 at the Chinese Service Centre for Scholarly Exchange, 62.56% have a master's degree, 29.83% have a bachelor's degree and only 6.24% have a doctorate. The 29,341 doctorates received their degrees in engineering (10,601, 36.13%), science (7,303, 24.89%), medicine (3,280, 11.18%), literature (1,779, 6.06%), economics (1,528, 5.21%), law (1,482, 5.05%), management science (1,394, 4.75%) and education (859, 2.93%), with the rest in agriculture, history and philosophy. Their doctorates came from 2,114 institutions. The top 11 schools awarding 12.05% of the doctorates are from Singapore (National University of Singapore, Nanyang Technological University), Japan (Tokyo, Kyushu, Tohoku, Nagoya, Hokudai, Kyoto and Tsukuba) and United Kingdom (Nottingham and Manchester). They received their doctorates from 67 countries, but the United States (8228, 28.04% of all the doctorates), Japan (6,140, 20.93%), United Kingdom (3,266, 11.13%), Korea (2,094, 7.14%), Germany (1,981, 6.75%), France (1,499, 5.11%), Singapore (1,240, 4.23%), Australia (823, 2.81%), Canada (767, 2.61%) and Russia (586, 2.00%) altogether awarded 90.75% of the doctorates. Top American universities whose graduates have sought degree certification include Illinois Institute of Technology, University of Illinois Urbana Champaign, University of Southern California, Columbia University, University of Illinois Chicago, Northeastern University, Missouri State University, Ohio State University, Boston University and University of Maryland College Park; but most of their graduates were in master's programs and a small number in doctoral programs.[28]

For comparison, between 2008 and 2014, the total number of PhD degrees that American universities had awarded to Chinese nationals was 30,362.[29] This suggests that most of the Chinese with American

---

[28] Chinese Service Center for Scholarly Exchange (comp.), *Report on the Certification of Educational Credentials Received from Institutions Outside China* (in Chinese), Beijing, People's Education Press, 2016, pp. 35–91.

[29] National Center for Science and Engineering Statistics, Directorate for Social, Behavioral and Economic Sciences (comp.), *2016 Doctorate Recipients from United States Universities*, NSF 18–304, Alexandria, VA, United States National Science Foundation, March 2018. Table 26. Doctorates awarded for 10 largest countries of origin of temporary

doctorates have yet to return. This corroborates the stay rates found among the Chinese who have earned American doctorates. Between 2012 and 2015, the vast majority of United States science and engineering (S&E) doctorate recipients from China (83%) reported plans to stay in the United States, and approximately half of these individuals reported accepting firm offers for employment or postdoctoral research in the United States. By country of citizenship at time of degree, China, the country that is the source of more S&E doctorate recipients than any other countries, has the highest 5- and 10-year stay rates. For 10,700 who received their doctorates in 2005, the 10-year stay rate was 90%; for 10,600 who received their doctorates in 2010, the 5-year stay rate was 85%, while the 5-year and 10-year stay rates for all the S&E PhDs were both 70% in 2015.[30] However, concerns about espionage involving Chinese in the United States may push some of them, including those Thousand Talent Program awardees, to return to China.[31]

Think outside the box?

There is the question of whether China can become an innovation-oriented nation without being open to different ways of thinking. This is more than just a philosophical question. While on the surface Chinese researchers and entrepreneurs are encouraged to think outside the box and not to be afraid of failure, at least equally important is that other ingredients of a true innovation culture — autonomy, free access to and flow of information, and especially dissent, scientific as well as

---

visa holders earning doctorates at United States colleges and universities, by country or economy of citizenship and field: 2006–2016.

[30] United States National Science Board, *Science & Engineering Indicators 2018*, p. 138.

For a particular graduating cohort of foreign-born non-citizen S&E doctorate recipients, the proportion of that cohort who report living in the United States a given number of years after receiving their degrees is an indicator of the cohort's long-term stay rate.

[31] American Institute of Physics, "New US Visa Screening Measures Target Chinese Citizens Studying 'Sensitive' Subjects", at <https://www.aip.org/fyi/2018/new-us-visa-screening-measures-target-chinese-citizens-studying-'sensitive'-subjects> (accessed 31 August 2018).

political — are not adequately applauded or tolerated. In the field of innovation, it is generally believed that tolerance is as critical as talent and technology in driving creativity and growth.[32]

In this regard, a puzzle raised by Qian Xuesen, a returnee from the United States in the mid-1950s and one of the most important contributors to China's missile and space program, seems to be most relevant.[33] In 2005, Qian told visiting Chinese Premier Wen Jiabao that one important reason that China has not turned out outstanding talent is that the nation does not have even one university that genuinely follows the model of nurturing scientific and creative talent and encourages unique innovation. Qian did not elaborate what he meant by his puzzle, thus leaving much room for interpretation, speculation and debate. However, given his thorough understanding of China's education and research system from his vantage point as well as his formative personal and professional life experience in the United States — he had studied and worked at the Massachusetts Institute of Technology and the California Institute of Technology for 20 years before being expelled in the mid-1950s amid the McCarthyism zeal — he was likely to imply the importance of such values as independent thinking, tolerance of dissent and freedom of inquiry.

Indeed, answers to the puzzle may have significant implications for China's endeavour to become an innovation-oriented nation amid internationalisation of China's human resources. Globalisation has brought China various practical benefits and advantages. However, they are not enough for greatness for science and innovation. The development of a high-quality talent pool is relatively easy to attain. The most difficult and important part is to nurture independent thinking and freedom of inquiry, while its absence in China has limited the

---

[32] Richard L. Florida, *The Rise of the Creative Class. And How It's Transforming Work, Leisure and Everyday Life*, New York, NY, Basic Books, 2002.

[33] The discussion on the Qian Xuesen puzzle draws from Cao Cong, "The Universal Value of Science and China's Nobel Prize Pursuit", *Minerva*, vol. 52, 2014, pp. 141–160.

pool of academic talent and stultified imagination and innovation. Therefore, to make its universities "world-class" and its talent pool more responsiveness to the challenge, the Chinese state needs to go beyond the pragmatism to treasure and uphold universal values of science and innovation. Only by doing so would China turn out world-class universities and disciplines and have its talent leapfrog to the international frontiers of research, as its scientific and political leadership has envisioned.

Therefore, allowing "blooming and contending" is more important than purely worshiping innovation as a new "religion". If the former is not allowed, the potential success of China's innovation strategy will be called into question. It is in this vein that China's innovation pursuits may be in conflict with the government's other goal, that is, the construction of a harmonious society, as innovation often requires running against the tide rather than simply going with the flow.

Where the Future Stands

In brief, while China's efforts to become an innovation-oriented nation certainly have the potential to change the complexion and landscape of the international S&TI regime, it is also the case that China faces numerous internal challenges that must be addressed sooner rather than later if the goals and objectives stated by the Chinese are to be realised. As indicated above, Chinese leaders and S&T policymakers should be given great credit for the substantial progress that China has made over these last three-plus decades. There is still a chance that China may be stuck in its current stage of S&TI development for a prolonged period of time. Nonetheless, more attention needs to be paid to the "software" side of the innovation equation so that a true "culture of creativity" can be inaugurated, implemented and nurtured across the full spectrum of national- and local-level Chinese S&T organisations and institutions. Only with this "culture of creativity" in place can China's efforts to reorient its economy and S&TI system acquire the needed traction and build the necessary forward momentum.

Acknowledgements

This research received partial support from the National Natural Science Foundation of China (71774091). This chapter draws materials from Cao Cong, Denis Fred Simon and Richard P. Suttmeier, "China's Innovation Challenge", *Innovation: Management, Policy & Practice*, vol. 11, 2009, pp. 253–259.

Chapter 7

Embracing the Era of Educational Finance 3.0

WANG Rong and TIAN Zhilei*

T he past decade or so since 2005 has witnessed the rapid growth of fiscal funding for education in China, and along with it tremendous efforts from the government to develop and improve the educational finance system. This chapter provides an analysis of the development of the country's educational finance system over time and seeks to add a layer of insight to the fundamental issues and challenges of the system in the future on the basis of a rough division of the development of China's educational finance system since the country's reform and opening up into three stages, namely 1978–2005, 2005–present and from the present forward.

1978–2005: The Era of Educational Finance 1.0

An examination of the system and policies in place at the time reveals that although governments at all levels, including the central government, were entrusted with the responsibility by law to manage education, the financial responsibilities of the various levels of government in

*WANG Rong is the Director and Professor at the China Institute for Educational Finance Research, Peking University. TIAN Zhilei is an Assistant Professor at the China Institute for Educational Finance Research, Peking University.

relation to education had not been delineated, a reality that remained fundamentally unchanged since the founding of the People's Republic of China up to the early 1990s. From the founding of the People's Republic of China up to the end of the last century, the relevant laws, regulations and financial practices established that the central government's educational expenditures would mainly be allocated towards institutions of higher education, specialised secondary schools set up by the central government, and primary and secondary schools affiliated with these institutions. The *decision of the state council on the implementation of the tax-sharing system* implemented in 1994 stipulated that "the central government shall bear the educational expenditures incurred at the central level" in a clause concerning the division of the authority of office, which showed little difference from the 1950 and 1951 regulations.

China's fiscal system constitutes the most decisive factor in the country's fiscal investment in education and corresponding institutional arrangements. The period beginning from China's reform and opening up up to 2005 witnessed two major reforms of its fiscal system, namely, the tax-sharing system reform implemented in 1994, and subsequently the rural tax-for-fee reform set in motion in 2000 and later implemented broadly across the country.

The main components of the tax-sharing system reform included the clear division of tax entitlements between central and local governments according to the different categories of taxes and the establishment of a transitional fiscal transfer payment system. The central government was mired in fiscal woes in the early 1990s. The situation was radically transformed as the central government's share of fiscal revenues increased to roughly 50% of the total after the implementation of the tax-sharing reform. However, because a sound fiscal transfer payment system was yet to be established, the ability of administrative authorities to adequately fund the corresponding stages of education at the local level was negatively impacted.

The rural tax-for-fee reform exposed the drawbacks of the original rural educational finance system, which were reflected by the fact that a severe lack of fiscal funding in rural education had resulted in schools' heavy reliance on extra-budgetary funds to maintain their operations, including non-personnel expenditures, teacher compensation and capital outlay expenditures.

In the realm of academic research, education finance scholars in China before 2005 reached consensus on the following points: first, the severe lack of educational funding constituted the most pressing concern; second, identifying the theoretical tools developed by the West — such concepts as public goods and externalities — as the intellectual framework for suggestions on government reforms and the improvement of educational finance system at all levels; third, analyses and discussions related to the equity and equality of compulsory education were centred on school input disparities between urban and rural areas and among regions, which were frequently examined in conjunction with institutional factors of the education finance system; fourth, scholars unanimously suggested that the implementation of a diversified financing system was a pragmatic choice based on the reality of a lack of educational funding in China; fifth, the central and provincial governments should increase their funding contributions to compulsory education. These discourses preluded the peak period of development of the educational finance system after 2005, providing the intellectual and theoretical groundwork for corresponding public policies.

It is particularly worth noting that the *"Reasonable Level of Government Expenditure on Education as a Percentage of GDP"* study, which was a key research project under the Sixth Five-Year Plan, and the *"Study on Educational Investment Decisions"*, another key research project under the Seventh Five-Year Plan, both carried out by a group of scholars from Peking University and Beijing Normal University, examined the global average public expenditure on education as a percentage of GDP given a certain level of economic development. The scholars' suggestions were finally adopted when, in 1993, *the Guidelines to China's Educational Reform and Development*, jointly issued by the CPC Central Committee and the State Council, proposed that "national fiscal expenditure on education as a percentage of GDP shall gradually increase and reach 4% at the end of the century." The Education Law of the People's Republic of China, promulgated and implemented in 1995, also delineated corresponding provisions. This model of institutional arrangement that links government expenditure on education with GDP and fiscal expenditures has since been referred to as the "linking mechanism".

2005–Present: The Era of Educational Finance 2.0

After 2005, expenditure on education as a percentage of GDP grew rapidly, first with the reform of the rural compulsory education funding guarantee mechanism, and subsequently as the 4% target was written into the *Outline of China's National Plan for Medium and Long-Term Education Reform and Development (2010–2020)*, the central government allocated the 4% funding responsibilities to local governments with strict accountability checking measures, resulting in the largest increase in educational expenditure in the 2010–2012 period since 1980. A series of milestone educational finance measures were introduced, including reform of the rural compulsory education funding guarantee mechanism, the establishment of a student financial aid system for underprivileged students in universities, colleges, polytechnics and secondary vocational schools, the implementation of free secondary vocational education and increasing financial support for the development of preschool education. From 2012 to 2016, the country's fiscal funding for education increased from 2.3 trillion yuan to 3.1 trillion yuan. State fiscal funding for education as a percentage of GDP remained above 4% for five consecutive years. According to the 2017 budgetary plan, expenditure on education as a percentage of public finance expenditure would reach 14.9%, the largest among all expenses. The timespan from 2005 to the present constitutes a peak period of development for the educational finance system following decades of fast and steady growth in fiscal expenditure on education after the founding of the People's Republic of China.

Specifically speaking, progress in major policies and institutional arrangements from 2005 to the present is mainly shown in the following aspects.

Key policy progress — achieving the "4% target"

The *Outline of China's National Plan for Medium and Long-Term Education Reform and Development (2010–2020)* clearly stated that national fiscal expenditure on education as a percentage of GDP shall reach 4% by 2012. In order to ensure the realisation of the "4% target", the *Opinions of the State Council on Further Increasing Fiscal Investment in Education* issued in 2011 puts forward the following two core requirements. First, governments at all levels were urged to effectively raise their fiscal expenditure on education as a percentage of public finance expenditure. To this end, the central government set individual targets for each province to adjust their fiscal spending makeup accordingly and monitored target implementation through supervision. Second, channels of funding for education were broadened with contributions and efforts by multiple parties. After adopting the above-mentioned high-pressure administrative means, the "4% target" was finally reached and exceeded in 2012, registering at 4.28%.

Building and improving the educational finance institutional mechanisms

The government has made tremendous efforts to build and improve the foundational and institutional mechanisms underlying the educational finance system, including the formulation of numerous normative documents, such as educational administrative regulations, policies and measures; the full incorporation of compulsory education into the scope of guaranteed public finance obligations and explorations with regard to the establishment of a funding guarantee mechanism for compulsory education; the incorporation of preschool education as a crucial public service into the scope of public financial support; the implementation of a funding mechanism for senior secondary education in which fiscal expenditure comprises the bulk of funding while other channels of funding play a supplementary role; guiding all localities in establishing and improving a funding system based on student numbers for secondary and higher vocational schools and universities; improving the budgetary appropriation mechanisms for universities affiliated with the central government; and establishing and improving the financial aid system for underprivileged students starting from preschool all the way through postgraduate education. With regard to the institutional dimension of the division of responsibilities between government and the market, the above-mentioned efforts have taken hold within the educational finance system across all levels of the government and categories of education.

Rapid expansion in the fiscal responsibilities of the central government in education

The landmark development in policy during this period was characterised by the implementation of free compulsory education, free secondary vocational education and by a series of major irreversible reforms of the educational finance system that fundamentally altered the division of fiscal responsibility between government and the market. In terms of intergovernmental institutional arrangements concerning the educational finance system, the reform of the rural compulsory education funding guarantee mechanism, introduced in 2005, proved to be a milestone breakthrough as it proposed for the first time that rural compulsory education shall be funded by "both the central and local governments" in a "project-specific and proportional fashion". Since then, with continuous growth in its financial resources, the central government has fully engaged itself fiscally in all levels of education from preschool to postgraduate programs.

An analysis of and reflection upon the achievements in educational finance policy in the past period can produce the following observations. First, the fundamental reason for the "4% target" having become an effective resource mobilisation strategy lies in the fact that it targeted the entire educational scene. Second, the implementation of the "4% target", the strengthening of the educational finance system and the rapid expansion of the central government's fiscal responsibilities are interrelated and mutually causal. Major education policies instituted after 2005 shared a common feature in design, that is, the central government attached great importance to resolving conflicts between the government and the people, and regarded the development and improvement of basic public services as a means to addressing the challenges, all the while establishing an ideological foundation that viewed local governments and professional groups as its target of work and the adjustment of local government behaviour and management of professional groups as a priority. The government's intervention in and support for basic public services have picked up continuously in both reach and volume, accompanied by increasing levels of centralisation. In this context, the funding strategies concerning education can be described in such terms as being project-specific, multileveled, system-wide and multidimensional.

"Project-specific" refers to the increasing importance of the vertical part of the "vertical–horizontal" bureaucratic dynamics in the process of educational funding as specially designated categorical grant projects become a concrete reflection of the will of the central government.

"Multilevel" refers to both the "4% target" for the system-wide funding efforts, but also for funding efforts for certain education subareas, such as preschool education, as well as the efforts to address specific prominent problems in certain types or levels of education, such as efforts for improving weak compulsory education schools.

"System-wide" refers to the comprehensive implementation of funding mobilisation strategies at all levels of education. For instance, preschool, postgraduate, special education and secondary vocational education, which had previously received little investment or attention from the central government, are now all covered by specially designated funding. Generally speaking, fiscal funding has been gradually reoriented and spread towards traditionally disadvantaged levels (categories, institutions) of education from traditionally prioritised levels (categories, institutions) of education. At the same time, the fiscal funding mechanism at the traditionally prioritised levels of education is evolving to become increasingly multidimensional. For instance, in higher education, in addition to the mainstream funding support, i.e. budgetary appropriations for the undergraduate teaching function, the student financial aid system, funding programs for graduate programs and budgetary appropriations for university-based basic research are examples of this development.

Since 2012, after the realisation of the "4% target", considerable policy discussions have continued to focus on relevant institutional issues within the governmental system, which is undoubtedly a reaction to the pressure for policy corrections after the institution of the "linking mechanism" intended to address the lack of incentives for local governments in funding education and corresponding centralised efforts. The view in favour of policy corrections has gradually gained ground with many believing that while the "linking mechanism" played a positive role in serving the intended cause during a specific historical period, it also inevitably led to the structural rigidity in fiscal spending and crippled the budgetary autonomy of local governments.

The past several years witnessed a series of efforts of policy corrections. The *decision of the central committee of the communist party of china on some major issues concerning comprehensively deepening the reform* adopted at the Third Plenary Session of the 18th Central Committee of the CPC stated that "we will clear up policy stipulations for priority spending areas that link expenditure increasing objectives to increases in financial revenues or GDP, and the mechanism of linking them up is not to be continued." In September 2014, the State Council issued the *decision on deepening the reform on budget management system*. A statement within the document on optimising the expenditure structure reiterated the decision of the Third Plenary Session. In the same year, the Budget Law of the People's Republic of China passed by the National People's Congress did not stipulate on the matter either.

After the linking mechanism was abolished, whether or not new rules can be established to ensure that basic public services such as education receive fiscal support in a sustainable fashion is a matter that the public hold dear to heart. The *Guiding Opinions of the State Council on Advancing the Reform of the Division of Financial Powers and Expenditure Responsibilities between the Central and the Local Governments* issued in 2016 marked the official launch of the reform framework for the division of decision-making authorities and expenditure responsibilities. In the coming months, what concrete policy measures are yet to unfold deserve close observation.

Embracing the Era of Educational Finance 3.0

In the eras of Educational Finance 1.0 and 2.0, addressing the inadequacy in local governments' fiscal capacity and incentives for education and securing the educational opportunities of rural residents and low-income groups constituted the call of the time. To this end, the central government employed a substantial amount of categorical grant programs and specially designated transfer payments to provide targeted financing to schools and, in the meantime, incentivised local fiscal investment in education through requirements for local financial counterpart funds combined with other policy measures of accountability checking. On the whole, institutional building in the Era of Educational Finance 2.0 answered fairly well the call of the era.

However, as the fundamentals of the demand and supply side of education evolved, the dividends that resulted from the series of educational fiscal policies instituted after 2005 have shown signs of depletion of late. New ideas and rules are urgently needed to cope with the ever-evolving and intensifying contradictions in the process of educational development and newly emerged realities. Major challenges are as follows.

Rethinking the boundary between government and the market in financing and providing education

In the past decade, policy research on educational finance has focused on problems within the governmental system, such as solidifying education's nature as a public good and a legitimate priority receiver of public finance support and a more reasonable delineation of expenditure responsibilities towards education between the various levels of government. However, marketised or market-oriented education providers have gradually gained a strong foothold in China in the past 10 years, a development much neglected by researchers during the period. These entities may bring forth a more diverse and complex roster of market players, such as the capital markets, towards which there is a lack of sufficient foresight and scope for analysis.

Building more flexibility in educational financing mechanisms

Even within the stages of education covered by China's free compulsory education policy, more scientific and detail-oriented calculations of the costs of education should be carried out, and the distinction between basic services and personalised services should be established. Budgetary appropriation standards towards basic services should be established, while institutional flexibility should be accorded to public schools in the area of increasing demand for personalised services on the principle that the individuals should shoulder costs thus incurred. In the meantime, the institutional mechanisms concerning the fiscal support and incentivisation of private education providers should be improved.

In summary, the core challenges of the Era of Educational Finance 3.0, especially the issue of how to properly handle the impact of market-oriented purveyors of education and the coordinated development of public and private education, will put to test the wisdom of policy researchers and makers.

Chapter 8

The Development of e-Commerce in China and the Implication for Southeast Asia

KONG Tuan Yuen*

The Contribution of E-commerce to China's Economic Growth

The Chinese market of e-commerce has grown rapidly and has become the largest global one in recent years. Based on the Chinese Ministry of Commerce data, the market size of Chinese e-commerce has tremendously increased almost five times from 6 trillion renminbi in 2011 to 29.2 trillion renminbi in 2017, accounting for nearly 40% of the worldwide share. It is noteworthy that e-commerce, especially e-retail has become one of the main drivers for China's economic growth. In 2011, e-retail accounted for 750 billion renminbi in size, but it expanded to 7.2 trillion renminbi, of which physical products accounted for 5.5 trillion renminbi, 15% of the total national retail in 2017,[1] and half of global retail e-commerce

* KONG Tuan Yuen is a Visiting Research Fellow at the East Asian Institute, National University of Singapore.

[1] The Ministry of Commerce of China, "The Report on E-commerce in China 2017", at <http://img.ec.com.cn/article/201806/1528093796188.pdf> (accessed 19 November 2018).

in 2017 is expected to occur in China.[2] Most importantly, e-commerce in China is not only developing in metropolitan areas due to convenient payment methods but also blooming in rural area due to efficient logistic arrangement. Both e-payments and logistics have together enhanced the cross-border online trade through internet settlement. Rural e-retail has reached 1.3 trillion renminbi, which increased 39.1% (YOY) faster than the growth rate of total e-retail (32.2%). The cross-border online trade is 90.2 billion renminbi, which has grown to 80.2% (YOY), including 33.6 billion renminbi in export and 56.6 billion renminbi in import.[3] According to the reports by the consulting firm *McKinsey*, the cross-border e-commerce of China may grow up 43% and reach 758 billion renminbi in 2018 and triple to 15% of the total e-commerce market in the next five years.[4]

There are many promotion methods being followed in China in the recent years to support e-commerce development. The Singles' Day Promotion (11 November) or Bachelor Day Promotion is one of the typical examples that expanded widely to contribute to the rapid development of China's e-commerce, and it became an important festival of consumption explosion similar to the Christmas season in western countries. The first Singles' Day Promotion Festival was held in 2009 and has since expanded and attracted more than 10,000 businesses who participated in the event on *Taobao.com* in 2012. The market size has rapidly grown, and other online e-commerce platforms followed in these footsteps to provide discounts or conduct promotions before or after 11 November in order to fight for the share of the flourishing e-commerce market. The website

---

[2] "China Will Account for Half of Global Retail Ecommerce Sales in 2017", *BizReport*, 5 July 2017, at <http://www.bizreport.com/2017/07/china-will-account-for-half-of-global-retail-ecommerce-sales.html> (accessed 12 August 2018).

[3] The Ministry of Commerce of China, "The Report on E-commerce in China 2017", at <http://img.ec.com.cn/article/201806/1528093796188.pdf> (accessed 19 November 2018).

[4] "A $60 Billion E-Commerce Loophole in China May Be Narrowing", *Bloomberg News*, 19 May 2017, at <https://www.bloomberg.com/news/articles/2017-05-18/a-60-billion-e-commerce-loophole-in-china-may-be-narrowing> (accessed 11 August 2018).

360buy held a one-month "Desert Storm" Promotion from 10 October; *Suning* held a "Zero Purchasing Within three hundred Yuan" Promotion, which offered a same value coupon once the purchase amount exceeded 300 yuan; and *Gome Online Mall* reduced its online prices by approximately 40%. Along with the expansion of online shops and retailers, many new logistics firms were set up to uphold the development of e-commerce in China.

Alibaba achieved a one-day transaction of 213.5 billion renminbi during the Singles' Day Promotion in 2018, which increased by 26.9% compared to the previous year and was about 4,270 times that of the first Singles' Day Promotion in 2009.[5] Besides, the logistics service created new history with a high of just over one billion renminbi. Alibaba believes that more than 180,000 branded companies over 200 countries were involved in the event. In addition, Alibaba's competitor, *JD.com*, held a similar event on 11 November and achieved sales of nearly 160 billion renminbi, which increased by 26% compared to the previous year.[6] Thus, the Singles' Day Promotion has not only become a special nationwide festival in China that was driven by major e-commerce platforms and supported by authorities, but also involved more and more retailers, businesses and consumers beyond the border, including entities that provided financial and logistic services.

Along with growing e-commerce developments, third-party online payment methods have been introduced to facilitate exchange transactions. AliPay, UnionPay and Tencent Finance are the three largest platforms of payment that accounted for nearly 60% of e-commerce in 2017.[7] It is well known that UnionPay is a state-owned enterprise

---

[5] "Alibaba Generates US$30.69 bn in Sales on Double Eleven", *Asia Times*, 12 November 2018, at <http://www.atimes.com/article/alibaba-generates-us30-69-bn-on-double-eleven/> (accessed 14 November 2018).

[6] "Alibaba Nets $30 billion in Singles' Day Haul", *The Japan News*, 12 November 2018, at <http://the-japan-news.com/news/article/0005343175> (accessed 14 November 2018).

[7] "China Third-Party Online/Mobile Payment Market Q4 2017", *China Internet Watch*, 29 May 2018, at <https://www.chinainternetwatch.com/24210/online-payment-market-q4-2017/> (accessed 20 November 2018).

which functions like the MasterCard or Visa, normally used in offline payments and transfers, even though it still holds a portion of the market share of payments in e-commerce. The online payment market is dominated by the internet giant Alibaba, and Tencent AliPay, which was created by the Alibaba group, is the most popular online payment platform in China. It just needs users to link their AliPay app with their local bank account to make online purchases. Tencent Finance, also called WeChat Pay, was incorporated in the social media WeChat with one billion monthly users and has expanded in recent years. It relied on QR codes that were found almost anywhere in China, including in rural areas and campuses, to process transfers and payments.

The excellent performance of e-commerce in China can not only be seen on the demand side but also in other aspects like infrastructure investments and related start-up venture capital. The major investment items included e-commerce infrastructure, e-commerce industrial park, e-commerce warehousing, O2O interaction (offline to online, online to offline), cross-border e-commerce and so on. The start-up venture capital for technologies such as Artificial Intelligence (AI) and Blockchain that are highly related to the exchange of online goods and services has significantly increased China's total investment in venture capital. In 2017, half of the world's 10 biggest venture capital investments were made in Chinese companies, especially in AI development. *Didi-Chuxing* and *Meituan-Dianping* accounted for about eight billion US dollars. Fundraising is supported by internet giants *Softbank* and *Tencent*, respectively, to promote the application of AI in e-commerce development. Furthermore, Alibaba has also raised 14 billion US dollors with major investors such as *Singapore Temasek Holdings* in the first half of 2018 to support *Ant Financial*'s development in fintech to explore businesses in e-payment and financial services.

Due to the promotion of the Mass Entrepreneurship policy, more than one-third of the firms have witnessed development in online sales and the market of e-commerce services reached about two trillion renminbi in 2015. According to *13th Five-Year Development Plan for e-Commerce*, there are about 26.9 million employees in e-commerce-related industries, whether they come from traditional industries and new types of businesses.[8] The Chinese government believes that cross-border e-commerce can significantly stir the growth rate of China's trade, which has slowed down in recent years.

The Scope of e-Commerce in China

The scope of e-commerce in China has evolved rapidly within last 30 years. Simply speaking, e-commerce literally means applying electronic tools or even information technology, such as internet and intranet, to carry out commercial activities. All electronic devices can be considered as tools of e-commerce, including telegraphs, phones, broadcasts, televisions and so on. At the beginning, the method of electronic data interchange (EDI) and electronic fund transfer (EFT) were initially introduced to accelerate information and money exchange in business. Credit cards, Automated Teller Machines (ATMs) and phone banking services were then accepted to change the mode of exchange in the traditionally commercial activities. This was the initial concept of e-commerce in the 1970s.

However, the common view of the development of e-commerce in China began from late 1990s. Notably, e-commerce has been widely explored not only in exchange methods but also in management of businesses itself in terms of physical distribution, capital flow and information exchange to support the entire business, including supply chain management, inventory management and customer relationship management, using information technology. Nowadays, the concept of e-commerce in China has developed further and broadened based on the evolutionary nature of the commercial activities. In a narrow sense, e-commerce in China is the transformation of the trading platform of conventional commercial activities through information technology. In a broad sense, e-commerce is the transformation of the whole

---

[8] Ministry of Commerce, "13th Five-Year Development Plan for E-commerce", 30 December 2016, at <http://www.mofcom.gov.cn/article/zt_dzsw135/> (accessed 12 November 2018).

process of conventional commercial activities through information technology.

There are at least three common modes that are always discussed to illustrate the development of e-commerce in China — Business-to-Business (B2B), Customer-to-Customer (C2C) and Business-to-Customer (B2C). With regard to China, internet technology was actively promoted for advancing the national information infrastructure and some e-commerce platforms were initially introduced in 1995, which are active even today. *China Yellow Page* (中国黄页), which was first established to provide information service for businesses, is considered as the beginning of B2B. *China Chemical Network*, which promoted and introduced chemical-related products and services, was next launched in 1997. Many e-commerce-related enterprises, such as *8848, Alibaba, Eachnet* and *Dangdang*, appeared one after another and extended the scope of e-commerce in China before the 2000s.

By early 2000s, the Dot.com bubble that led to negative shock in the global economy also seriously affected the development of Chinese e-commerce, especially the C2C mode of e-commerce enterprises. The popularity of internet and information technology in China did not completely support the advancement of e-commerce in these periods. Thousands of Chinese e-commerce enterprises, *8848* for example, suffered heavy loss and left the market. According to a survey conducted by the China B2B research centre, the websites of e-commerce-related enterprises between 2000 and 2002 only accounted for 12.1% of those available at present.[9]

Chinese e-commerce gradually recovered in 2003, which was also when *Alibaba* (B2B) established *Taobao.com* to compete with *Eachnet* (易趣网) that later was sold to eBay, an American e-commerce giant, in the C2C market. In order to simplify the exchange method for trading, *Alibaba group* further built the *Alipay system* (阿里支付) to provide third-party online payment services. Along with the improvement of

---

[9] "The Survey of China's E-commerce between 1997 and 2009", *Toocle China B2B Research Centre*. 2009, at <http://www.100ec.cn/zt/1997/> (accessed 17 August, 2017)

information technology, Alibaba then proceeded to move their business of *Taobao and Alipay system* into mobile devices. *Tencent* (腾讯) also introduced the network of *PaiPai* based on its social network *QQ* to enter the C2C market, but it was sold to *JD.com* (京东商城) and closed in 2016.

Actually, the most common type of e-commerce is (B2C, where related enterprises expanded their business from conventionally displaying the physical goods in real shops to virtually creating a website and email, and using online payment methods for trading; however, most of them are small and medium enterprises who find it hard to survive or just act as a supplement for real shops. In terms of market size, *JD.com* is one of the most successful B2C companies which focuses on *3C* products. Besides, *Alibaba* expanded the business model from B2B to C2C, and then B2C in 2008 by creating *Tmall.com* (天猫商城) to sell their own goods directly. *Sunning.com* (苏宁易购), which is based in Nanjing and was developed earlier in 1990s, also holds a part of the market share, but it was merged with *Tmall.com* in 2012.

The website *1688.com* (阿里巴巴批发网), one of the businesses in *Alibaba group* that provides consultation and services in domains such as purchasing, wholesale and logistics, for small–medium companies, is now the biggest B2B enterprise in China. *HC360.com* (慧聪网) is another leading organization and was the first company listed on the Chinese stock market. There are some B2B enterprises that only concern a single industry or particular function that have developed rapidly. For example, *made-in-china.com* focuses on providing matching services in the manufacturing industry. Others include *Gongchang.com* (世界工厂网), *Zhaomei.com* (找煤网), *Njw88.com* (农集网) and so on.

Apparently, *Alibaba group* has gradually been playing a leading role in the development of Chinese e-commerce in almost all aspects, even though there are some influential companies which share the market. The advantage of *Alibaba group* not only comes from the implementation of advanced information technology and rapid resource integration in processes, such as supply chain management for saving operational costs and work efficiency, but also from continuously providing new business models and solutions to explore new customers and create new markets.

Apart from *Taobao.com* (C2C), *Tmall.com* (B2C) and *1688.com* (B2B), there are at least three other types of major businesses in the *Alibaba group* that mutually support each other. The first type consists of extended and overseas-oriented subsidiaries, including *AliExpress* (全球速卖通) for global consumers to directly purchase Chinese products and *Alibaba.com* (阿里巴巴国际交易市场) as a worldwide version of *1688.com* for global trading and wholesaling. The second type comprises technology solution-based subsidiaries, including *Alimama.com* (阿里妈妈) that provides consultation for e-commerce enterprises in digital marketing, *Alibabacloud.com* (阿里云) that offers cloud computing services, *Ant Financial* (蚂蚁金服) that provides financial services to small enterprises and consumers, and *CaiNiao* (菜鸟) that uncovers the logistic data for current e-commerce companies to improve their business or the potential ones to create a new line.

The Supporting Policies

From 1990s, the Chinese central government has gradually realised that information technology is one of the major elements to support national economic growth. Some prospective projects were implemented to enhance the infrastructure for the development of information technology, including four golden plans (golden bridge, golden gate, golden card and golden tax), and the first batch of internet (*Chinanet, ChinaGBN, Cernet, Cstnet* and *CNNIC*). Even so, most of these projects were just for academic purposes at the very beginning.

However, the widespread use of internet led the State Council to announce the Interim Regulation of the People's Republic of China on the Management of International networking of Computer Information in 1996 to satisfy the increasing requirement of regulation for internet activities. It was very clear from Article 1 from the amendment in 1997 that the purpose of the regulation was not only to strengthen the management of international networking of computer information but also to develop heathier international exchange of computer information. Based on the amendment, the Measures for Security Protection Administration of the International Networking of Computer Information Networks was promulgated to emphasise the security protection to avoid social instability at the end of the same year.[10]

After the implementation of the initial internet regulations, the Ministry of Foreign Trade and Economic cooperation of China established a website in 1998 to promote the regulation of trade and provided information on international and local trade, especially to assist Chinese companies entering foreign markets via the internet. The website of China Import and Export Fair was also launched in the following year to support online trading activities. Meanwhile, the Chinese central government set up the Department of International Electronic Commerce as a window for local and foreign companies to carry out e-commerce.

The comprehensive promotion of e-commerce by the Chinese central government could be tracked back to the 10th Five-Year Plan (2001–2005). One of the key parts of the plan is to push forward the information technology industry and hold up the development of e-commerce.[11] The white paper regarding Chinese e-commerce, namely The Internet Application and e-commerce of Chinese Enterprises (2000–2001), was simultaneously published to provide the guideline for current and potential e-commerce enterprises to engage in e-commerce activities.

In the second half of 2000s, the Ministry of Commerce of China began to provide several influential suggestions and regulations to enhance e-commerce. The major documents included the Law of Electronic Signature (2004), the opinion on accelerating the e-commerce's development (2004), the guideline for e-payment (2005),

---

[10] "Measures for Security Protection Administration of the International Networking of Computer Information Networks", *CNNIC*, at <http://www.cnnic.cn/ggfw/fwzxxgzcfg/2009/201207/t20120720_32433.htm> (accessed 24 August 2017).

[11] "The Outline of Tenth Five-Year Plan for National Economic and Social Development of the People's Republic of China", The State Council of The People's Republic of China, at <http://www.gov.cn/gongbao/content/2001/content_60699.htm> (accessed 23 August 2017).

the opinion for online trading (2006), the regulation of e-commerce (2008), the e-commerce's development for 11th Five-Years Plan (2007), the Regulation of e-shopping (2008), the opinion for speeding up the logistics for e-commerce (2009), the rules of e-payment services for non-financial sector (2010) and so on.

The policies for e-commerce-related elements such as third-party payment systems were continuously established in 2010s. The Chinese Ministry of Commerce enacted the rules of third-party exchange platform (2011) to build a fair and trustworthy environment to protect the legal interest of both consumers and enterprises. It also provided suggestions on the establishment, maintenance and monitoring of credit systems by creating the Guideline of Credit System Construction of e-Commerce in 12th Five-Year Plan (2011). In addition, advanced topics, including the demonstration cities on e-commerce, e-logistic, financial IC card, transborder e-commerce, etc., had been discussed and form the e-commerce-related policies.

Internet broadband applications were officially studied from late 1990s and implemented in 2000s. The State Council of China announced the Strategy of Broadband China in 2013, emphasising the need to speed up web surfing and internet efficiency, especially targeting on increasing the number of users in rural areas, small–medium enterprises and regional coordination. From 2014, it also introduced the list of demonstrated cities to extend the broadband application from first-tier cities to second- and third-tier ones every year.

There are four major polices that have been advocated to promote the supporting environment of e-commerce under the administration of Chinese President Xi Jinping since 2013 — Internet Plus Action Plan, Made in China 2025, Mass Innovation and Entrepreneurship, and the Belt and Road Initiative. Broadly speaking, the aims of the Internet Plus Action Plan are constructing free and easy bases for internet development, intensifying the innovation-driven cyberspace, expanding the e-commerce market, enhancing the capacity and ability of intelligence, and organising the implementing agency.

Made in China 2025 supports e-commerce from the perspective of industrial development. There are 10 sectors which were expanded from Seven Strategic Emerging Industries. The new generation of information technology industries, which includes the environmental establishment and technological application of e-commerce, is one of the sectors that the Chinese government is highly concerned with.

By pushing forward the economic structural reform and adjustment in China, the Chinese government brought forward the idea of Mass Innovation and Entrepreneurship to encourage people to do business by various innovative ways and incubate creative ideas online. The internet has become the most important channel to try an own business, which can flourish with the development of e-commerce. The current development of e-commerce was highly hastened by the Belt and Road Initiative which shifted the interest of e-commerce from the local level to across borders. The Belt and Road Initiative encouraged the Chinese companies and individuals not only to strengthen the engagement with foreign counterparts along the routes but also to provide opportunities for both sides to widen the scope of e-commerce via the internet.

The Implication for Southeast Asia

China is the pioneer of e-commerce development in the region; so other countries, especially the Association of Southeast Asian Nations (ASEAN), are keen to learn from and cooperate with China to promote e-commerce. The relatively successful practice of China's e-commerce gave ASEAN countries a good model to follow. ASEAN has initiated ASEAN Economic Community (AEC) Blueprint 2025 that consists of five interrelated and mutually reinforcing cooperation thrusts, including: (i) A Highly Integrated and Cohesive Economy; (ii) A Competitive, Innovative, and Dynamic ASEAN; (iii) Enhanced Connectivity and Sectoral Cooperation; (iv) A Resilient, Inclusive, People-Oriented, and People-Centred ASEAN; and (v) A Global ASEAN. In line and directly related to the above-mentioned first three thrusts of promoting a more integrated economy, innovation and connectivity, e-commerce collaboration was considered as a new source of regional growth.

It is envisaged that regional cooperation on e-commerce can also eventually promote the last two thrusts of a people-oriented and people-centred ASEAN, and a global ASEAN by enabling more individuals and enterprises to achieve greater access to markets and facilitate more cross-border transactions. Also, e-commerce is in line with the overall focus in 2018 that sees ASEAN and China working together to jointly commemorate the 15th anniversary of the establishment of the strategic partnership between ASEAN and China, and celebrate the China–ASEAN Year of Innovation.

E-commerce is widely considered crucial for economic development nowadays. It is not only pushing the development of infrastructure and logistics that would lead to greater connectivity among ASEAN–China countries but also driving the cross-border trade and investment that would strengthen greater regional economic integration. In the long run, e-commerce also brings along the rise of the sharing economy and the widespread use of the e-payment method, which would improve and lead to the growth of the new economy together. Inevitably, flourishing e-commerce may create short-term adjustment costs that might sway some existing commercial sectors. For example, shopping malls would be forced to close and many small conventional traders, especially in informal sectors, would lose opportunities to explore their businesses through the traditional way. It leads to potentially high social costs for the less-developed ASEAN countries.

Southeast Asian countries explore how to nurture their e-commerce capabilities and promote collaboration in this area so as to help individuals or companies more easily access new markets and overseas customers. In Southeast Asia countries, despite their diversity and different stages of growth, the governments also realise the importance of e-commerce that leverages on technology and know-how to not only spur economic growth but also promote social considerations, such as greater distribution of wealth through new employment opportunities and easier access to markets.

According to the research findings commissioned by *Google* and *Temasek Holdings*, the value of internet economy in Southeast Asia will be over US$ 240 billion by 2025, a fifth higher than the previous estimation.[12] Furthermore, 1.7 million jobs will be created and 200,000 highly skilled jobs, such as software engineering and data scientists, will emerge to help the companies expand their businesses or create new opportunities in different areas, especially e-commerce logistics, ride-hailing, and online travel and food delivery. The same study also reports that the investment in the internet economy hit US$ 24 billion in 2015 and targets to receive US$ 40 billion to US$ 50 billion capital by 2025. The internet economy of Southeast Asia could be seen world-wide as one of the fastest growing, and it is attracting investors to participate in e-commerce development.

The development of e-commerce in Southeast Asian countries has witnessed moderate growth in recent years (Table 1). Among the Southeast Asian countries' population of close to 650 million, over 370 million or 58% have become internet users. This means that more than half of Southeast Asian countries' population, roughly equal to half of internet users in China, have the potential to participate in online commercial activity. Even though data for Brunei, Cambodia, Laos and Myanmar are not available, the total value of the e-commerce market in terms of consumer goods in this region has reached nearly US$ 18 billion, especially Indonesia (7 billion) due to the population base. The total value of the e-commerce market as a proportion of Southeast Asian countries' population is still tiny. In contrast, China's e-commerce market for consumer goods was close to US$ 500 billion in market value in 2017. Simply speaking, China has nearly 28 times the Southeast Asian countries' e-commerce market value with only double the internet users. The e-commerce penetration has grown rapidly, in particular, in Southeast Asian countries like Singapore (51%), Malaysia (45%) and Vietnam (35%).

Table 1 also shows that most Southeast Asian countries are still plagued by the problem of "digital divide", between the urban and

---

[12] "Internet Economy to Create 1.7 million Full-Time Jobs in Southeast Asia by 2025: Study", *Channel NewsAsia*, 19 November 2018, at <https://www.channelnewsasia.com/news/technology/internet-economy-to-create-1-7-million-full-time-jobs-in-10946012> (accessed 20 November 2018).

Table 1: The Comparison between China and Southeast Asian Countries in E-Commerce Development (2017)

	Population Person (millions)	Urbanisation (%)	Internet Penetration Person (millions)	Internet Penetration (%)	E-Commerce Penetration Person (millions)	E-Commerce Penetration (%)	E-Commerce (Consumer Goods) Value (USD billions)
China	1412.0	58	751.0	53	581.5	41	499.1
Indonesia	265.4	56	132.7	50	28.1	11	7.1
Singapore	5.8	100	4.8	84	3.1	54	3.3
Thailand	69.1	53	57.0	82	11.9	17	3.0
Vietnam	96.0	35	64.0	67	35.1	37	2.2
Philippines	105.7	44	67.0	63	33.8	32	1.2
Malaysia	31.8	76	25.1	79	15.2	48	1.1
Brunei	0.4	78	0.4	95	n.a.	n.a.	n.a.
Cambodia	16.1	21	8.0	50	n.a.	n.a.	n.a.
Laos	6.9	41	2.4	35	n.a.	n.a.	n.a.
Myanmar	53.6	36	18.0	34	n.a.	n.a.	n.a.
ASEAN	640.8		371.7	58			

Source: Listed from *We are Social, Hootsuite* (2018).

rural areas, and between the higher and lower income groups. The e-commerce development may reduce this gap because it offers rural populations a real incentive to be more digitalised. China provides a good example of this. Following the latest information released by the China's Ministry of Commerce in 2017, the amount of rural e-retail is 1.2 trillion renminbi, which is an increase of 39.1% (YOY), and rural internet users have reached 200 million, an increase of 35.4% (YOY).[13] On the other hand, the companies in the Southeast Asian countries in general have not sufficiently utilised the internet to engage in commercial activities, in terms of using email with clients/suppliers or having a dedicated website in Asia to promote their businesses, which lags behind most of other countries in the Asian region and is just on par with the South Asian countries (Asian Development Bank, 2016) (Figure 1).

In China, the e-commerce industry has made rapid progress over the decades and has become a mainstay of the economy. The Chinese government has identified innovation in general and digital economy (of which e-commerce is an integral part) in particular as key engines of growth. At the commercial level, some of the giant internet Chinese enterprises such as Baidu, Alibaba and Tencent are at the cutting edge of innovation and have already secured a large domestic market share in niche areas. They have also heralded a new business model that offers useful references for other countries.

The growth of e-commerce may in the short run disrupt some urban business, but it will also lead to new employment opportunities. More significantly, it may ultimately promote rural development and eventually narrow the urban–rural income disparity, a big problem in most developing countries. Additionally, e-commerce may lead rural areas to upgrade their infrastructure, such as electricity and bandwidths for facilitating the network transaction (B2B, B2C, C2C and so on), and

---

[13] The Ministry of Commerce of China, "The Report on E-commerce in China 2017", at <http://img.ec.com.cn/article/201806/1528093796188.pdf> (accessed 19 November 2018).

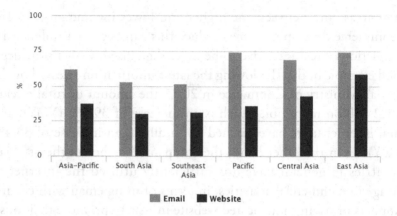

Figure 1:   Share of Companies that Use Email with Clients/Suppliers, Have Own Website in Asia (% by Region)
Source: Enterprise Survey 2016, World Bank

also establish a convenient transportation system for increasing fresh and early food exchange.

The Southeast Asian Countries' e-Commerce Policy

There is huge potential for Southeast Asia to boost its growth and catch up with countries on cutting edge e-commerce when its internet users are willing to jump into various e-commerce activities and its companies are keen to broaden their businesses via online technology. The complementarity between Southeast Asian countries and China in online technology and the e-commerce market could provide many collaborative opportunities for mutual benefit. This is the reason Southeast Asia countries are keen to create a digital policy to help the development of e-commerce.

Most of the Southeast Asian countries started their e-commerce policies by digital infrastructure improvement. The main digital policy in Indonesia is the Indonesian Broadband Plan 2014–2019, which is a part of both the Master Plan for the Acceleration and Expansion of

Indonesian Economic Development, and the National Medium-Term Development Plan 2015–2019, which aims to promote nationwide broadband for enhancing digital connectivity in Indonesia, spanning from Sabang in Aceh to Merauke in Papua. The digital policy in Indonesia has been initiated by the Parliament. The non-profit organisations and civil society movements, such as the Indonesian Internet Service Providers Association, Telecommunication Society, Internet Domain Name Managers Indonesia, Society of Creative Industries Information Technology and Communications Indonesia, Friends for Fair Information and Communications (SIKA) and higher education institutions/universities, will also participate individually in the process of digital policymaking.

In Philippines, the Department of Trade and Industry formulated the first Philippine e-Commerce Roadmap 2016–2020 in order to point out the important role of e-commerce for national development and to review the achievements and prospects after the enactment of the Electronic Commerce Act 2000.[14] The Roadmap has followed the APEC Digital Prosperity Checklist to enhance Philippines's e-commerce development by strengthening six *"I"*s — *infrastructure* (need for appropriate supply chain and communication), *investment* (promotion from FDI to capital flow), *innovation* (enhancement from supporting policy to R&D protection), *intellectual capital* (accumulation such as e-commerce skill and training from technological to linguistic to entrepreneurship), *information flow* (by promoting privacy and a trusted internet environment) and digital *integration* (between domestic industries to global production network and market).

In the 11th Malaysia Plan (2016–2020), infrastructure development in the form of, for example, digital access is the major policy to support sustainable economic growth. The new government after the 14th general election has also pushed hard for broadband penetration with lower price in Malaysia. Since 2016, the National e-Commerce Strategic Roadmap of Malaysia aimed to double Malaysia's e-commerce

---

[14] Philippines Department of Trade and Industry "E-commerce Roadmap", at <https://www.dti.gov.ph/roadmap> (accessed 16 November 2018).

growth rate by 2020 by encouraging small–medium enterprises involved in e-commerce businesses through e-payment innovations, logistic facilitation and e-marketplaces. Most significantly, the Malaysian government has cooperated with the Chinese e-commerce giant Alibaba's Jack Ma, to develop the Digital Free-Trade Zone for connecting all the small businesses through online trade.

The Digital Thailand 4.0 Plan was introduced in 2016. The aims of the plan was not only to set up a countrywide digital infrastructure to push forward the economy with digital technology but also to create a knowledge-based digital government and society and to build the digital workforce. The plan was highlighted to strengthen the internet adoption of businesses, especially to encourage small–medium enterprises from the rural and remote areas to market their products and develop a payment channel through the internet. The Thai government is working hard to form a digital economy and society, and is expected to become one of the digital leaders within the ASEAN economic community.

The Singapore government agencies work very closely to make businesses transform into e-commerce environments. Several industry initiatives were introduced to promote e-commerce development in Singapore.[15] The Economic Development Board has collaborated with the Info-communications Media Development Authority (IMDA) to standardise IT facilitation and B2B documents exchange to form an e-commerce-friendly cluster for companies under the Industry 21 blueprint. They aimed to develop an internationally linked e-commerce infrastructure to uphold Singapore as an e-commerce hub and to encourage its strategic businesses applications and promote public e-commerce penetration. The Action Community for Entrepreneurship, Enterprise Singapore and JTC Corporation provide coinnovation programmes to facilitate the corporates and start-ups to access local and

---

[15] Economic Development Board of Singapore, "Singapore Industry Initiatives for E-commerce", 9 July 2018, at <https://www.edb.gov.sg/en/news-and-resources/insights/innovation/singapore-industry-initiatives-for-e-commerce.html> (accessed 16 November 2018).

global online markets through digital technology and knowledge support. The Inland Revenue Authority of Singapore also introduced the Networked Trade Platform to support companies in the trade and logistics industry to development e-commerce where importers and exporters need online services from all related government agencies.

Part 3

Reform and Reorganisation of the State Sector

Chapter 9

Financialisation of the State Sector in China

Barry NAUGHTON*

S ince 2013, changes in the governance of state firms in China has resulted in the entire state sector becoming increasingly "financialised." In a purely definitional sense, this means that control over state firms is increasingly exercised by financial means, operating at a distance, through corporate governance institutions similar to those in other economies. However, it must be emphasised from the outset that this financialisation has taken place in a particular context. After decades in which the Chinese government was primarily withdrawing from direct management of the economy (through market-oriented economic reforms, 1978 to about 2006), China has begun to re-emphasise the primacy of government-defined national goals. Crucially, though, these goals are mainly pursued through financial means. The result has been an increasingly interventionist government, steering increasingly important state firms, through financial instruments. Changes introduced as part of the broad reform package of the 2013 Third Plenum have, perhaps unexpectedly, been an important part of this phenomenon.

*Barry NAUGHTON is the So Kwanlok Professor at the School of Global Policy and Strategy, University of California, San Diego.

This chapter begins with a description of the background of the important shift to financialisation, emphasising its evolutionary development out of multiple elements from diverse agendas. The main body of the chapter describes the changes in terms of three different levels: from the top-down exercise of ownership rights; the proliferation of government-managed funds, especially "industrial guidance funds"; and the evolution of "mixed ownership" firms at the grass-roots. In the third section, I make a preliminary assessment of these changes. I argue that the financialisation of the state sector, in and of itself, likely provides some efficiency gains by reducing the importance of bureaucratic management and oversight in the state sector. However, the fact that financialisation has been accompanied by increased government steerage and Communist Party oversight is likely to vitiate many of those efficiency gains. Ultimately, the different outcomes and effects are part and parcel of a single set of policy changes. The desire to steer the economy to continued high growth and a high-technology future, for now at least, has the highest priority with Chinese policymakers. In this context, financialisation provides a means to use state-owned firms to achieve these objectives, while attempting to minimise the associated efficiency losses. This amounts to an enormous wager on the success of industrial policies, and it is not at all clear that China's leaders will win this gamble.

The Evolution of a Financialised State Sector

One of the most enduring images of the state-owned enterprise (SOE) is that of a giant steel mill. Based on the Soviet model, the steel mill was the classic "dinosaur", enormous but slow-moving and inefficient. Moreover, these dinosaurs — in China as well as in the Soviet Union — were controlled primarily through quantitative targets and top-down allocation of inputs and output. Financial controls existed, but they were purely passive accounting devices used to prevent corruption and diversion of resources. The traditional SOE, in other words, was specifically "de-financialised," a plant in a gigantic government-run industrial complex, without its own financial intelligence or financial interest.

Such old-style SOEs disappeared in China during the 1990s.[1] Traditional planning with output targets and quantitative rationing was abolished. However, the conversion to something new was incomplete. The Company Law of 1995 envisaged the gradual conversion of traditional SOEs into corporations, which would enable them to develop a straightforward financial calculus and lay the groundwork for diversified ownership. This process went quickly for one category of SOEs — profitable firms that could be listed on domestic or international stock exchanges — but went very much more slowly for less-profitable firms and, especially, for the rather opaque "apex corporations" under the central SASAC. These 100-odd firms were still somewhat bureaucratic and non-transparent, had often held on to money-losing subsidiaries, and a late as 2010, less than half had been corporatised. The corporate governance foundation for financialisation was not generally in place in the state sector, 20 years after the promulgation of the Company Law. The SOE reform slowed down, and as a result SOEs were stuck in a partially bureaucratic, partially business environment. Meanwhile, private businesses surged ahead with the introduction of venture capital, new corporate forms and explosive, innovative firm development.[2] As a result, the industrial sector was increasingly dominated by private firms. By the end of 2017, only 17.8% of industrial employment was in state-controlled firms.[3]

While SOEs were becoming much less important in industrial sectors, state ownership continued to dominate the financial sector itself.

---

[1] John Wong, *Zhu Rongji and China's Economic Take-off*, London, Imperial College Press, 2016.

[2] For accessible accounts, see David Sheff, *China Dawn: Culture and Conflict in China's Business Revolution*, New York, Harper Business, 2002; and Porter Erisman, *Alibaba's World: How a Remarkable Chinese Company is Changing the Face of Global Business*, New York, Palgrave Macmillan, 2015.

[3] National Bureau of Statistics, *China Statistical Yearbook 2018*, Tables 13-3 and 13-5. This covers industrial enterprises with revenue above 20 million yuan (about USD$3 million). The state-controlled enterprise share of assets is much higher, 39% at the end of 2017, while the state share of industrial workers would be significantly lower if small-scale firms (essentially all private) were included.

Hard information about the financial sector is much less available than is the case for industry.[4] However, about 98% of banking system assets in China are in state-owned banks.[5] The state-owned financial sector was frequently a poor match with the increasingly dynamic private sector. Small private firms still depended primarily on internal earnings and informal borrowing to grow, finding dealing with the state banks costly and difficult. State banks, in turn, often preferred to deal with state firms, even though those firms are substantially less profitable than their private-sector counterparts. Thus, a large state-owned financial sector has long been established in China, but the effort to genuinely spread financial markets and financial decision-making to the public and private goods-producing economy has proceeded by fits and starts. This chapter describes the extension of those financial principles to the rest of the state sector through the creation of an intermediary layer of financial funds.

A big milestone in the evolution of SOEs was the 2013 Third Plenum, which laid out a broad program of renewed economic reforms in which the state sector played a prominent role. It called for completing the long-overdue conversion of traditional SOEs into corporations, which was mostly accomplished by 2018, laying the basis for financialisation. It called on SOEs to develop mixed-ownership systems, including allowing (exceptional) cases in which private parties take controlling stakes in existing state enterprises. It said that the exercise of state ownership should transition from "asset management" to "capital management", that is, to a kind of arms-length wealth management. Though vague, this could in itself potentially imply financialisation, since it called for the establishment of several separate state investment funds, and transfer of some ownership to the social security fund (eventually 10% stakes were transferred). Thus, the Third Plenum

---

[4] Detailed information on the financial sector was redacted from the published 2013 Third Economic Census.

[5] See the discussion in Barry Naughton, *The Chinese Economy: Adaptation and Growth*, Cambridge, MA, MIT Press, 2017, pp. 488–492. Only 1.3% of bank assets in 2015 were in foreign banks, and a few pilot private domestic banks were approved in 2014. Only the rapidly growing fintech operations of the Internet giants Alibaba and Tencent modify this general picture.

made extensive proposals for altering the system of managing state ownership, but was very imprecise as to how these changes were to play out.

In fact, the implementation of reforms laid out at the Third Plenum was extremely uneven, and on balance disappointing. A broad pattern emerged that when reforms ran into difficult patches, during which they threatened to destabilise the economy or slow growth, reforms were quickly frozen or withdrawn. The most obvious cases of this were the stock market in 2015 and RMB internationalisation and capital account liberalisation in 2016. The stock market in 2015 soared on the back of promising reforms and encouragement in the official media; when an inevitable pullback occurred in the summer, policymakers poured money into market stabilisation through government-backed funds and restricted various kinds of selling. Capital account liberalisation in 2016 led to the loss of almost one trillion dollars in official foreign exchange reserves, in this case, forcing the government to reimpose controls on capital outflows. Other reforms also fit into this general pattern, including reforms of the taxation system (2014–2015). As a result, a broader capital market liberalisation did not take shape in the years after 2013, at least through the end of 2018. It is not that reforms were a complete failure, but rather that a particular pattern of partial success and partial failure became evident. The outcome was a state sector that was in fact adapted towards financial controls without a broader financial market liberalisation. This outcome was largely the result of the preference of Chinese policymakers for control and stability, and their desire to shape development outcomes in their preferred way. The end result was a strengthened set of instruments giving policymakers the potential to steer state enterprise development and decisions.

State Capital Investment and Operation Funds

From the beginning of the post-2013 reform process, the mechanism proposed to begin the financialisation process from the top-down was the creation of new state capital investment and operations companies (SCIOs). These new funds or holding companies were to be inserted directly under the existing government ownership agencies, central (SASAC) State Asset Supervision and Administration Commission and the local SASACs. SASAC was a legacy and hybrid agency, cobbled together from various bureaucratic agencies. It had the legal authority to exercise government ownership, but also substantial regulatory responsibilities. It had little in the way of financial expertise. The objective, then, was to insert SCIOs underneath SASAC in order to create a layer focused on financial return, possessing financial expertise and even, possibility in competition with other SCIOs over return. This had the potential to create a real incentive for change and restructuring in the state sector, but it took quite a while to work out the forms and permissible modes, which was only resolved after two years of debate and discussion in an authoritative top-level document in late 2015.[6]

The approach ultimately adopted was to convert a few existing SOEs under the control of central and local SASACs into SCIOs and gradually transfer authority to them. Ultimately, after the experiments proved successful, SASAC could be abolished. The SCIOs are explicitly instructed to maximise investment returns, but also to exercise control functions more effectively. Thus, the SCIOs have turned out to be much more like investment banks or development funds than wealth funds. By 2017, central SASAC had created 10 pilot SCIOs, each of them created by granting expanded powers to an existing SASAC firm. Even before that time, the hundred or so "apex" firms directly under SASAC had special status as "investment capable" entities and presided over corporate empires with hundreds of subsidiaries. Now they were being encouraged to diversify further according to financial principles and transform themselves into something more like financial holding companies. Provincial and municipal SASACs created 122 subordinate SCIOs by late 2018. (There are some minor differences between state

---

[6] Communist Party of China (CPC) and State Council, "Guiding opinions of the Central Committee of the Chinese Communist Party and the State Council on deepening the reform of state-owned enterprises", [in Chinese], Xinhuanet, 24 August 2015, at <news. xinhuanet.com/politics/2015-09/13/c_1116547305.htm>. Ultimately, the more radical proposal to create government wealth funds, like Temasek in Singapore, was set aside.

capital investment companies and state capital operations companies, which are here treated together as SCIOs.) At the central level, SASAC chose familiar subordinate firms to become SCIOs, because they had experience with restructuring and the exercise of control rights, but also because they are closely tied to SASAC and fit comfortably into the existing hierarchy of control. Whether local SASACs have carried out more radical experiments with independent SCIOs must be determined by future research.

SCIOs clearly have developmental functions. That is, they are not instructed simply to maximise returns, but rather to develop new industries in line with government development plans and priorities. This is explicitly stated in the enabling legislation: they should "Push state capital into important industries and key sectors that affect national security, the commanding heights of the national economy and the people's livelihood … and fully bring into play the core and exemplary function of SOEs in realizing the strategy of innovation-driven development and become a manufacturing power", among other things.[7] Local-level SCIOs are often happy to support the specific priorities laid out in local development plans.

Industrial Guidance Funds

The next level down is more operational in implementing government policies and developmental strategies. These are the "industrial guidance funds", which basically seek to replicate the United States experience with venture capital funds and other types of investment entities. Crucially, these funds are set up to be "specialised", both in their objectives and in their organisational form. There is a managing partner specialised in running the fund's specific investments, and a number of

---

[7] Communist Party of China (CPC) and State Council, "Guiding opinions of the Central Committee of the Chinese Communist Party and the State Council on deepening the reform of state-owned enterprises", Article 14. Wang Lu and Sun Shaohua, "Speeding up the pilot reform of state capital investment and operations companies," *Jingji Cankaobao.* December 10, 2018, pp. 1, 3.

limited partners who provide funding without participating directly in management.[8] The funds are generally either limited partnerships — with an SOE or government agency as the primary sponsor and managing partner — or a non-listed joint stock corporation. SASAC, or a local government, authorises and establishes the basic framework for the fund, but does not directly participate in the creation of the fund or its management. That is, governments and ministries act as "initiators" of industrial guidance funds (IGFs) but should normally delegate that actual investment in the fund to a corporate entity. This is where SCIOs come in: frequently, SCIOs create the managing partner that will fund the fund. Therefore, one description of the IGFs is as follows: "the government sets up a platform; central SOEs serve as sponsors; the [state] banks come in close behind; and social capital will follow."[9] Here, "SOEs" usually refer to SCIOs, that is, those SOEs that have been given expanded investment rights. It can immediately be seen that IGFs are intended to leverage their initial capital, attracting investment from multiple limited partners.

Every fund has a "purpose." Upon establishment, it declares the investment strategy it will follow (for example, angel investing, venture capital, fund of funds) and the sectoral priorities it will follow. These strategies are a matter of public record, and the registrations show that most funds intend to invest in a relatively broad range of high-tech, strategic or "new growth driver" sectors. In principle, IGFs could be set up to invest in whatever they want, but in practice China is engaged in a vast, government-supported program to foster high-tech industrialisation. The various specific programs are grouped under the government's umbrella "Innovation-Driven Development Strategy" (IDDS),

---

[8] Xiao Yaqing (Head of SASAC) quoted in Xinhua News Agency, "Make state capital operation more prominent; a three-level system of innovation development funds for central SOEs is rapidly coming together", *Xinhua*, 24 May 2017, at <http://www.gov.cn/xinwen/2017-05/24/content_5196474.htm>

[9] Chen Yanpeng, "Uncovering the mystery of the SOE Reform Fund: Where does 550 billion RMB come from and where will it be invested?", *Huaxia Daily*, 27 May 2015, at <http://fund.eastmoney.com/news/1593,20170527742275031.html>

a top-level document adopted in May 2016.[10] Not surprisingly, the vast majority of IGFs post investment strategies that are in line with the IDDS. One of the oldest and best-known of these funds is the Integrated Circuit (IC) Industry Fund, which the Ministry of Finance describes as "an organic combination of national strategy and the market mechanism."[11] The professionals who run the funds are given clear incentive contracts, with relatively high-powered rewards for good performance.

Industrial guidance funds are new, but are already enormous. At the end of 2014, the total value of "guidance funds" was only a couple of hundred billion renminbi, not much more than the value of the National IC Development Fund (first round) which was set up in that year. By the end of the second quarter of 2018, the value of the funds had reached an astonishing 10.3 trillion renminbi, roughly US$1.5 trillion.[12] The value is a stock, rather than a flow: it is the total fund-raising scope designated in the articles of agreement creating individual fund. The figure is significantly larger than the flow of investment into projects during the course of the year and, more important, not all the funds have raised all the money specified in the agreements. In this sense, the figures may overstate the size of the financial resources mobilised. Yet the National IC Development Fund did succeed in raising and disbursing the entire value of its first round of fundraising by 2017, and launched a second round.

Table 1 provides a list of the largest of these funds. There are several huge central-government-run funds. The largest is the SOE Structural Adjustment Fund, which can provide funding both for the high-tech industry and to restructure and shrink traditional industries, as

---

[10] Chinese Communist Party and State Council, "Outline of the Innovation-Driven Development Strategy [in Chinese]", Xinhua News Agency, 19 May 2016, at <http://www.xinhuanet.com/politics/2Xin016-05/19/c_1118898033.htm>

[11] Ministry of Finance, Economic Construction Division, "The Operation and Investments of the National Integrated Circuit Industry Fund are Running Smoothly", at <http://jjs.mof.gov.cn/zhengwuxinxi/gongzuodongtai/201508/t20150828_1438798.html> (accessed 25 August 2018).

[12] These data come from the commercial database maintained by Zero2IPO.

Table 1: Largest Industrial Guidance Funds

Fund Name	Level	Scale (billion RMB)
Central SOE Structural Adjustment Fund	Central	350
National Strategic Emerging Industries Fund	Central	300
Qingdao New Growth Drivers	Municipal	300
National IC Fund (Rounds One & Two)	Central	289
Jinan New Growth Drivers	Municipal	250
China Optical Valley (Wuhan)	Municipal	250
Sichuan Sector Development	Province	200
Gansu Highway Fund	Province	200
Guangzhou Urban Renewal	Municipal	200
China Innovation Fund	Central	150
Guoxin Central SOE Operational Fund	Central	150

envisaged in the Supply-side Structural Reform initiative introduced in 2016. The new Strategic Emerging Industries (SEI) Fund, established in 2017, is already the second largest fund, and the two rounds of funding in the IC Industry Development Fund together add up to 289 billion. In fact, the giant central government funds only account for 22% of total funding. The bulk of the funding is at the local level: provincial funds are 32% of the total and municipal funds 46%. Among the local-level funds, the municipal funds from the cities of Qingdao, Jinan, Wuhan and Guangzhou stand out for their huge size.

IGFs make up an intermediate layer. Above them are the SCIOs, or sometimes governments acting directly. They invest "downward" in grass-roots firms, which will often be of "mixed ownership" (discussed in the following section). An example helps clarify the relationship among entities at different levels. One of central SASAC's apex firms is Guoxin (or China Reform Holdings). It has long had a special status among SASAC firms as a specialist in firm restructuring, and has now been designated a SCIO, a state capital operations company. Its expanded responsibilities have included raising several "industrial guidance funds", sometimes in collaboration with other SCIOs, that carry out direct investments. Among the IGFs Guoxin has established is one China Venture Capital (Guofengtou). Guoxin provided China Venture Capital with its managing partner, and it raised additional money from several limited partners (including the finance subsidiary of China Construction Bank and the local government of Shenzhen, where it is headquartered). True to its name, China Venture Capital invests both in start-up firms and in acquisitions. It is the sole owner of a Silicon Valley-based venture capital firm called Canyon Bridge Capital Partners, which in 2017 made a takeover bid for an American firm called Lattice Semiconductor. Clearly, Guoxin has seized substantial financial autonomy and has used it in creative ways. Equally clearly, that autonomy is implicitly or explicitly conditional on Guoxin serving as an instrument for government policy — in this case, building up China's semiconductor industry through foreign acquisitions. In pursuit of that objective, nearly any kind of activity is permitted.[13] This case also shows an SCIO exercising developmental policy through fully financialised instruments. All of Guoxin's subsidiaries, including China Venture Capital, are independent entities with fully articulated corporate governance structures and clear incentives and responsibilities for the managing partner and the limited partners. Even Guoxin itself is largely financialised, since it exercises a financial ownership stake in many firms without having any of the additional regulatory and command-and-control functions that SASAC had.

Upon establishment, IGFs bring in a group of limited partners or equity shareholders. The largest central government IGF, the Central SOE Structural Adjustment Fund, is relatively new, initiated in September 2016 by the Chengtong Corporation, a central government SOE converted into an SCIO. All of this fund's limited partners are SOEs. This is also true of the National IC Fund, at least in its first round of fundraising. The biggest contributors to the National IC Fund are the state budget and the China Development Bank, that is, fiscal and quasi-fiscal institutions, respectively. The next biggest is the

---

[13] The acquisition was blocked by the US government's Committee on Foreign Investment in the US (CFIUS).

Tobacco Monopoly (which contributed 11 billion renminbi), followed by three local government-controlled entities from Beijing, Wuhan and Shanghai. It is obvious that these "stakeholders" were corralled into investing in these funds either because they had money — that is, they were cash-rich members of the "national team", like the Tobacco Monopoly — or because they were local government entities that were, in essence, bidding for a piece of the action.

At the local level, the fundraising process is similar to the national case, except that the city government plays a much stronger overall role. For example, Wuhan is one of four areas designated by the national plan to develop the IC industry. The Wuhan (city) Economic Development Investment Corporation is the initiator of a 30 million renminbi fund, called the Hubei (province) IC Industry Fund. Fiscal agencies at the province (Hubei), city (Wuhan) and local development zone (Eastlake High technology New Zone) all contribute as initiators.[14] The fund then brings in multiple investors and has also signed a strategic cooperation agreement with CDB Capital, a subsidiary of China Development Bank. Nanjing city government has an even more ambitious program, involving the attraction of multiple foreign companies, including Cadence and Synopsis among EDA companies and a fab set up as a subsidiary of TSMC, the Taiwan Semiconductor Corporation. Some of the local funds claim to have private participants, but information on partner identities is scarce and the amounts certainly small.

It should be clear that there are multiple channels of subsidisation built into the IGF structure. Patient initial capital is provided by the government which is willing to accept a low rate of return. Once an IGF is established, low-interest loans are often provided by government development banks. There are implicit — and occasionally explicit — guarantees that suggest that investors may get bailed out if investments go sour. Private firms are explicitly encouraged to participate in IGFs as

---

[14] "30 Billion Renminbi Hubei IC Industry Investment Fund Set up in Optical Valley", *Zhongguo Ribao*, 5 August 2015, at <http://china.chinadaily.com.cn/2015-08/05/content_21511324.htm>

limited partners. Indeed, IGFs have repeatedly been praised by policy-makers as a vehicle that can draw in private funds and "mobilise social capital." Yet, so far, there are few cases of private firm participation.

Mixed Ownership

"Mixed ownership" has been a high-profile element component of the current wave of SOE reforms since 2013, without ever having been clearly or consistently defined. To be clear, mixed ownership has been a feature of the Chinese state sector for a long time, ever since state firms began to be listed on the stock market in the 1990s. Since the 2013 Third Plenum, a multistranded program of expanding "mixed ownership" to new spheres has gradually been put in place. Strategic "private" investors are to be attracted into previously monopolised state sectors, and public–private partnerships have been advocated as a way of diversifying funding for infrastructure investments. In cases where SOEs are deemed to be operating in fully competitive sectors of the economy, private investors are invited to increase their stakes in former SOEs, and might even take a controlling stake (although the govern-ment stake may not be sold off; the private participant can take control only if it adds to its investment, diluting the government share). An example of the potential of mixed ownership reform is provided by a local pilot, Yunnan Baiyao. This provincially controlled healthcare and pharmaceutical firm, which developed from a century-old traditional Chinese medicine company, took on two private strategic investors as part of a dramatic restructuring and expansion. The state share declined to 49%, giving the firm far greater autonomy.[15]

Mixed ownership does not necessarily imply purely private partici-pation. An interesting element has been the decision to allocate 10% of the existing state ownership to the Social Security Fund. Initiated in a few pilots in 2017, this program was being rolled out as an

---

[15] M. Chu, W. C. Kirby, N. Hua Dai and Y. Wang, "Yunnan Baiyao: Transforming a Chinese State-owned Enterprise", Harvard Business School Case N2-318-078, Boston, Harvard Business School (revised 20 March 2018).

implementation in all SOEs and financial institutions beginning in 2018.[16] The significance of this for corporate governance is that it introduces a passive financial investor into the ownership structure who ought to have an interest purely in maximising the share value. Another potentially important variant of mixed ownership has been the enthusiasm displayed for employee stock ownership. Employee stock ownership programs (ESOPs) were begun in 2013–2014, but then screeched to a halt at the end of 2014. Since 2016, 10 ESOP pilots have been moving forward again, and could grow into something significant. Although employee financial interests are not necessarily aligned with those of financial investors, different policies would presumably be hashed out in the Board of Directors on the basis of ownership stakes.

"Mixed ownership" also includes SOEs taking stakes in private firms. This element was included in the 2013 reform program, but did not seem likely to be an important element until recently. Clearly, there was always a danger that SOEs, with access to abundant cheap capital, could use mixed ownership as a justification for expanding their control in the economy. However, it was really with the acceleration of industrial and technology policy that this aspect of mixed ownership grew in importance. The IGFs, in particular, are encouraged to take stakes in technologically promising private companies, in order to allow them to scale up more rapidly, and to bear some of the risk. The intention is to "support" the private firm's growth. Yet one can see that there are clear risks here. Private firms that are "supported" by the injection of capital and the purchase of a significant ownership stake by the state clearly experience a diminution of their own control rights. There is a fine line between the "support" for private firms and the "renationalisation" of formerly private firms. These tensions, always apparent, have become more prominent during 2018 as fairly tight financial conditions have emerged as the government seeks to "de-leverage", that is control the

---

[16] State Council, "Notice of the State Council on Printing and Distributing the Implementation Plan of Transferring Some State-owned Capital to Enrich Social Security Funds", [in Chinese], Guofa (49), 18 November 2017, at <www.gov.cn/zhengce/content/2017-11/18/content_5240652.htm>

aggregate level of debt in the economy. Since SOEs continue to have access to cheap credit from state banks, much of the stress of de-leveraging falls on private firms. In this context, there were in 2018 more than 20 cases of government firms taking controlling stakes in listed private firms, in order to assist them in making it through the difficult times.

A particular example of the dynamic at work with this side of mixed ownership is provided by the state firm Tsinghua Unigroup. A highly entrepreneurial, but majority state-owned corporation, Tsinghua Unigroup, has made its name leveraging various kinds of state and market capital. Most dramatically, Tsinghua Unigroup bought out two of China's most dynamic private IC design firms, Spreadtrum (Shanghai) and RDA (Beijing). These two firms had very different specialties and corporate cultures. Spreadtrum was a classic "fast follower", which specialised in producing versions of complex communications chips that are the core of a sophisticated cell phone (it was, in other words, a fast follower of Qualcomm in the United States and Mediatek in Taiwan). RDA, on the other hand, specialised in Bluetooth and other subsidiary communications chips, with an ultra-cheap and practical mentality. Tsinghua Unigroup thought that by buying both and combining them, they would have the basis for a communications IC giant. However, the experience has not been very successful. The entrepreneurial founders of both firms ended up leaving, and the merged firm has turned out to be much less dynamic than the two original private firms had been.

The Chinese government is entirely willing to make it worthwhile for private firms to participate in IGFs and priority sectors, and they do not shrink from providing benefits directly to private firms, but they do not seem to have found a way to do so. A policy on encouraging private investment (not just in IGFs) was adopted by the State Council Office in September 2017, and it quickly gets to the point, after saying that private firms should be brought into industrial policy priority sectors: "We should bring into play the function of fiscal funds in spurring [private sector investment], using diverse methods such as investment subsidies, capital injection, or setting up investment funds, to attract a broad swathe of social capital, support enterprises in increasing the magnitude of their technological effort, in order to increase the input into key point projects in critical areas like IC or in [technological] weak links."[17] In other words, private firms are welcome to participate as investors in the funds and the funds are encouraged to invest in private firms in pursuit of their objectives, so long as this fits national government priorities. Mixed ownership, in this sense, has become a way for government financial influence to spread to new corners of the economy. A special example of this comes in the new civil–military fusion plan, which invites private firms into the defence industry (previously reserved for state firms) and provides financial support for both SOEs and private firms to move into sophisticated dual-use sectors.[18]

Discussion

We can clearly see an extension of government financial influence throughout the economy, using financial resources and exercising financial controls in order to shape economic outcomes. This means a more important role for both SOEs in the real economy and for new types of state-dominated financial vehicles. The pattern of financialisation is clearly shaped by the importance that top Chinese policymakers give to the developmental missions assigned to SOEs. Xi Jinping has been extremely consistent with this approach. In mid-2018, Xi insisted that the standards by which SOE reforms should be judged were whether they contributed to the preservation and growth of state

---

[17] State Council Office, "Guiding Opinions on Further Stimulating Effective Private [minjian] Investment Activity to Promote Continued Healthy Economic Development", 79, 1 September 2017, at <http://www.gov.cn/zhengce/content/2017-09/15/content_5225395.htm>. This document specifically encourages private participation in railroad equipment, Internet Plus, Big data and robotics, on the grounds that these sectors involve long and complex production chains. It also welcomes private participation in "Made in China 2025" demonstration zones and projects.

[18] Tai Ming Cheung, *The Chinese Techno-Security State and the Pursuit of Power, Innovation, and Global Leadership*. Forthcoming.

capital, improved SOE competitiveness, and improved the functionality of state capital. More tellingly, Xi described SOEs as strong forces that could be relied upon by the Party and government, which would carry out strategic Communist Party directives, and strengthen comprehensive national strength and the people's well-being.[19] Clearly, this view constrains the path of SOE reforms and is consistent with the failure of broader capital market liberalisation and the strengthening of institutions to steer SOEs. This is the context in which financialisation is developing.

Financialisation, then, is not so much a reform in and of itself as it is an adaptation of instruments to a new world of government steerage and reliance on SOEs to help achieve state and Party objectives. Clearly, financial instruments are not as *inefficient* in achieving such goals as administrative or bureaucratic commands would be. They distort decision-making less than bureaucratic commands do. They make macroeconomic imbalances less likely by encouraging the government to provide resources, instead of imposing unfunded mandates without resources. Moreover, this relatively "market-driven" approach supports a pragmatic commitment to using multiple avenues and approaches to achieve industrial policy goals. Really, nothing is ruled out at the outset. Thus, there is significant room for multiple, competing strategies and actors, including competing regional champions. The strategic approach is opportunistic: try foreign acquisitions, and if that doesn't work, shift to something else. Moreover, policymakers are happy to pick winners after the event, backing already successful firms in order to grow them to be national champions. A variety of strategic approaches will also be guaranteed by the difference in resources and incentives at the local and central government levels. Local governments play a big role, and national strategy (the IDDS) specifically says governments at all levels should play a part.

---

[19] "How should SOEs be reformed? These words by Xi Jinping make it perfectly clear", [in Chinese], *Central Television News*, 17 July 2018, at <http://www.ce.cn/xwzx/gnsz/gdxw/201807/17/t20180717_29774806.shtml>

However, the benefits of financial instruments does not mean that these instruments are sufficient to achieve results with market-like efficiency. Instead, there are many obstacles to the smooth operation of this new financialised system. It is sufficient to flag three. First, although the managing partner has, in theory, high-powered incentives, we have many indications that IGFs target extremely low rates of return. A Shanghai fund manager has been quoted as saying that as long as the fund gets its money back, it doesn't matter if it makes a profit. The National IC Fund is known to have targeted a 5% rate of return. However, according to industry sources, the Fund had to acknowledge that it wouldn't be able to make such a return, and it set up a separate "Strategic" subfund with a target rate of return of 0%, along with the "Commercial" subfund which retained the 5% target rate of return. This seriously distorts the incentives fund managers have because they can survive by making safe investments, whereas a true venture capital fund must produce at least a few big winners.

Second, incentives are highly asymmetric. That is, fund managers get rewarded if they produce a substantial return, but probably are not punished if they fail to achieve a positive return. As shown earlier, the Chinese government induces investment in IGFs by means of a very strong message of government support. This profoundly erodes the credibility of the government's statements that investments will be undertaken on market principles, since it implies that government will stand ready to bail out bad investments. Indeed, the government explicitly states that it *will* bail out specific types of investors, such as the (government) insurance company that has invested in preferred stock at the National IC Fund, and has even made provisions for budgetary set-asides for this bail out. Clearly, the government's implicit promise to bail out preferred stockholders — but not ordinary shareholders — is based on an artificially clear distinction that is unlikely to be credible in the marketplace.

In fact, we have seen that the government intentionally diffuses risk and responsibility among a variety of limited partners. Having induced these wealthy public entities to invest, is it credible that the government will impose losses on them in the event of catastrophically bad investments? It is not. The parties all know the government is the driver. In fact, the government has intentionally created a "convoy system", such as that in Japan in the 1990s, in which all of the biggest firms (*keiretsu* in Japan) supported each other and the government allowed nobody to go bankrupt.

Finally, there is a risk that the large sums flowing into a relatively restricted range of high-priority sectors is creating a "bubble", and that there will be huge overcapacity problems when the bubble bursts. China has an extraordinary number of immature electric vehicle manufacturers. Most will go bankrupt. Policymakers know this fact and accept the risk, arguing that they are indeed like venture capital firms, and will be happy if 1 out of 10 of their investments pays off. But this assumes that they can also handle the macroeconomic risks created, writing off the financial debts and closing down the physical capacity of overbuilt sectors. "Financialisation" is, without doubt, a double-edged sword. While as a single instrument, it is clearly more effective than old-style bureaucratic coordination, as an economy-wide choice it may produce new and large risks. The Chinese government is making a large gamble on the effectiveness of financialisation in driving the economy in directions of its choice, but it will take a while to see whether they have fully understood the risks in creating a new wave of financial excess.

Chapter 10

Reforming China's State-owned Enterprises: Recent Development and Prospect

Sarah Y TONG*

Introduction

The year 2018 marks the 40th Anniversary of China's economic reform and opening up. Reforming China's large and hugely diverse state sector has been among the most important and difficult tasks. Since the late 2013, when the Communist Party of China (CPC) Central Committee promulgated a grand reform blueprint, the "Decision on Major Issues Concerning Comprehensively Deepening Reforms" (hereafter, the Decision), the issue of reforming China's state-owned enterprises (SOEs) have attracted renewed attention. Five years on, an effort is warranted to examine and update what has been accomplished, after the announcement of the Decision, and what challenges remain.

In the 2013 Decision, the Chinese government has, for the first time, pledged to allow the market to play a decisive role in allocating resources, suggesting that direct government intervention in the economy shall weaken and that the importance of SOEs may decline. Meanwhile, it

---

* Sarah Y TONG is a Senior Research Fellow at the East Asian Institute, National University of Singapore.

seems that the Chinese leadership remains highly wary of relinquishing its control over the economy and is uncertain of the interplay between the state and the market. Although the SOE reform tops the overall reform agenda, the Decision provides no clear direction pertaining to the role SOEs should play in the Chinese economy and society.

More importantly, Chinese SOEs are a complicated lot. There are large numbers of SOEs, of varying sizes, sectors and administrative arrangements. At the central government-level, there are some 130 enterprise groups, of which around 100 are owned by SASAS, as a representative for state ownership, and the remaining by the Ministry of Finance. Meanwhile, there are considerably more SOEs under various government ministries and local governments.[1] Reforming these SOEs that would involve different government institutions in various locations will inevitably be complicated. Another complication concerning SOE governance and reform is the role of the CPC and its organisations in SOEs' corporate governance, as well as its relations with government agencies and the management teams.

Since 2015, SOE reforms have gained renewed significance and urgency. Despite the stimulus package launched by the government since 2009 that enabled a strong short-term rebound, economic growth started to decelerate in 2012, and the government struggled to address several serious problems, such as production overcapacity and surging corporate debt. These problems are closely linked to China's SOEs and solving them requires effective reforms of China's large and bloated state sector.

---

[1] There is not a clear breakup of central and local SOEs, which include both state-owned and state-controlled firms. According to the National Bureau of Statistics, there is a total of 2,459 state-owned enterprises in 2016, of which 554 are centrally owned (Source: China Industry Statistical Year Book 2017). If state-controlled enterprises are included, the total number was about 19,000. However, it is not clear how many of these 19,000 are under the central administration. Meanwhile, the data from the Ministry of Finance show that in 2016, a total of around 57,000 firms (as independent accounting unit) were managed by central governments and 116,000 by local authorities. Of the 57,000 centrally administered ones, about one quarter are under various ministries (*Source*: Finance Yearbook of China 2017).

On 13 September 2015, the CPC Central Committee and the State Council jointly announced the "Guideline to Deepen Reforms of the State-owned Enterprises (SOEs)" (hereafter, the Guideline), nearly two years after the grand reform blueprint, also known as the Decision, was promulgated in late 2013. Indeed, the delay in the release of the document and the joint appearance of representatives of five government agencies at the press conference[2] are indicative of the difficulties of pursuing further SOE reforms.

Following the promulgation of the Guideline, which is considered the top design of China's SOE reforms, the State-owned Assets Supervision and Administration Commission (SASAC) and other government agencies followed up with a series of supplementary policies that form the so-called 1+N SOE reform programme. It is, however, noteworthy that the government has not stated how many or listed the names of the supplementary documents it intends to formulate. Dozens of government documents that are relevant to SOE reforms have been issued by the State Council as well as other branches of the government. Examples include the "Opinions of the State Council on the Development of Mixed-ownership Reform of SOEs", announced in September 2015; "Opinions of the State Council on Reforming and Improving Sate-Owned Capital Management System", announced in November 2015; and "Opinions on Adhering to Party Leadership and Strengthening Party Building while Deepening the Reforms of SOEs", announced in September 2015.[3]

While the Guideline has not been able to clarify the role of the state sector in the Chinese economy, it has stipulated certain new approaches to SOE reforms this time around. For example, the Guideline highlights the introduction of a dual-track system that applies to both the

---

[2] Representatives from SASAC, National Development and Reform Commission, Ministry of Finance, Ministry of Industry and Information Technology, Communications, and Ministry of Human Resources and Social Security were at the press conference to brief the public about the Guideline, See <http://finance.people.com.cn/n/2015/0915/c1004-27583225.html> (accessed 24 September 2015).

[3] Please refer to Appendix A for a list of major documents concerning SOE reforms from September 2015 onwards.

firms and the management teams to improve the SOE governance. In particular, the SOEs will be categorised into two groups: the commercial ones and those in public services. Commercial SOEs are further classified into two types: those in competitive sectors and in various special sectors. Top managers are likewise recruited from the market or through Party and government recommendations, and are offered different pay packages and career prospects.

Another focus of the ongoing SOE reforms is to transition from asset management to capital management by setting up state capital investment and state capital management companies. By inserting a layer of investment companies between SOEs and government agencies like the SASAC, the reform aims to enhance SOEs' market orientation and reduce bureaucratic meddling.

A third aspect is to encourage the diversification of SOEs' ownership structure, also known as the mixed ownership reform, through public offerings, share sales to employees, and SOE asset acquisition by non-state companies utilising convertible bonds, rights swaps and other means.

Since the issuance of the Guideline, there have been significant progress in policy deliberation. At the central level, the government ministries and Party organisation have joined the SASAC to formulate policy directives in various aspects of SOE reforms. Local governments have also announced plans to experiment on various reforms.

Uncertainty remains on the future of China's current round of SOE reforms for several reasons. Most importantly, the conceptual dilemma regarding the role of the SOEs seems to be unresolved. Moreover, as SOE conglomerates become larger and more influential with entrenched interest groups, any serious reform will become operationally difficult and politically risky. Reforms could also be sidetracked by either bureaucratic infighting or indifference since China's SOEs are under the management of many different organs and at different levels of government.

Overall, for SOE reforms to succeed, two related issues need to be resolved. The first is to draw a distinction between the state and the market. This is important for all SOEs, particularly the central SOEs.

Classifying SOEs into different functional groups is a move in the right direction but the follow-up steps are essential. Combining two huge companies into a giant is the easy part. The real challenge is to effectively restructure and reorganise. The second main issue concerns corporate government and personnel management, relating to the role of the Party, executive recruitment, incentive structure and board of director reforms. In this respect, recent developments does not look too encouraging, as it is unclear how strengthening Party-building in SOEs and the Party's direct involvement in business operation is conducive to improving corporate governance.

This chapter examines China's SOE reforms since the late 1970s, focusing on the latest efforts since 2013. The discussion is covered in four sections. The first section introduces and provides an overview. The second section reviews the previous reforms between the 1970s and 2000s, and highlights the various features and key outcomes. The third section examines the latest reform programme, including both policy deliberation and various experiments at the central and local levels. The final section draws preliminary conclusions of the reform efforts.

Previous SOE Reforms and the Pitfalls

Reforming the large and relatively inefficient state sector has been a key part of China's overall reform agenda from the late 1970s and significant progress has been achieved since. Prior to the early 2010s, the government has over time carried out numerous experiments to reform the SOEs, from introducing a contract system in the 1980s to corporatisation in the 1990s. While the number of SOEs has reduced significantly, the state sector remains powerful and retains its dominance in certain sectors. Meanwhile, SOEs remain comparatively inefficient.

During the early phase of the reforms, between the late 1970s and early 1990s, the key task was to provide SOEs with managerial autonomy and introduce market incentives to managers and employees. The government then implemented pilot experiments for the contract system, with success similar to the household responsibility system in rural reforms introduced in the 1990s. During the period, external market conditions had changed considerably, with non-state players such as township and village enterprises and foreign-invested enterprises entering the market. Intense market competition had thereby led to operation difficulties.

A more comprehensive SOE reform was promulgated in 1993 when the "Decision on the Establishment of a Socialist Market Economic System" was approved at the Third Plenum of CPC's 14th Central Committee. The objective specified therein is to establish a modern corporate system with "well-defined property rights, clear responsibilities, separation of business management from political affairs, and scientific management".[4] In 1994, it was further stipulated that the government would focus on enhancing the state sector by "grasping the large and deregulating the small". Most significantly, the "Decision of CPC's Central Committee on Major Issues Concerning SOE Reform and Development" (the 1999 Decision) was announced in late 1999.

The two immediate objectives of the 1999 Decision were to pull the large number of loss-making SOEs out of their difficulties, and to introduce modern corporate systems in major large and medium-sized SOEs.[5] Meanwhile, the government also identified several mid- to long-term goals — e.g. to restructure the SOEs, to improve efficiency, to enhance technological capability of SOEs and to enable the state sector to play a leading role in the Chinese economy. Interestingly, for the first time, the 1999 Decision advocated certain bold reforms, such as eliminating the equivalent ranking of SOEs and their leaders.

Compared to the previous attempts, the reforms in the late 1990s had produced more pronounced results. While tens of millions of SOE employees were laid off and non-performing assets amounting to trillions of dollars separated from the SOEs, the reforms turned around two-thirds of the loss-making SOEs. Large SOEs were consolidated,

---

[4] See <http://cpc.people.com.cn/GB/64162/134902/8092314.html> (accessed 20 August 2018).

[5] See <http://cpc.people.com.cn/GB/64162/71380/71382/71386/4837883.html> (accessed 20 August 2018).

slashing the number of SOEs and firms with state control in the industrial sector from 65,000 in 1998 to 27,000 in 2005, or from 39% to 10% in percentage share.[6]

The reform agenda of the late 1990s were not fully implemented due in part to fierce criticism of certain practices. For example, some SOE managers obtained state assets through management buyout (MBO) schemes at a very low cost, raising serious concerns about asset stripping of SOEs. Since the mid-2000s, although certain changes continued to take place in the state sector, implementation of significant reforms had virtually stopped.

One significant development was the establishment of the SASAC[7] in 2003 under the State Council. The SASAC was tasked with three responsibilities as the owner and the regulator of the SOEs, and also as the institution responsible for promoting SOE reforms. While large industrial state-owned industrial conglomerates[8] were placed under the supervision of the SASAC, provincial SASACs were set up to oversee SOEs at different localities.

The SASAC can be said to have largely failed in all three areas of responsibilities as the three roles provide conflicting incentives. First, as a representative of state ownership, the SASAC has not strongly pushed profitable SOEs to surrender more of their profits to the state treasury, even as many centrally administered SOEs have become hugely profitable. This is partly due to the lack of clarity in stipulating which institutions would be apportioned with the profits submitted.

Prior to 2007, SOEs were not required to pay dividends to the state. While this has been changed, with the joint announcement of the "Interim Measures for the Administration of State-owned Capital

---

[6] Sarah Y Tong and Huang Yanjie, "China's State-owned Enterprises in the Post-crisis Era: Development and Dilemma", *EAI Background Brief*, East Asian Institute, National University of Singapore, no. 694, 3 February 2012.

[7] SOEs in the industry and construction sectors are under the regulation of SASAC, while those in the financial sector are under the supervision of the China Banking Regulatory Commission or China Insurance Regulatory Commission.

[8] Many of these conglomerates were industrial ministry-turned-corporations, which kept their ministerial rankings for the companies and their leaders.

Income Collection of Central Enterprises" in late 2007 by the Ministry of Finance and the SASAC, the rates remain relatively low. In the 2007 document, the rates of submission were set at between 0% and 10%, depending on which sectors the SOEs were in. They were subsequently raised to between 0% and 15% in 2010, and further to between 0% and 25% in 2014.

Second, as a regulator, the SASAC and its leaders were not given adequate authority to supervise the few powerful SOEs for two reasons. First, the ranking of the SASAC and its leaders at the ministerial level places them on an equal ranking as some of the central SOEs. Second, some of the top executives of the SASAC were recruited and appointed by the Party's Organisation Department, not by the SASAC.

Third, as the supervisor of the SOEs, the SASAC has little incentive to push for reforms that may reduce the size and influence of the SOEs under their supervision. Indeed, the amount of profits generated by SOEs, especially the centrally administered ones, has expanded significantly since the early 2000s (Figure 1). This is largely attributed to their monopolistic position and generous financing by state banks.

Between 2002 and 2014, for example, SOEs' total profit rose by nearly 17% a year, from RMB377 trillion to RMB2,477 billion. Of which, nearly 70% were those of the centrally managed SOEs. Following a two-year contraction, the amount of profit by SOEs rose in 2017, hitting a record high, thanks to the restructuring that has eliminated excess industrial capacity and to the improving commodity prices. Meanwhile, SOEs and state-controlled firms have also expanded in size. The average number of employees more than doubled from less than 500 in 1996 to more than 1,000 in 2013.[9] Total asset per firm surged even more drastically, from about RMB60 billion in 1996 to RMB2.3 trillion in 2017.[10]

However, on the whole, SOEs remained inefficiently managed, compared to non-SOEs. As is shown in Table 1, between 2000 and

---

[9] The number of SOEs and state-controlled firms had increased by over 2,200 between 2011 and 2015, while the average number of employees declined.

[10] *Source*: CEIC Data Manager.

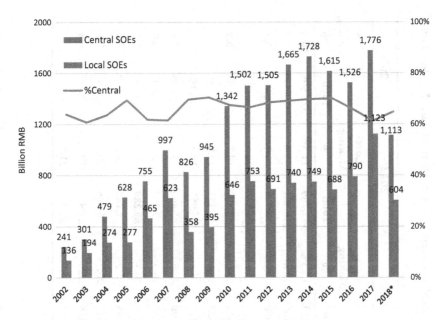

Figure 1: Profit of Centrally and Locally Managed SOEs

Note: Data available for 2018 are those from January to June.

Source: Ministry of Finance of PRC, and Sarah Y. Tong and Huang Yanjie, "China's State-owned Enterprises in the Post-Crisis Era: Development and Dilemma", EAI Background Brief No. 694, East Asian Institute, National University of Singapore, 3 February 2012.

2016, the number of industrial enterprises had more than doubled, while the share of loss-making firms had more than halved, from 23.4% to 10.8%. Among the various groups of firms defined by ownership types, the state sector fared the worst. In particular, the share of loss-making firms among those of sole state ownership remains high at 27%.

In 2011, loss-making firms constituted 22% of SOEs and 21% of limited liability corporations with sole state ownership. The values compared very unfavourably to domestic firms at 8% and private firms at 6% for the same year. The situation has since further worsened. In 2016, 26% of SOEs and 27% of limited liability corporations with sole state ownership were making a loss. Meanwhile, 10% and 8% of all domestic firms and private firms, respectively, were loss-making (Table 1). Total losses by loss-making SOEs in 2015 and 2016

Table 1: China's Industrial Enterprises by Types of Ownership: Total Numbers and the Share of Loss-Making Firms, 2000–2016

	2000		2004		2008		2012		2016	
	Total	Loss-Making %	Total	Loss-Making %	Total	Loss-Making %	Total	Loss-Making %	Total	Loss-Making %
All firms	**162,885**	**23.4%**	**276,474**	**21.1%**	**426,113**	**15.3%**	**343,769**	**11.5%**	**378,599**	**10.8%**
Domestic	134,440	22.6	219,309	19.2	348,266	12.8	286,861	9.8	329,045	9.7
SOEs	42,426	36.4	23,417	42.6	9,682	29.7	6,770	25.5	2,459	26.2
Collectives	37,841	15.9	18,095	16.5	11,737	14.6	4,814	10.6	2,092	12.4
Cooperatives	10,852	15.5	8,215	14.5	5,612	13.7	2,397	10.2	946	8.9
Joint ownership	2,510	19.4	1,439	21.2	833	18.6	481	14.8	110	10.9
Limited liability	13,215	21.8	41,234	21.6	62,835	17.5	66,955	13.5	96,240	13.1
Sole state ownership	1,226	27.2	1,449	34.2	1,398	27.8	1,444	24.2	3,434	27.1
Shareholding	5,086	19.2	7,171	19.5	9,422	16.3	9,012	12.4	12,007	13.0
Private	22,128	12.6	119,357	14.6	245,850	10.7	189,289	7.8	214,309	7.8
Others	382	36.1	381	17.3	2,295	11.2	7,143	8.6	882	5.4
Non-mainland	28,445	26.8	57,165	28	77,847	26.7	56,908	20.2	49,554	17.7
HKMCTW	16,490	27.1	28,399	28.4	35,578	26.6	25,935	19.3	23,429	16.8
Other FIEs	11,955	26.4	28,766	27.5	42,269	26.7	30,973	21.1	26,125	18.5

Note: Values in gray tint indicate firms with 100% state ownership.

Source: CEIC Data Manager.

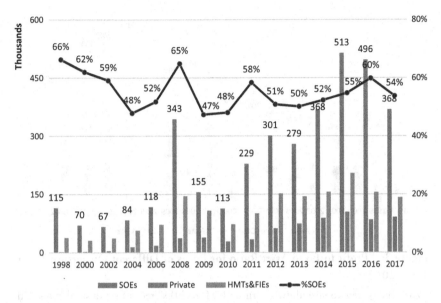

Figure 2: Total Amount of Losses by Loss-Making Firms of Different Groups, 1998–2017

Source: CEIC Data Manager.

amounted to RMB513 billion and RMB496 billion, respectively, nearly 50% higher than that in 2008 during the global economic crisis (Figure 2).

Investments in the state sector thus generated the least amount of profit, compared to those in private firms and foreign-invested enterprises. Figure 3 shows that SOE reforms in the late 1990s had indeed improved the overall profitability of the state sector. However, the state sector's overall performance remains unsatisfactory in recent years. While the state sector has yet to recover to its pre-2008 peak, it is significantly less capable than private and foreign-invested firms in generating profit from the investment.[11]

---

[11] According to a study by the UniRule Institute of Economics, "The Nature, Performance and Reform of the State-owned Enterprises" published in 2011, the real rate of return to capital for China SOEs was not only low but sometimes negative, if full-scale subsidies, including capital, land and energy, are taken into account.

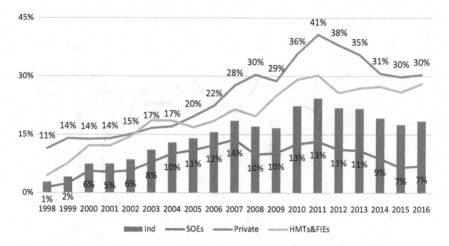

Figure 3: Profit to Fixed Asset Ratio for Firms of Different Ownership Types, 1998–2016

Note: "Ind" refers to all industrial firms. "HMTs&FIEs" refers to industrial firms with investment from investors outside mainland China, including Hong Kong, Macao, Taiwan and foreign investors.

Overall, SOE reforms between 1980s and the mid-2000s had made achievements in terms of profit generation and reduction in the number of SOEs. In what can be attributed to the government's shift towards "making the SOEs larger and stronger" since the mid-2000s, SOEs have absorbed large amount of investments that are relatively less efficient. However, little progress was made in certain important reforms identified in the 1999 Decision, such as further "separation of enterprises from government". Likewise, the administrative ranking of top SOE executives remained intact.

The Renewed Push to Reform the State Sector

There were high expectations of a new round of SOE reforms in late 2013, when the Decision was announced. Regarded as the Party's efforts to reconfigure the relationship between the state and the market, the Decision placed strong emphasis on SOE reforms. Since then, there have been substantive ongoing policy discussions in the public domain as the government makes policy announcements. Despite the conceptual ambiguities and the uncertainties in specific reform tactics, some progress has been made via pilot programmes implemented in different areas and different localities.

Ambiguities and contradictions

Despite the comprehensive coverage and eloquent deliberation of the Decision, i.e. the 2013 all-inclusive comprehensive reform plan, it largely remains a conceptual design, leaving many questions related to SOE reforms unanswered. The Guideline (to Deepen Reforms of the SOEs) announced two years later in September 2015, with the aim to provide clearer direction and further details, also failed to clarify doubts and boost confidence. In fact, it may have generated new anxieties on whether the leadership is committed and serious about SOE reforms. Several factors have contributed to the lack of enthusiasm in the prospect of this new round of SOE reforms.

First, both documents sent conflicting signals on the role of the market and the state: while encouraging the market to play a decisive role in the allocation of resources, the documents stress that the state sector would remain the pillar of the economy. The Decision proclaimed for the first time that the market would play a "decisive role" in the allocation of resources and the state would refrain from exercising excessive intervention in the economy. However, it also emphasised that the state sector will remain the pillar of the economy and it would "continually strengthen the vitality, control and influence of the public sector". The Decision further stated that "China's basic economic system is one with public ownership as its main body but allowing for the development of all types of ownership". Such ambiguity has caused confusion and serious doubt.

Second, both documents identified "new" emphases for SOE reforms, such as transitioning from asset management to capital management and promoting mixed ownership, which are not entirely new. The lack of specific measures raised doubts about the reforms in overcoming difficulties encountered in previous reform efforts. Third, it remains unclear whether SOEs are purely business entities or whether they have to also shoulder certain political responsibilities, such as exercising administrative control over the strategic industries.

The type of role that the Party plays in SOEs is also a key concern. The Guideline indicates that the Chinese authority intends to curb corruption by strengthening the Party's influence and direct participation in SOEs' governance. This seems to be inconsistent with the overall reform direction, which is to reinforce the market's decisive role and to enable the SOEs to be more adaptive, more market-oriented, more modern and international.

The Guideline calls for "the full play of Party organisation's political central role in the SOEs and a clear designation of Party organisation's legal status in SOEs' corporate governance structure". More specifically, it proposes the principle of "four simultaneous and two cross-overs". The "four simultaneous" literally means "the SOEs reforms will be promoted while insisting on simultaneous planning of Party-building, on simultaneous establishment of the Party organisation and working bodies, on simultaneous assignment of Party branch leaders and staff, and on simultaneous launch of Party work".

In addition, the government aims to "uphold and improve the two-way access and the cross-representation system for SOEs leadership". The Guideline states that "eligible members of the Party leadership can be members of SOEs' board of directors, board of supervisors, or managers, through legal procedures". Conversely, "members of the board of directors, board of supervisors, and top executives can have an appropriate degree of cross-representation with members of SOEs' party leadership". "Generally, SOEs' Party secretary general and the chairman of the board are to be held by the same person."

Such consolidation of the Party's direct participation in SOEs' governance appears to be inconsistent with the overall reform direction. It is also unclear how widely applicable these principles will be as the government also promotes mixed ownership reforms for SOEs. In fact, the Guideline stipulates that "the establishment of Party organisations and the execution of Party work is the prerequisite for SOEs' mixed ownership reforms".

Meanwhile, "the type of establishment, the allocation of responsibilities, and the mode of management for these Party organisation will be determined scientifically according to the characteristics of the mixed ownership SOEs". Such rules will undoubtedly cause greater anxiety in private entrepreneurs with concerns about these SOEs with mixed ownership and their ability to avoid the Party's administrative interference. Moreover, it is also uncertain how these rules could help curb corruption in SOEs without transparency.

An article published in *Qiu shi* (*Seeking Truth*) in May 2016 further triggered heated debate on the direction of China's SOE reforms. This article, titled *Strengthen Party-Building in the Comprehensive Deepening of SOE Reforms*, was authored by the SASAC's Party committee.[12] The assertion that "major decisions (of the SOEs) must first be examined by the Party committees (or leading Party group) of the enterprises, which then propose their opinions and suggestions. SOEs' major operational and managerial matters involving regulations of national macroeconomy, national strategies, national security and so on must first be discussed and approved by their Party committees (or leading Party groups), before a decision is made by the board of directors and the executive team" is the most conspicuous. Such writing, by suggesting that SOEs will remain to be under the direct control of the Party, rather than business entities with business objectives, undoubtedly amplifies concerns.

Progress and the reform programmes

Despite public disappointment in SOE reform, the two documents indicated positive changes in several areas, including promoting a rules-based corporate governance in order to reduce excessive government interference in SOEs' business operations and introducing a dual-track system that is applicable to both firms and management teams in SOE governance.

---

[12] See <http://www.qstheory.cn/dukan/qs/2016-05/31/c_1118938354.htm> (accessed 26 June 2016).

In particular, the SOEs will be categorised into commercial and public service. Commercial SOEs are made up of those in competitive sectors and in various special sectors. Top managers of commercial SOEs are also recruited from the market or via Party and government recommendations, and are offered different pay packages and career prospects.

The shift from asset management to capital management has witnessed some progress with the setting up of state capital investment and state capital management companies. By inserting a layer of investment companies between SOEs and government agencies like the SASAC, the reform aims to enhance SOEs' market orientation and reduce bureaucratic meddling. Since the announcement of the Guideline in 2015, a series of documents, the so-called "SOE reform 1+N framework", has been issued by various government agencies.

Furthermore, in February 2016, the government had identified 10 areas of reform experiments — i.e. the role of board of directors, market-based management recruitment, the system of professional managers, reforms of corporate compensation schemes, state-owned capital investment and management companies, mergers and acquisitions of central SOEs, mixed ownership reform, employee shareholding reforms, SOE information disclosure, and resolving legacy problems of separating SOEs' social functions from business operations — in SOE reforms.

Since 2015, SOE reforms have focused on the following select few areas. The first is classifying SOEs into two categories: for profit and public service. The government, on the one hand, aims to improve performance of for-profit SOEs, particularly the centrally administered SOEs, through mergers and restructuring. On the other, the government removes the SOEs' legacy assets related to the social functions they previously performed.

The second area pertains to developing a modern corporate system. Four measures, in particular, have been identified: to implement the board of directors system and specify director's powers and authority, to hire and remunerate managers by the market mechanism approach, to gradually replace bureaucrats with professional managers as SOEs' managers, and to implement differentiated allocation in reforming the remuneration system reform.[13]

The third area involves transitioning from asset management to capital management in order to improve supervision. While the government needs to clearly define the powers of supervisory agencies, it should also focus on setting up and operating state capital investment and management companies. It also stipulates a target for SOEs to submit 30% of their profits to the central government by 2020.

The fourth area pertains to the development of a mixed ownership economy. More specifically, the government encourages non-state capital to hold stakes in SOEs and likewise supports SOEs to have a stake in firms in the fast-growing private sector. Employee stock incentive compensation is also another strategic measure to explore.

The fifth area focuses on enhancing the Party leadership of SOEs. The goal is to incorporate Party leadership into SOEs' corporate governance structure and to strengthen corporate governance with Party discipline. Since 2016, SOEs have been ordered to revise their corporate charters to support and clarify the Party committees' role in corporate governance. In addition, the 19th Party Congress in 2017 had changed the Party constitution to affirm the Party committee's responsibility to play a leadership role in SOE governance.

Pilot programmes and local experiments

Given the large number and diversity of China's SOEs, reforming them will be complex and difficult. It is therefore logical to adopt various approaches in the management and reform of SOEs since central and local SOEs differ considerably, and SOEs at different localities also vary. The implementation of pilot programmes have since begun as early as in 2014 and expanded considerably.

In making the shift to state capital investment and management, about 10 companies were identified to participate in the pilot experiments. In 2014, the State Development and Investment Corporation,

---

[13] See *China: Accelerating SOE Reforms*, DBS Asian Insights, June 2016.

China National Cereals, Oils and Foodstuffs Corporate were designated as trial cases for state capital investment. Six more companies — Shenhua Group, Baowu Group, China Minmetals, China Merchants Group, China Communications Group and Poly Group — were added to the list in 2016. Meanwhile, two other companies, Chengtong Group and China Guoxin, were identified to participate in pilots for state capital management. State capital investment and state capital management companies at provincial levels have also been established. There are reportedly over 100 such companies at the central and local levels.[14]

More recently, in July 2018, the State Council announced the "Implementation Opinions of Pilot Reforms to Promote State-owned Capital Investment and State Capital Management Companies". In this document, the government stipulates the objectives of setting up state capital investment and management entities. First, the government aims to improve the state capital management system by separating state ownership from the day-to-day management of the companies and by allowing the market to play a role in the operation of the state capital investment and management. Second, it aims to steer these companies towards the state development directions, so that they concentrate their investments on key strategic sectors and areas, and on potential firms.

Another important area of the reform experiment is promoting the concept of mixed ownership. In September 2015, the State Council issued the "Opinions on Developing Mixed Ownership Economy through State-owned Enterprises Reforms". In December 2016, the Central Economic Work Conference stated that mixed ownership reform serves as an important breakthrough for SOE reforms. It further identified the following seven industries — electricity, oil, natural gas, railway, civil aviation, telecommunications and military industries — and also specified concrete steps to be taken for the implementation of mixed ownership reforms.

---

[14] See <http://www.xinhuanet.com/finance/2018-08/02/c_1123210350.htm> (accessed 16 August 2018).

The experiments kicked off in 2014 when two private capital companies — China National Pharmaceutical Group Corp (Sinopharm) and China National Building Materials Group Corp (CNBM) — were selected and invited for partial ownership trial. By the end of 2017, with seven key industries identified, 19 centrally administered SOEs have been included in the first batch of experiments.[15] The employee shareholding scheme is one aspect of the mixed ownership reform, and the government had released a guiding principle, the "Opinions on the Pilot Project of Employee Stock Ownership in State-owned Mixed Ownership Enterprises", in August 2016. It is reported that 10 third-tier companies in centrally administered SOEs were chosen to carry out the experiments.

The mixed ownership reform of China Unicom indicates an important step forward. In August 2017, the company announced its plan, and introduced Tencent, Baidu, Jingdong, Alibaba and China Life as its investors. By streamlining the organisation, the number of departments and personnel at the headquarters were reduced by one-third and by more than half, respectively. Meanwhile, the company's board of directors composition has been adjusted to include more outsiders as non-independents.

Also in 2014, the government launched pilot programmes to allow company boards greater autonomy. Four companies — China National Pharmaceutical Group Corp, China National Building Materials Group Corp, China Energy Conservation and Environmental protection Group and Xinxing Cathay International Group — were chosen for this experiment that entitles company boards of directors, rather than the SASAC, the rights to appoint senior management and set performance metrics. In 2016, two more companies, China Railway Signal and Communication Corp and State Development and Investment Corp, participated in the pilot program. The next three companies in the pilot

---

[15] "Deepening Mixed Ownership Reforms of State-owned Enterprises" (in Chinese), at <http://www.gov.cn/xinwen/2017-12/19/content_5248342.htm> (accessed 16 August 2018).

reform timetable are Baowu Group, State Development and Investment Corp, and China General Nuclear Power Group.

In April 2017, the State Council announced the "Program for Functional Transformation of the SASAC toward Capital Management". The programme aims to free SOEs from excessive government interference in business operations. As such, many regulations would be eliminated, deregulated or reassigned.

In response to the SASAC's shift towards capital management, numerous funds have been set up. In 2016, four Industry Guidance Funds, founded and established by China Aerospace Science and Technology Corporation, China Merchants Group, China Reform Holdings Corporation, and China Development Bank Capital of China Development Bank, aim to support the development of innovative enterprises in various fields and sectors. For example, the National Clean Energy Equity Investment Fund (Guoxie qingjie nengyuan guquan touzi jijin) was set up jointly by China Insurance Investment Fund and China Merchants Capital Investment LLC to explore new energy. Guotong Fund , set up in November 2016 and approved by the SASAC, was funded by over a dozen companies including China Reform Holdings Corporation Ltd and Postal Savings Bank of China to support Chinese companies' global ventures in the "One Belt, One Road" initiative and in international production capacity cooperation. The China Reform Fund (Guoxin jijin), established by China Reform Holdings, aims to support the SASAC's efforts to restructure China's central SOEs and facilitate the development of strategic emerging industries. China Reform Holdings had led the establishment of the State-owned Capital Venture Capital Fund in August 2016 that provides support to the development of innovative firms. In September 2016, China Chengtong Group established the SOE Structural Adjustment Fund to support SOE restructuring.

While the central government actively conducts various reform experiments, it also implements numerous local programmes. Through these experiments, new trends are emerging. For example, some local SOEs have transferred the control rights to non-state investors. Pudong Science Investment and Yunnan Baiyao are two such examples.

Moreover, the government of Tianjin municipality has also been open about maintaining minority shareholding in some of its companies.

Different localities have different emphases in implementing their reform plans. By early 2017, 28 provincial-level localities have developed roadmaps and timetable for SOE reforms. In Shanghai, two platforms were established for state-owned capital investment and management, namely Guosheng Group and Shanghai International Group. Some of the indicative reform cases in Shanghai are employee shareholding reform in Shanghai International Port Group, and stock exchange listings of Greenland Group, Shanghai Xian Dai Architectural Design Group, Shanghai Urban Construction Group and Huayi Group.

The Shandong government also announced its comprehensive reform plans. In particular, it proposed to transfer 30% of capital belonging to 470 local SOEs to the Shandong Social Security Fund. In addition, two companies, Shandong Lucion Investment Holdings Group and Shandong State-owned Assets Investment Holdings, were approved by the SASAC to carry out reforms related to state capital investment and management.

State-owned capital investment and management companies were also established in various other localities, including Chongqing, Jiangxi and Shenzhen. Many localities, such as Jiangxi and Shenzhen, put great emphasis on the implementation of mixed ownership reform. Moreover, Shenzhen established an SOE Reform and Strategic Development Fund to support the SOEs to enhance their core competitiveness and production chain.

The Prospects of Future Development: An Assessment

It has been nearly five years since the government released its ambitions reform blueprint in 2013 and about three years after the announcement of the comprehensive plan on SOE reform plan. Major uncertainties surrounding the outcome of the government's new efforts to transform SOEs remain and this could be attributed to a few important factors.

Most significantly, the conceptual dilemma of the role of SOEs remains unresolved. Maintaining a balance between direct control over a segment of the economy and indirect management of marketplace to preserve its openness and transparency is still challenging for the government. Having the state capital investment and state capital management companies as the buffer layer between the SASAC and SOEs is deemed a feasible endeavour to achieve a better balance. Categorising SOEs into different groups is another approach to achieve the balance.

The extent to which such efforts could succeed is unclear. In the case of state capital investment and state capital management companies which only care about commercial returns, the success of reforms will depend essentially on whether SOEs operate under the market discipline. There are of course exceptions, e.g. SOEs in strategic industries and those with public interest. The challenges are: first, it will take time to build a marketplace where SOEs and non-SOEs compete as equals; and second, it is unclear which institution is of authority and how it will determine which sector to grant SOEs more privileges. For instance, SOEs in profitable industries will have strong incentives to stay in monopoly and stake a claim for their strategic significance. It is also difficult to envisage how the Party and Party organisations' increased role in the SOEs could help enhance their competitiveness and efficiency.

China's economy has encountered mounting difficulties in sustaining growth momentum since 2012, and in turn affected SOEs' performance. The ongoing SOE reforms and restructuring could bring painful consequences like employee retrenchment and local fiscal difficulties, thus leading to strong resistance and policy setbacks. Nevertheless, economic difficulties could serve to facilitate SOE reforms, particularly at the local level, as a way to reduce fiscal burden to the governments.

Despite many concerns and difficulties, SOE reforms have moved forward, as evident in the implementation of pilot programmes and local experiments, and then the announcement of plans with clearer directions and details. Some tentative conclusions can be drawn from these developments. It becomes apparent that the government views the strengthened Party-building in SOEs as an important instrument to safeguard the reforms and the government's control of state assets, especially at the central level. At the local levels, active local innovations are tolerated, and may lead to encouraging outcomes in various localities.

To Chinese leaders, SOEs, particularly the centrally administered ones, will continue to shoulder the responsibility of fulfilling not only economic but also social and strategic objectives. As a result, a considerable proportion of these firms will remain in tight control of the government, which strives to grow them larger and stronger. Reforms of central SOEs therefore primarily involve mergers and acquisition, as well as restructuring and reorganisation. Since 2015, there have been a number of reorganisation of central SOEs. As of August 2018, the number of central SOEs has declined to 96.

Meanwhile, reforms related to board directorship and internal corporate governance have not made much progress, particularly in central SOEs. For example, the approach to recruit SOE executives through market channels is barely considered. There were only rules to limit executives' pay.

There are also issues concerning the mixed ownership reform for SOEs. First, non-state investors have the misgivings that they may not enjoy the same rights as the state investors. With the lack of transparency and effective monitoring, there is also no guarantee that private investors' interests are protected. Second, the state reserves the more profitable businesses to the state sector, leaving the less attractive investment opportunities to private investors. With strong state presence in the economy and limited alternative investment opportunities, private investors face limited choices. Reform efforts of local SOEs could nonetheless lead to fruitful outcomes. These SOEs do not have to be responsible for national development strategies and they only have to deal with competition from SOEs of other localities. Third, amid challenging times in the economy and difficulties faced by many SOEs, local governments may take bolder measures in their reform efforts.

Appendix A: 1+N Government Documents on SOE Reforms (September 2015–May 2018)

Overall Guidance

- Guiding Opinions of the CPC Central Committee and the State Council on Deepening the Reform of State-owned Enterprises (September 2015)

Classification and Assessment by Functional Classifications of SOEs

- Guiding Opinions on the Functional Definition and Categorisation of State-owned Enterprises (December 2015)
- Implementation Plan on Improving the Assessment of Centrally-Administered SOEs by Functional Classifications (September 2016)

Development Mixed Ownership Economy

- Opinions of the State Council on Mixed Ownership Reforms of State-owned Enterprises (September 2015)
- Guiding Opinions on Encouraging and Regulating Non-state Capital into SOEs' Investment Projects (October 2015)
- Opinions on State-controlled Mixed Ownership Enterprises' Implementation of the Pilot Employee Stock Ownership Program (August 2016)

Enhancing Modern Corporate Governance

- Opinions on Deepening the Reform of the Salary System of Managers of Centrally Administered Enterprises (December 2015)
- Opinions on Comprehensively Promoting the Construction of Rule of Law in Centrally Administered Enterprises (January 2016)
- Interim Measures for the Equity and Dividend Incentives for State-owned Scientific and Technological Enterprises (February 2016)
- Methods for Assessing the Performance of Persons in Charge of Centrally Administered Enterprises (December 2016)
- Guiding opinions of the General Office of the State Council on Improving the Corporate Governance Structure (April 2017)
- Notice on Printing and Distributing the Provisions on the Responsibilities of the Principal Responsible Persons in Centrally Administered Enterprises (July 2017)
- State Council's Opinions on Reforming the Salary Decision Mechanism in State-owned Enterprises (May 2018)

Enhancing State Capital Management

- Opinions of State Council on Reforming and Improving State-Owned Capital Management System (November 2015)
- Guiding Opinions of the General Office of the State Council on Promoting the Structural Adjustment and Reorganisation of Centrally Administered Enterprises (July 2016)
- Notice of the General Office of the State Council on Forwarding the Transformation Plan of the SASAC Toward Capital Management (April 2017)

(Continued)

Appendix A: (*Continued*)

Strengthen Supervision and Prevent the Loss of State Assets

- Opinions of the General Office of the State Council on Strengthening and Improving the Supervision of the State-owned Assets of Enterprises and Preventing the Loss of State-Owned Assets (November 2015)
- Measures for the Supervision and Administration of the Transactions of State-owned Assets of Enterprises (July 2016)
- Opinions of the General Office of the State Council on Establishing a System of Investigating the Responsibility of State-owned Enterprises for Violating Business Investment (August 2016)
- Measures for the Supervision and Administration of Overseas Investment by Centrally Administered Enterprises (January 2017)
- Centrally Administered Enterprise Investment Supervision and Administration Measures (January 2017)
- Measures for the Supervision and Administration of State-owned Shares of Listed Companies (May 2018)

Strengthen and Improve Party Leadership Over SOEs

- Opinions on Adhering to Party Leadership and Strengthening Party Building while Deepening the Reforms of State-owned Enterprises (September 2015)

Create Environment Conducive for SOE Reforms

- The National Development and Reform Commission's Review and Suggestions on Polity Support for SOE Reforms (September 2015)
- Notice on Distributing the Working Plan to Accelerate the Relief of SOEs' Obligations to Operate Social Programs and Resolution of Legacy Issues (May 2016)

Source: Compiled by the author from online sources.

Chapter 11

The Role of the Party Committee within Large State-owned Enterprises in China: A Theoretical Investigation

Jim SHEN Huangnan and ZHANG Jun*

Introduction

The reform of large state-owned enterprises (SOEs) in China is one of the most debated topics among Chinese economists. Indeed, various aspects of SOE reforms range from external market competition to ownership incentives to corporate governance. Among these reforms, power delegation reforms within large SOEs have become one of the most important factors affecting the efficiency implication of firms. Since the 1980s, power delegation reforms had been undertaken in several ways, including the household responsibility system, lease management system and joint-stock reform.[1] *Ex post* agency inefficiencies, however, especially with reference to insider

*Jim SHEN Huangnan is affiliated with the Department of Economics, SOAS University of London, contact email: hs63@soas.ac.uk; and ZHANG Jun is affiliated with the China Centre for Economic Studies, School of Economics, Fudan University, contact email: junzh_2000@fudan.edu.cn
[1] H. Wang, "The Study on the Reforming Progress of SOEs in China 1979–2003", *Chinese Economic History Research Journal*, vol. 3, 2005.

control of SOEs, emerged after the implementation of power delegation reforms.[2] The insider control problem inevitably led to lower efficiencies of large SOEs in China.[3] Under such context, in the late 1990s, the central government in China retightened its political control over large SOEs by further strengthening the status of the party committee in the firms.

To date, however, most of the conventional literature has argued that an anti-efficiency effect of internal bureaucratic control over large SOEs exists as a result of its dampening effect on SOE managers and CEO initiatives to exert full effort.[4] In this chapter, we illustrate the relevance of why the function of the party committee within large SOEs might, to some extent, mitigate the *ex post* agency inefficiencies, such as preventing empire-building activities by monitoring CEO behaviour. This chapter does not intend to tell a one-sided story. We also demonstrated that imposing the party committee control within large SOEs could undermine incentives for the CEOs and SEO managers to exert full effort. Therefore, we suggested that a trade-off exists between internal bureaucratic control and loss of CEO initiatives.

---

[2] J. Wu, *Contemporary Chinese Economic Reform*, Shanghai Far East Press, 2003; Y. Qian, "Enterprise Reform in China: Agency Problems and Political Control", *Economics of Transition*, vol. 4, no. 2, 1996, pp. 427–447.

[3] M. Aoki, "The Contingent Governance of Teams: Analysis of Institutional Complementarity", *International Economic Review*, vol. 35, no. 3, 1994, pp. 657–676; C. Zhang, "On the Discussions of Reforms of Governance Mechanism of SOE from the Perspective of Funding Financing", *Reform*, vol. 3, 1995.

[4] HuangNan Shen, Lei Fang and Kent Deng, "Rise of 'Red Zaibatsu' in China: Entrenchment and Expansion of Large State-owned Enterprises, 1990–2016", Economic History Working Papers, No. 260, Department of Economic History, London School of Economics and Political Science, London, UK, 2017; Justin, Yifu Lin, Fang Cai and Zhou Li, *The China Miracle: Development Strategy and Economic Reform*, Hong Kong, The Chinese University of Hong Kong Press, 2003. Justin Yifu Lin, Fang Cai and Zhou Li, "The Lessons of China's Transition to a Market Economy", *Cato Journal*, vol. 16, no. 2, 1996, pp. 201–232; Y. Qian, "Enterprise Reform in China: Agency Problems and Political Control", pp. 427–447; Colin Lixin Xu, Tian Zhu and Yi-min Lin, "Politician Control, Agency Problems and Ownership Reform, Evidence from China", *Economics of Transition*, vol. 13, no. 1, 2005, pp. 1–24.

The result of such a trade-off is that SOE agents, such as CEOs and managers, have to be heavily compensated because of the loss of incentives such that the party committee formal authority could dominate the CEO's or the agent's formal authority allocation within large SOEs. The formal authority allocation here refers to the case under whether SOE party committee or SOE CEO has the ultimate decision-making authority within large SOEs. This is to say, the party committee secretary could not extract all of the benefit from the centralisation of internal control over large SOEs; otherwise, CEOs and managers would not follow a party committee formal authority's allocation contract.

The rest of this chapter is organised as follows. The following section is the literature review. The section "A Simple Model" explains the theoretical model. The section "Policy Implications" discusses the corresponding policy implications of this chapter. The final section provides concluding remarks.

Literature Review
Ownership incentives

The most conventional view in the mainstream literature to resolve problems of insider control within large SOEs in China is to give ownership incentives to SOE managers such that they become the real owners of the firms.[5] Researchers have argued that even after the state delegates the power and decision-making authority to large SOE managers, because of the absence of real owners of firms, no effective mechanism is available to monitor the *ex post* behaviour of SOE

---

[5] W. Zhang, "Decision Rights, Residual Claim and Performance: A Theory of How the Chinese State Enterprise Reform Works", *China Economic Review*, vol. 8, no. 1, 1997, pp. 67–82; W. Zhang and Ma. Jie, "The Ownership Foundation of Yardstick Competition", *Economic Research Journal*, vol. 6, 1999; J. Kornai, *The Socialist System: The Political Economy of Communism*, Oxford, Clarendon Press, 1992; A. Shleifer and R. W. Vishny, "Officials and Firms", *The Quarterly Journal of Economics*, vol. 109, no. 4, 1994, pp. 995–1025; A. Shleifer and R. W. Vishny, "A Survey of Corporate Governance", *The Journal of Finance*, vol. 52, no. 2, 1997, pp. 737–783.

managers and CEOs. As a result, SOEs have a high level of agency costs. These high agency costs might stem from empire-building activities, perk consumption or favouritism. In general, SOE managers are not real owners, and therefore, their interests normally are misaligned with the SOE as a whole. Therefore, the solution they offer is achieved through the privatisation of SOEs such that SOEs will have real owners. The problem with this line of thought, however, according to Shen, Fang, Zhang and Jefferson, is that it considers principal–agent relations within SOEs only through the ownership angle.[6] This approach did not take into account the complex power division structure within large SOEs, and also neglected to take into account the political feasibility of implementing outright privatisation of large SOEs in China. For instance, regarding the monitoring mechanism, during the era of pre-SOE reforms, the so-called old three meetings (*lao san hui*) existed, which included party committee, workers committee and trade union, which could monitor the SOE manager and people who were in charge of the firms. After the SOE reforms were initiated in the 1980s, the so-called new three meetings (*Xin san hui*) emerged, which included the board of directors, shareholders committee and board of supervisors. Both the old three meetings and new three meetings could be regarded as providing the important function of monitoring the SOE CEOs. Therefore, views with respect to the absence of monitoring mechanism within large SOEs appear to neglect the inherent organisational structure of firms. According to the research by Ma *et al.*,[7] the party committee within large SOEs could actually lower *ex post* agency costs and, to some degree, even improve the efficiency of large SOEs. This chapter aligns with the spirit of Ma *et al.*, but takes a step further by arguing that there are also downsides for

---

[6] Jim HuangNan Shen, Lei Fang, Jun Zhang and Gary Jefferson, "The Partial Reform Equilibrium of China's Large SOEs: A Nash Bargaining Approach", at SSRN, <https://papers.ssrn.com/sol3/papers.cfm?abstract_id=3092373>

[7] Ma. L, Yuanfang Wang and Xiao xiu Shen, "Research on Governance Effects of China's State-owned Companies' Party Organization — A Perspective Based on Insiders Control", *China Industrial Economics*, vol. 8, no. 293, 2012.

imposing party committee control over large SOEs — that is, the undermining of manager incentives.

Corporate governance

The second prevailing view to resolve problems of insider control within large SOEs in China is to create a so-called stakeholder joint governance system. This view was first proposed by Yang and Zhou.[8] They argued that the shareholder primacy theory, stemming from modern corporate governance literature, which has been the guiding thought of power delegation reforms of Chinese SOEs, fails to take into account the following three possible problems. (a) Due to the absence of real owners of large SOEs, SOE managers would be interested in only their benefits. This interest misalignment between SOE managers and the general population, which constitutionally is denoted as the shareholders of large SOEs, could lead to a situation in which SOE managers would easily infringe on the rights of shareholders. (b) Although the shareholder primacy theory suggests that SOE CEOs or managers as the agents should manage the state assets on behalf of shareholders, collective decision-making is often required in large SOEs in China because all of the state assets are constitutionally owned by the general population. This would lead to the free-rider problems of SOE managers as they could ascribe the poor performance of large SOEs to the result of poor collective decision-making rather than personal responsibility. (c) The shareholder primacy governance system would lead to the ignorance of other stakeholders involved in the process of SOE reforms, such as workers. The solutions offered have included the establishment of an independent workers' committee as well as a bank committee to protect worker and minority shareholder interests. Unlike previous work, although we recognise the absence of a benefit protection mechanism for stakeholders, we do not agree with the solutions offered by previous studies. We argue that under

---

[8] R. Yang and Yean Zhou, "On the Joint Governance Mechanism of Firms under the Logic of Relevant Stakeholders", *China Industrial Economics,* vol. 1, 1998.

the particular context of social-political institutions in China, it is politically infeasible to establish an independent workers' committee or let the representatives of workers enter the board of directors. Therefore, a compromise is needed, such as a party committee that could care about the overall interest of all of the relevant stakeholders within large SOEs. Additionally, any unilateral interest pursuit ought to be banned.

External competition

The third prevailing view to resolve problems of insider control within large SOEs in China is to create an externally competitive market structure.[9] According to this view, rather than examining the efficiency implication of large SOEs from the internal governance structure, it is more plausible to use the criteria of market competition to assess whether or not the SOE managers perform well. Researchers have argued that a perfect competitive market will include a guideline for the average profitability level that a viable firm ought to obtain to survive in the market. On the basis of this average level of profitability, one could easily assess whether or not an SOE performed efficiently. Therefore, in this case, one could obtain a sufficient amount of information regarding the quality of internal corporate governance of SOEs. If an SOE could not survive under a perfect competitive market or earned profits below the average profitability level generated by the perfect competition market structure, then one could argue that SOE managers as agents of firms were not doing competent work. Succinctly put, the presence of a perfectly competitive market plays an important role in disciplining and monitoring the behaviour of SOE managers. This results in the fact that the information asymmetry between SOE agents (managers) and SOE principals could be undermined to a large degree. This argument has two pitfalls. The first one is that the degree of competition in the market could be endogenous to the ownership structure

---

[9] Justin Yifu Lin, Cai Fang and Li Zhou, "Competition, Policy Burdens, and State-owned Enterprise Reform", *The American Economic Review*, vol. 88, no. 2, Papers and Proceedings of the Hundred and Tenth Annual Meeting of the American Economic Association, May 1998, pp. 422–427; Justin Yifu Lin, "Viability, Economic Transition and Reflections on Neo-Classical Economics", *Kyklos*, vol. 58, no. 2, 2005, pp. 239–264.

of firms. In accordance with Zhang and Ma, the SOE-dominated industries in China experienced yardstick competition,[10] which resulted into welfare losses and profit losses for SOEs.[11] Therefore, if the market is experiencing yardstick competition, the profitability level no longer would provide sufficient information to reflect the true performance of firms. Second, an overemphasis on the role of external market structure in disciplining the managerial behaviour of SOEs would lead to the misperception that an internal corporate governance structure was not important. The work by Zhang[12] actually showed that the relaxation of entry barriers of the industries that initially were dominated by SOEs that have not been restructured would lead to an overentry problem, which finally would erode the total profitability of the industries.

A Simple Model

The model developed in this section aligns with the spirit of Aghion and Tirole.[13] Assume a political hierarchy composed of a principal (party committee secretary) and an agent (board of directors or CEO). Within this hierarchy, the party committee secretary is responsible for deciding to invest in some projects that are necessary to maximise the benefits of the SOE as a whole.[14] These projects could include the construction of infrastructure, social aid and market stabilisation. The basic idea is that the party committee secretary could have two ways of organising the agents to implement the projects. Under the principal formal authority case, the party committee would mandatorily force the CEO to collect the information and to implement

---

[10] The yardstick competition refers to the situation under which there exits the excessive level of competition in the market among firms.

[11] Weiying Zhang and Jie Ma, "The Ownership Foundation of Yardstick Competition", *Economic Research Journal*, vol. 6, 1999.

[12] Jun Zhang, "Demand, Scale Effect and the Losses of China's State-owned Industries — An Industrial Organization Approach", *Economic Research Journal*, vol. 6, 1998.

[13] P. Aghion and J. Tirole, "Formal and Real Authority in Organizations", *Journal of Political Economy*, vol. 105, no. 1, 1997, pp. 1–29.

[14] The case under which the party committee secretary and chairman of board of directors are the same person is not considered here and is beyond the scope of this research.

projects. Under the agent formal authority case, the CEO would refer the implementation of these projects to mid-level SOE mangers and have them collect the required information.

Projects: The CEO screens $n \geq 3$ potential and *a priori* identical projects on behalf of the party committee secretary. Each project k $\in \{1,2,3,\ldots,n\}$ would generate a verified monetary gain or profit B_k for the party committee secretary and b_k for the CEO.[15] B_k is generated according to the party committee secretary's capacity to implement each project. The CEO's private benefit stems from the referral of implementation of projects to mid-level managers. The value of b_k also reflects the extent to which the CEO could have the autonomy to refer the projects to the managers. The more effectively that managers implement the projects, the more private benefits that could be yielded for CEOs. This is to say, once the CEOs are given more autonomy, they might be interested in only those projects that could maximise their own private benefits, which could deviate from the general interest of the organisation as a whole. If no project is implemented, the benefit for the party secretary and the CEO would be zero, which could be denoted as $B_0 = b_0 = 0$.

For each party, at least one ineffective project yields a "sufficiently negative" payoff. This indicates that an uninformed CEO prefers to recommend inaction rather than to refer certain project to managers. Similarly, an uninformed party secretary would not select a project that delivers a negative payoff.

The preferred projects of the party committee yield known profit B. Similarly, the CEO's preferred project yields known profit b. This is to say, the projects implemented by the party committee might generate different benefits if delegated to CEO. For instance, in terms of the selection of investment projects, a CEO might invest in some projects with which the personal interests are given greater priority than the party secretary.[16] In this case, if the party committee secretary's preferred

---

[15] As noted, these projects could include infrastructure investment or the provision of aid.

[16] In some situations, CEOs might be less aggressive in investing in some projects. This is because CEOs could behave like empire builders in which they are not interested in profit maximisation, but rather in sales revenue maximisation. In this case, CEOs prefer more investments than the party secretary committee.

project is chosen, the CEO receives expected benefit βb.[17] Likewise, if the CEO's preferred project is chosen, the party secretary receives expected benefit αB. The congruence parameter β and α measure the degree to which the preference of the party secretary is aligned with the CEO. In this case, both β and α belong to [0,1]. Here, α measures the extent to which the party secretary's preferred project is also preferred by the CEO. Likewise, β measures the degree to which the CEO's preferred project is also preferred by the party secretary. In addition, $b > 1$, $B > 1$.

In terms of the misalignment of the interest between the party secretary and the CEO, it is a well-known fact that the party secretary is more inclined to invest in some projects that might benefit the interests of the SOE as a whole. The party secretary is the representative of the interest of the party, and SOEs are one of the most important sources of economic and political benefits for the communist party in China.[18] Nonetheless, CEOs are more prone to maximise private control of benefits, such as compensations, ranking promotions, empire building and perk consumption. These personal interests might deviate from or harm the interest of the SOE as a whole, which raises the *ex post* agency problems, such as moral hazard or insider control. In addition, the party secretary may favour giving more autonomy to CEOs. Party secretaries are not knowledgeable of the local economic conditions of SOEs and therefore have the incentive to decentralise the power such that CEO could take more initiative. Nevertheless, the recentralisation of power by the party secretary (the pick of the party secretary's preferred projects) would necessarily be misaligned with the CEOs' preferred projects because those CEOs could no longer pursue the empire-building activities that might support their interests.

---

[17] In line with P. Aghion and J. Tirole, "Formal and Real Authority in Organizations", pp. 1–29, the expectation refers to the *ex ante* uninformed situation in which all of the projects are alike.

[18] HuangNan Shen, Lei Fang and Kent Deng, "Rise of 'Red Zaibatsu' in China: Entrenchment and Expansion of Large State-owned Enterprises, 1990–2016". *Economic History Working Papers*, No. 260, Department of Economic History, London School of Economics and Political Science, London, UK, 2017.

Assumption 1: $\begin{cases} \alpha < \frac{1}{2} \\ \beta > \frac{1}{2} \end{cases}$

Preferences: The party secretary is risk neutral and has utility $B_k - R(E)$ if project k is chosen, and $R(E)$ are the losses for the party secretary arising from the additional investment made by the CEO. The party secretary is protected by limited liability condition, indicating that $R(E)$ could not be negative. The CEO's utility is then $b_k + R(e)$. Here, $R(e)$ is the benefit derived from the additional amount of investments, which could be treated as the empire-building activities undertaken by the CEO. Note that the empire-building benefits are both functions of probability E and e. This chapter assumed that the higher probability that the party secretary is informed (higher value of E), the lower the amount of losses incurred by the CEO's empire-building investment. The opposite is true for a lower value of E. In contrast, when the CEO is more likely to be informed, higher benefits could be obtained from the empire-building activities. The functional form for $R(E)$ is linear, which could be written as $R(E) = -dE + R_{min}$, where $d > 1$ and R_{min} is the minimum level of benefits received by the party secretary — that is, when the party secretary is fully uninformed, what is the minimum level of benefits that could be obtained? Similarly, the functional form for $R(e)$ is also linear, which could be expressed as follows: $R(e) = fe + R_{max}$, where $f > 1$ and R_{max} is the maximum level of benefits that CEO could obtain when fully uninformed. Moreover, this chapter assumed that the party secretary would be more inclined to derive benefits from the CEO's empire-building activities than the CEO would be inclined to transfer those benefits to the party secretary. Although the party committee secretary had weaker information than the CEO about the details of the internal corporate governance of the SOEs, the secretary would be able to fully recentralise the decision-making authority because of stronger political legitimacy. As a result, the party secretary would be better able to extract the benefits from the CEO's empire-building activities. The CEO would have obtained all of the empire-building benefits in the absence of centralisation by the party committee. Conversely, from the CEO's viewpoint, to maintain political loyalty to the party, it is more likely that the CEO would share the benefits of these empire-building activities with the party secretary rather than retaining these benefits. On the basis of this fact, we have the second assumption in this chapter:

Assumption 2: $\frac{dR(e)}{de} < \left| \frac{dR(E)}{dE} \right|$ [19]

Information: We assume that the nature of projects' payoffs is initially unknown to both the party secretary and the CEO, such that it could reflect the non-routine nature of the decision over which authority may be delegated to the CEO.[20] The CEO acquires information in a binary form. At private cost, $g_A(e) = \frac{ke^2}{2}$, the CEO perfectly learns the payoffs of all of the candidate projects with probability e. Here, k is the positive effort parameter for CEO. This probability occurs when the CEO could adapt to local information of different projects using the information collected by SOE managers. With probability $(1-e)$, the CEO learns nothing and still treats all of the candidate projects as identical. This happens when the CEO does not refer the implementation of projects to SOE managers.

Likewise, the central state decides how much effort to devote to learning payoffs. With probability E, the state becomes perfectly informed about the payoffs of the projects. Its effort cost function could be denoted as, $g_p(E) = \frac{hE^2}{2}$, where h is the positive effort parameter value for central state. With probability $(1-E)$, the central state learns nothing. The disutilities of effort $g_A(\cdot)$ and $g_p(\cdot)$ are increasing and strictly convex and satisfy $g_i(0) = 0$, $g_i'(0) = 0$, and $g_i'(1) = 1$, $i = A, P$. In addition, it is assumed that $h < b$, as once the CEO obtains benefit from picking preferred projects, it has to be strictly larger than the marginal cost of effort of principals. This is to say that the project would gain more than the cost for which the party secretary seeks for being informed. If it is converse, then the party secretary could gain sufficient benefit from the CEO's referral of the projects to managers, which would undermine the degree of CEO's incentives.

---

[19] This assumption also implies that $f < d$.

[20] P. Aghion and J. Tirole, "Formal and Real Authority in Organizations", pp. 1–29.

Authority: If the party secretary has formal authority, the party secretary may always overrule the CEO. The party secretary would do so if it has been perfectly informed and if the CEO's preferred projects are incongruent. In this case, the party secretary has the formal and real authority over the choice of project and can fully dispense the CEO's information and recommendation. Otherwise, given $\alpha > 0$, the CEO would have the real authority to decide which project to pick and such authority would have to be admitted by the party secretary.

If the CEO has formal authority, the independent CEO is perfectly informed as a result of referral of the projects to managers. In this case, the CEO could select the preferred projects and this decision could not be overruled by the party committee.

Contracts: In line with the incomplete contract theory approach by Grossman and Hart,[21] we assumed that projects cannot be described and contracted *ex ante*. The initial contracts would specify the allocation of formal authority to only one of the parties.

The timing would be as follows: (a) The party secretary offers a contract that specifies the formal authority to it or the CEO over the future choice of the projects, (b) both parties privately collect the information regarding n projects' payoffs; (c) the party that does not have the formal authority communicates the information about what is learned about the subset of preferred projects choices, and (d) the controlling party chooses a project (or none) on the basis of the collected information and the information communicated by the other non-controlling party.

Payoffs under two allocations of formal authority

Under the case of party secretary formal authority, the utilities for the party secretary and CEO are as follows, respectively:

$$u_p = EB + (1 - E)e\alpha B - g_p(E) - R(E) \tag{1}$$

---

[21] O. Hart and S. Grossman, 'The Costs and Benefits of Ownership: A Theory of Vertical and Lateral Integration, *Journal of Political Economy*, vol. 94, no. 4, 1986.

$$u_a = E\beta b + (1-E)eb - g_a(e) + R(e) \tag{2}$$

Based on Eqs. (1) and (2), we could seek the following two reactions for the CEO and the party secretary:

$$\begin{cases} B(1-e\alpha) = g'_p(E) + R'(E) & (3) \\ b(1-E) = g'_a(e) - R'(e) & (4) \end{cases}$$

By plugging the effort cost function into Eqs. (3) and (4), we obtain the following Nash equilibrium (E, e):

$$\begin{cases} E = \dfrac{B\alpha(b+f) - k(B+d)}{bB\alpha - kh} \\ e = \dfrac{b(d+B-h) - hf}{B\alpha b - hk} \end{cases}$$

Under CEO formal authority, when informed by the SOE managers, the CEO simply chooses a preferred project. When the CEO is uninformed and the party secretary is informed, the party secretary suggests a preferred project, which then is implemented by the CEO. So, the utilities for both the party secretary and CEO, respectively, could be expressed as follows:

$$u_p^d = e\alpha B(1-e)EB - g_p(E) - R(E) \tag{5}$$

$$u_A^d = eb + (1-e)E\beta b - g_A(e) + R(e) \tag{6}$$

From Eqs. (5) and (6), we could derive the respective reaction function for the CEO and the party secretary under the case of CEO formal authority:

$$\begin{cases} B(1-e) = g'_p(E) + R'(E) & (7) \\ b(1-E\beta) = g'_A(e) - R'(e) & (8) \end{cases}$$

By plugging the convex cost function forms for Eqs. (7) and (8), we could obtain the following Nash equilibrium (E_d, e_d):

$$
\begin{cases}
E_d = \dfrac{B(f-k-b)-kd}{B\beta b - kh} & (9) \\[3mm]
e_d = \dfrac{\beta(d+B)-(f-b)}{B\beta - k} & (10)
\end{cases}
$$

Based on Eqs. (5), (6), (9) and (10), it could be derived that the agent is less likely to be informed and the principal is more likely to be informed under the case of party secretary formal authority if and only if the following two conditions are satisfied:

$$
\begin{cases}
E_d < E \\
e_d > e
\end{cases}
$$

If these two conditions hold, it could be ensured that the party committee formal authority case would dominate the CEO formal authority case.

From these two conditions, this chapter makes the following proposition:

Proposition 1: *The party secretary would be more likely to be informed under the contract of party committee formal authority if and only if the benefit arising from picking its preferred project cannot be sufficiently large such that it could compensate for the loss of CEO initiatives. That is,*
$B > \frac{kh[\alpha(f+b)-(f-b)]}{b^2\alpha[\beta(f+1)+(1-f)]}.$

Proof of Proposition 1:

Step 1.
To have, it must be the case that

$$
\frac{B(f-k-b)-kd}{B\beta b - kh} < \frac{B\alpha(b+f)-k(B+d)}{bB\alpha - kh} \qquad (11)
$$

Rearranging Eq. (11), we obtain the following:

$$\left[B\left(f - k - b\right) - kd \right]\left(bB\alpha - kh\right)$$
$$< \left(B\beta b - kh\right)\left[B\alpha \left(b + f\right) - k\left(B + d\right)\right] \tag{12}$$

Expanding Eq. (12) and rearrange it, we derive the following:

$$\left(Bf - Bk - Bb - kd\right)\left(bB\alpha - kh\right)$$
$$< \left(B\alpha b + B\alpha f - kB - kd\right)\left(B\beta b - kh\right) \tag{13}$$

Equation (13) could be further reduced to the following:

$$Bfb\alpha - fkh - Bkb\alpha - Bb^2\alpha + bkh - kdb\alpha$$
$$< B\beta\alpha b^2 - \alpha bkh + B\alpha f\beta b - \alpha fkh - kB\beta b - kd\beta b \tag{14}$$

We could further write Eq. (14) as follows:

$$Bfb\alpha - B\alpha f\beta b - fkh + \alpha fkh - Bb^2\alpha - B\beta\alpha b^2 + bkh + \alpha bkh$$
$$< -kB\beta b - kd\beta b + Bkb\alpha + kdb\alpha \tag{15}$$

This implies that

$$Bfb\alpha \left(1 - \beta\right) + fkh\left(\alpha - 1\right) - Bb^2\alpha \left(1 + \beta\right) + bkh\left(1 + \alpha\right) + kb\left(B\beta - B\alpha\right)$$
$$< kdb\left(\alpha - \beta\right) \tag{16}$$

According to Assumption 1, we know that

$$Bfb\alpha \left(1 - \beta\right) + fkh\left(\alpha - 1\right) - Bb^2\alpha \left(1 + \beta\right) + bkh\left(1 + \alpha\right) + kb\left(B\beta - B\alpha\right)$$
$$< kdb\left(\alpha - \beta\right) < 0$$

Based on the sandwich theorem, we know that

$$Bfb\alpha \left(1 - \beta\right) + fkh\left(\alpha - 1\right) - Bb^2\alpha \left(1 + \beta\right) + bkh\left(1 + \alpha\right)$$
$$+ kb\left(B\beta - B\alpha\right) < 0 \tag{17}$$

From Eq. (17), it could be derived that

$$Bfb\alpha\left(1-\beta\right)+fkh\left(\alpha-1\right)-Bb^{2}\alpha\left(1+\beta\right)+bkh\left(1+\alpha\right)$$
$$<-kb\left(B\beta-B\alpha\right) \tag{18}$$

From Eq. (18), we know that

$$Bfb\alpha\left(1-\beta\right)+fkh\left(\alpha-1\right)-Bb^{2}\alpha\left(1+\beta\right)+bkh\left(1+\alpha\right)$$
$$<-kb\left(B\beta-B\alpha\right)<0 \tag{19}$$

By sandwich theorem, this means

$$Bfb\alpha\left(1-\beta\right)+fkh\left(\alpha-1\right)-Bb^{2}\alpha\left(1+\beta\right)+bkh\left(1+\alpha\right)<0 \tag{20}$$

After rearranging Eq. (20), we obtain the following:

$$Bb\alpha[\beta\left(f+b\right)+\left(b-f\right)>kh\left[\alpha\left(f+b\right)-\left(f-b\right)\right]$$

$$B>\frac{kh\left[\alpha\left(f+b\right)-\left(f-b\right)\right]}{b\alpha\left[\beta\left(f+b\right)+\left(b-f\right)\right]}$$

Proof completes

Proposition 1 implies that under the party committee formal authority, the party secretary's benefits derived from the preferred projects should be sufficiently high because the secretary has more incentives to make effort caused by the power centralisation within large SOEs. This is to say, when the party secretary picks some preferred projects, the secretary could extract all of the benefits. To a large degree, however, this would undermine the incentives of the CEO, which might harm the interests of SOEs as a whole. This reveals the trade-off between gaining control and losing incentives.

Proposition 2: *The CEO would be less likely to be informed (shrink the effort) under the case of party committee formal authority, but still follows* *this contract if and only if the benefit arising from picking the preferred project is sufficiently large. Namely, $b > \frac{hf}{B+d}$.*

Proof of Proposition 2:

To make $e_d < e$, we must have the following:

$$\frac{\beta(d+B)-(f-b)}{B\beta - k} < \frac{b(d+B-h)-hf}{B\alpha b - hk} \tag{21}$$

Rearranging Eq. (21), we have the following:

$$\left[(d+B)-(f-b)\right](B\alpha b - hk) < (B\beta - k)\left[b(d+B-h)-hf\right] \tag{22}$$

Rearranging Eq. (22), we would derive the following:

$$B\alpha bd + B^2\alpha b - B\alpha bf + B\alpha b^2 - B\beta bd - B^2\beta b + B\beta hf - 2hkb$$
$$< dk(h-b) \tag{23}$$

Because $dk(h - b) < 0$, then it must be the case that

$$B\alpha bd + B^2\alpha b - B\alpha bf + B\alpha b^2 - B\beta bd - B^2\beta b + B\beta hf < 0 \tag{24}$$

which is to say,

$$\alpha bd + B\alpha b - \alpha bf + \alpha b^2 - \beta bd - B\beta b + \beta hf < 0 \tag{25}$$

This means

$$\alpha bd + B\alpha b - \alpha bf + \alpha b^2 < B\beta b + \beta bd - \beta hf \tag{26}$$

It could be demonstrated that

$$\alpha bd + B\alpha b - \alpha bf + \alpha b^2 < \beta(Bb + bd - hf)$$

This is to say,

$$\beta > \frac{\alpha bd + B\alpha b - \alpha bf + \alpha b^2}{(Bb + bd - hf)}$$

Since $\beta < 1$, this implies that

$$\frac{\alpha bd + B\alpha b - \alpha bf + \alpha b^2}{\left(Bb + bd - hf\right)} < 1 \tag{27}$$

From Eq. (27), it implies that

$$\alpha bd + B\alpha b - \alpha bf + \alpha b^2 < \left(Bb + bd - hf\right)$$

Therefore,

$$ab\left(d + B - f + b\right) < \left(Bb + bd - hf\right) \tag{28}$$

Since $0 < ab < \frac{(Bb + bd - hf)}{(d + B - f + b)}$, then by sandwich theorem,

$$\frac{\left(Bb + bd - hf\right)}{\left(d + B - f + b\right)} > 0 \tag{29}$$

Based on the Assumption 2, $(d + B - f + b) > 0$, it must be the case that $(Bb + bd - hf) > 0$.

This implies that

$$b > \frac{hf}{B + d}$$

Proof completes

Proposition 2 implies that to make the party committee formal authority work, the CEO must be compensated heavily such that it could offset the losses of initiatives of the CEO when the party committee has a substantial amount of bureaucratic control over large SOEs.

Policy Implications

The theories proposed by our model have far-reaching implications on the corporate governance issues of large SOEs in China. First, according to our model, an optimal level of bureaucratic control must exist over large SOEs because of the trade-off between loss of control by the party committee and the lower *ex-post* agency cost, such as eliminating the empire-building activities by SOE CEOs. According to our analysis, it is not always efficient to impose full party-committee control over SOEs, as this inevitably would undermine the incentives of CEOs to work hard. The CEO has to obtain a certain level of benefits such that they could accept the party committee authority within large SOEs. Nonetheless, if SOE managers are given full autonomy, then *ex-post*-agency inefficiencies would arise, such as empire-building activities and perk consumption, which would conflict with the overall interest of a firm. In advanced economies, the way in which firm shareholders monitor the SOE CEO normally is through the introduction of an independent board of directors, which consists of the representatives of employees, shareholders and other level of managers. This is apparently politically infeasible in China, as China's SOEs are under direct party control. Therefore, the role of the party committee might to some degree substitute the role of an independent board of directors, which could sufficiently monitor the SOE agents (CEO and managers). The downside of indefinitely imposing party committee control over large SOEs is that this could undermine the incentives for CEOs to exert full effort.

Conclusions

This chapter constructed a theoretical model to illustrate the relevance of the costs and benefits of the role of the party committee within large SOEs. We determined that a trade-off exists between internal bureaucratic control and loss of incentives for managers to exert full effort. Recognising this trade-off, we derived the condition under which the party committee's formal authority always dominates. We argued that the party committee's formal authority dominates if and only if CEOs' loss of incentives could be heavily compensated such that they would accept such formal authority allocation. In other words, the party committee secretary could not extract the full surplus from such formal authority allocation, as this would cause a loss of incentives for CEOs to exert full effort. Thus, an optimal degree of bureaucratic control exists over large SOEs in China. The conclusions drawn from this chapter have far-reaching implications for the current debate about the role of the party committee within China's large SOEs.

Acknowledgement

We are particularly thankful for the comments from Tian Zhu and Wan-Wen Chu.

Part 4

Regional Development and Trade Restructuring

Chapter 12

Trends of Regional Development and Shifts of Fiscal Power in China

LU Ding*

Introduction

China is a continental country of vast territory with the world's largest population. In the past four decades, China has achieved remarkable economic growth and lifted itself from a poor, underdeveloped economy to a fairly well-developed global power. Forty years ago, the size of the Chinese economy, measured by gross domestic product (GDP) in US dollars, was only 8% of the then United States economy, ranked as the 11th largest economy in the world. Nowadays, China has become the world's second largest economy, with its annual GDP equivalent to over 60% that of the United States. In 1980, China was counted as a low-income economy with about $200 per capita annual income. By 2015, China's per capita gross national income (GNI) reached $7,900, making it an upper-middle-income country according to World Bank's classification.[1]

---

*LU Ding is the Vice Dean and Professor at the School of Entrepreneurship and Management, ShanghaiTech University.
[1] By the World Bank's classification, "low-income economies are those with a GNI per capita of $1,025 or less in 2015. Lower-middle-income economies are those with a GNI per capita of $1,026–$4,035. Upper-middle-income economies are those with a GNI per capita of $4,036–$12,475. High-income economies are those with a GNI per capita of

China's economic development is, however, highly uneven across regions. In most years during the rapid-growth decades, interregional income inequality had increased. The coastal provinces generally enjoyed advantages of engaging with the market opening process earlier than the inland provinces. In the later years, a catching-up process has been observed among many inland areas. The dynamics of regional development in China has motivated prolific literature on the study of regional economic convergence. Empirical tests using cross-sectional or panel data at provincial, prefectural and county levels have been carried out to verify whether conditional or unconditional convergence has occurred across different parts of China. Those studies have exposed the patterns of unbalanced spatial development and revealed various factors that have driven or constrained economic convergence.[2]

The disparity of regional development has important implications on subnational fiscal arrangements. China's multilevel fiscal structure features a hierarchic system where the local governments hold independent budgets, share main tax revenues with the central government and carry out assigned responsibilities of providing local public goods and infrastructure. Many studies have examined the effectiveness and efficiency of this system of fiscal federalism. For instance, Fan and Wan, Ping and Bai, and Liu and Ma have evaluated the effects of fiscal incentives, transfers or fiscal decentralisation on local public spending and

---

$12,476 or more." World Bank, *World Development Indicators* 2017, Washington D.C., World Bank, 2017, p. xvii.

[2] Subrata Ghatak and Li Hong, "Economic Growth and Convergence in China's Provinces: Theory and Evidence", Economics Discussion Papers, 2002; Celine Bonnefond, "Growth Dynamics and Conditional Convergence among Chinese Provinces: A Panel Data Investigation using System GMM Estimator", *Journal of Economic Development*, vol. 39, no. 4, 2014, pp. 1–25; Françoise Lemoine, Sandra Poncet, and Deniz Ünal, "Spatial Rebalancing and Industrial Convergence in China", *China Economic Review*, vol. 34, 2015, pp. 39–63; Cheong Tsun Se and Wu Yanrui, "Convergence and Transitional Dynamics of China's Industrial Output: A County-Level Study Using a New Framework of Distribution Dynamics Analysis", *China Economic Review*, vol. 48, 2018, pp. 125–138.

public good provision.[3] Wang, Shen and Zou analysed provincial taxation performance and estimated that there was potential room for additional taxation.[4] Pan, Huang and Chiang investigated how local government fiscal deficits may have impacted land finance and real estate market.[5] Bai, Hsieh and Song looked into the role of off-balance-sheet spending by local governments in financing the post-2008 fiscal expansion.[6]

The primary focus of this chapter is to discuss about changing distribution of fiscal power across China's provincial economies. An examination of cross-province concentration of domestic production and population from 1995 to 2016 indicates a pattern of changing developmental convergence. A similar pattern of changes is observed in the distribution of gross fiscal contributions by the provincial economies to the central government's revenue. Using estimated net fiscal positions of provincial economies, however, this study reveals a trend of fiscal power concentration in later years. This trend has profound implications on intergovernmental political–economic relationship.

The rest of this chapter is arranged as follows. The section "Concentration and Convergence of the Provincial Economies" discusses the geographic dynamics of (provincial) economic sizes and its consequential impact on development convergence. The section "The

---

[3] Fan Ziying and Wan Guanghua, "The Fiscal Risk of Local Government Revenue in the People's Republic of China", *ADBI Working Papers*, 2016; Ping Xin-Qiao and Bai Jie, "Fiscal Decentralisation and Local Public Good Provision in China", Finance Working Papers, June 2005; Liu Chang and Ma Guangrong, "Taxation without Representation: Local Fiscal Response to Intergovernmental Transfers in China", *International Tax and Public Finance*, vol. 23, no. 5, 2016, pp. 854–874.

[4] Wang Qian, Shen Chunli, and Zou Heng-fu, "Local Government Tax Effort in China: An Analysis of Provincial Tax Performance", *Region & Development*, vol. 29, 2009, pp. 203–236.

[5] Pan Jiun-Nan, Huang Jr-Tsung and Chiang Tsun-Feng, "Empirical Study of the Local Government Deficit, Land Finance and Real Estate Markets in China", *China Economic Review*, vol. 32, 2015, pp. 57–67.

[6] Bai Chong-En, Hsieh Chang-Tai and Song Zheng Michael, "The Long Shadow of a Fiscal Expansion", *Brookings Papers on Economic Activity*, vol. 47, no. 2, 2016, pp. 129–181.

Changing Economic Landscape in a Global Perspective" presents the changing ranking of large provincial economies in a global perspective. The section "Estimation of Provincial Fiscal Power" provides the estimation of provincial distribution of fiscal power by measuring local governments' net fiscal positions. The final section discusses trends of fiscal power distribution in contrast to development convergence and comments on its political–economic implications.

Concentration and Convergence of the Provincial Economies

The Chinese mainland territory consists of 31 provincial administrations. Over the past decades, economic growth has taken place at various rates across regions, changing the relative sizes of China's provincial economies. As shown in Table 1, the shares of the 4, 8, 10, 12 and 16 largest provincial economies in China's GDP all increased from 1995 to 2005, suggesting that the larger provincial economies tended to

Table 1: Concentration of GDP in Largest Provincial Economies

	1995	2000	2005	2010	2016
CR-4	32.0%	33.7%	38.9%	37.4%	36.8%
CR-8	50.1%	53.2%	59.2%	56.5%	55.4%
CR-10	61.0%	64.4%	70.4%	68.4%	67.3%
CR-12	67.7%	71.1%	77.4%	75.4%	74.0%
CR-16	75.5%	79.2%	85.4%	83.7%	82.1%
HHI (GDP)	0.0457	0.0507	0.0620	0.0590	0.0574
HHI (Population)	0.0449	0.0451	0.0438	0.0447	0.0448
GDP–Population Correlation	0.7486	0.7587	0.7703	0.8324	0.8458

Note: CR-n is the concentration ratio (or share of GDP) of the largest nth provincial economies.

Source: Compiled and calculated based on data from China's National Bureau of Statistics.

grow faster than the smaller ones during the period. Measured by the Herfindahl–Hirschman Index (HHI),[7] the cross-province concentration of domestic production rose by 35.6% from 0.0457 to 0.0620 through these years.

In the period 2005–2016, however, all the concentration ratios declined as well as the HHI, which fell by 8%, indicating that the cross-province concentration of domestic production has been somewhat moderated. All the measures of concentration have still remained significantly higher than they were in 1995 and 2000.

By definition, an economy's size is

$$\text{GDP}_i = \text{Per capita GDP}_i \times \text{Population}_i \qquad (1)$$

A province may increase its economic size relative to others either by raising per capita GDP faster than others or by increasing its population size relative to others. The latter can be the result of a relatively higher natural rate of population growth, a relatively higher net immigration rate or a combination of both. As shown in Table 1, the HHI for population did not change much over the decades, while the statistical correlation between GDP and population has monotonically increased through the years. The rising correlation implies that provinces with higher shares of GDP but lower shares of population have gained their shares of population while those with lower shares of GDP but higher shares of population have lost their shares of population. Given that natural rates of population growth were not higher in richer regions, the rising correlation must have been caused by immigration to provinces with higher per capita GDP levels.

The closer correlation between shares of GDP and shares of population also indicates economic convergence across regions. If per capita

---

[7] The HHI is typically a measure of concentration of all firms' shares in a market. Since it is the sum of squared values of all firms' shares, its value ranges from zero (indicating perfectly deconcentrated market) to one (indicating a monopoly with 100% concentration of shares). Here, we borrow the index to measure the concentration of domestic production across provincial economies.

Table 2:   Share-of-GDP to Share-of-Population Ratio

	1995	2000	2005	2010	2016
Median	0.74	0.79	0.87	0.88	0.86
Mean	1.02	1.07	1.13	1.07	1.05
Max	3.49	3.75	3.42	2.42	2.20
Min	0.36	0.35	0.38	0.43	0.51
Std. dev.	0.66	0.74	0.75	0.54	0.48

Source: Calculated based on data from China's National Bureau of Statistics.

GDP were equal everywhere, the share of GDP and share of population would also be the same in every region, or in mathematical form[8]:

$$\frac{\text{share of GDP}}{\text{share of population}} = 1 \qquad (2)$$

In Table 2, we can see the changes of the share of GDP to share of population ratios over years. The gap between the maximum ratio and the minimum ratio increased from 1995 to 2000, while the standard deviation of the ratio rose sharply. These changes suggest that the growth across the regions was not converging in the period. The standard deviation of the ratios, which shows how diverse the ratios are, reached its peak in 2005. Between 2005 and 2016, both the standard deviation and the gap between the maximum and minimum ratios have fallen sharply. The mean value of the ratios first rose from 1995 to 2005, but has since declined. All these imply that convergence has occurred since 2005.

Figure 1 plots the shares of GDP against shares of population for the years 1995, 2005 and 2016. A nonlinear relationship between the two is established by a second-order polynomial function estimated for

---

[8] Divide both sides of equation (1) by national GDP and assume that $PCGDP_i$ equals national $PCGDP$, it follows that *share of GDP* must also equal to *share of population*.

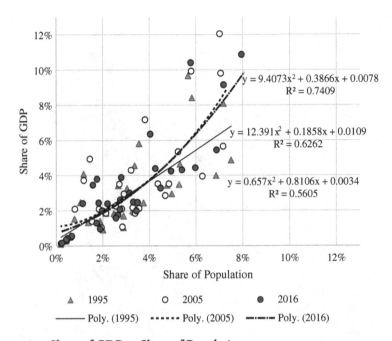

$$y = 9.4073x^2 + 0.3866x + 0.0078$$
$$R^2 = 0.7409$$

$$y = 12.391x^2 + 0.1858x + 0.0109$$
$$R^2 = 0.6262$$

$$y = 0.657x^2 + 0.8106x + 0.0034$$
$$R^2 = 0.5605$$

Figure 1:   Share of GDP vs Share of Population

Source: Compiled from data of China's National Bureau of Statistics.

each year. Between 1995 and 2005, most of the provinces with larger GDP shares had raised their shares of GDP relative to their shares of population, causing the polynomial function curve to bend upwards at the higher end. This change indicates a higher disparity of incomes across the region. During the decade 2005–2016, that bend was straightened just a little bit while the *R*-square of the curve increased, suggesting a better fit of the function to the data.

As can be seen from Figure 2, the richest three municipalities — Shanghai, Beijing and Tianjin — have the highest share-of-GDP to share-of-population ratios above 1.80. (For example, Shanghai's share of GDP is 3.8%, more than double its share of population by 1.8%.) The poorest provinces are Gansu and Yunnan, whose shares of GDP are 1.0% and 2.0% with shares of population being 1.9% and 3.5%, respectively.

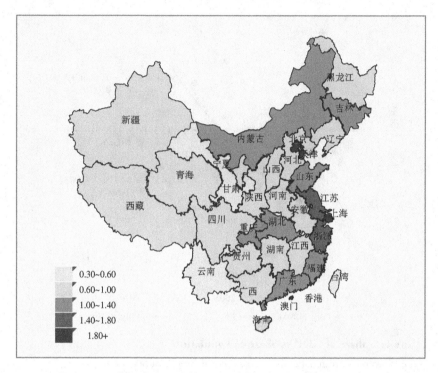

Figure 2: **Geography of Share of GDP to Share of Population Ratios (2016)**
Source: Compiled from data of China's National Bureau of Statistics.

In summary, measured by economic size at the provincial level, the Chinese economy became more concentrated during the decade 1995–2005, but the concentration has since then been moderated in the last decade. The convergence of provincial economic development has also experienced a turning point around 2005: growth was more divergent before that year and has become more convergent afterwards.

The Changing Economic Landscape in a Global Perspective

The dynamics of regional development has an inevitable impact on the landscape of the regional economies. Table 3 shows the ranking of

Table 3: Ranking of the Largest 12 Provincial Economies

Rank	1995			2005			2016		
	Provinces	GDP % of Total	Population % of Total	Provinces	GDP % of Total	Population % of Total	Provinces	GDP % of Total	Population % of Total
1	Guangdong	9.7	5.7	Guangdong	12.0	7.0	Guangdong	10.9	8.0
2	Jiangsu	8.4	5.8	Jiangsu	9.9	5.8	Jiangsu	10.4	5.8
3	Shandong	8.1	7.2	Shandong	9.8	7.1	Shandong	9.1	7.2
4	Zhejiang	5.8	3.6	Zhejiang	7.2	3.8	Zhejiang	6.4	4.0
5	Henan	4.9	7.5	Henan	5.7	7.2	Henan	5.4	6.9
6	Hebei	4.6	5.3	Hebei	5.3	5.2	Sichuan (↑3)	4.4	6.0
7	Liaoning	4.6	3.4	Shanghai (↑1)	4.9	1.4	Hubei (↑5)	4.4	4.3
8	Shanghai	4.1	1.2	Liaoning (↓1)	4.3	3.2	Hebei (↓2)	4.3	5.4
9	Sichuan	4.0	6.9	Sichuan	3.9	6.3	Hunan (↑1)	4.2	4.9
10	Hunan	3.5	5.3	Beijing (↑5)	3.7	1.2	Fujian (↑3)	3.9	2.8
11	Hubei	3.4	4.8	Hunan (↓1)	3.5	4.8	Shanghai (↓4)	3.8	1.8
12	Fujian	3.4	2.7	Hubei (↓1)	3.5	4.4	Beijing (↓2)	3.5	1.6

Note: The arrow and number indicate the change of ranking position as compared to the previous ranking.

Source: Compiled from data of China's National Bureau of Statistics.

the largest 12 provincial economies through years 1995–2016. What is remarkable is the fairly stable ranking of the largest provincial economies over the two decades: there has been "no" change in the ranking of the largest five at all! Meanwhile, all the largest 12 economies in 1995 except for Liaoning remain at the same rank two decades later.

Partially thanks to the converging trend since 2005, Beijing and Shanghai, the two provincial economies with a share of GDP much higher than share of population, had their ranking demoted in 2016. Meanwhile, Sichuan, Hubei and Hunan, whose shares of GDP were much lower than their share of population in 2005, saw their ranking rise by 2016.

In a global perspective, the ranking of these Chinese provinces rose quickly as compared with other countries during these decades. In Table 4, we place China's largest three provincial economies on the global ranking of economies during the years 1995–2016.

In 1995, China was the world's eighth largest economy, ranked below Italy and Brazil. Meanwhile, Hong Kong and Singapore, the two city–state economies with a majority Chinese population, were ranked 28th and 38th in the world economy, bigger than any of the Chinese provinces measured by GDP. China's largest three provinces by economic size — Guangdong, Jiangsu and Shandong — were ranked 42nd, 45th and 47th, respectively, in the world.

By 2016, China had already been the world's second largest economy for six years. The economic sizes of Guangdong, Jiangsu and Shandong, the largest three among the Chinese provinces, were equivalent to those of Australia, Mexico and Indonesia, ranked 14th, 15th and 16th in the world. In contrast, Hong Kong is now ranked 32nd in the world by its GDP, which was less than that of Liaoning, the 14th largest provincial economy in China. Singapore's economy, ranked 37th in the world, was about the size of Shaanxi's, the 15th in China. In fact, 24 of the Chinese provinces have reached economic sizes that make them comparable to the world's 14th to 50th largest economies.

Table 4: Rank of the Largest Three Provincial Economies in the World Economy
(Unit: 100 million renminbi)

	1995				2016		
Rank	Economy	Chinese Province	GDP	Rank	Economy	Chinese Province	GDP
28	Hong Kong		12,080	10	Canada		102,010
29	Saudi Arabia		11,971	11	Korea, Rep.		93,739
—	—		—	12	Russian Federation		85,232
37	Malaysia		7,408	13	Spain		82,182
38	Singapore		7,340	14	Australia	Guangdong	80,014
39	Venezuela, RB		6,255	15	Mexico	Jiangsu	69,540
40	Philippines		6,190	16	Indonesia	Shandong	61,923
41	Chile		6,134	17	Turkey		57,370
42	Ireland	Guangdong	5,781	—	—		—
43	United Arab Emirates		5,490	32	Hong Kong	Liaoning/14th	21,316
44	New Zealand		5,338	33	Israel		21,106
45	Pakistan	Jiangsu	5,064	34	Denmark		20,385
46	Egypt		5,024	35	Philippines		20,253
47	Czech Republic	Shandong	4,992	36	Ireland		20,247
48	Peru		4,452	37	Singapore	Shaanxi/15th	19,726

Note: GDP figures are current-year nominal values converted to RMB by annual exchange rate.

Source: Compiled from World Bank national accounts data and OECD National Accounts data files.

Estimation of Provincial Fiscal Power

In a system of fiscal federalism, what really counts is not a local economy's size but its fiscal power. The foundation of China's contemporary fiscal revenue system was laid down by a major fiscal reform in 1994. Before that reform, the central–local government fiscal relationship was defined by the "fiscal contract responsibility system" evolved in the 1980s. Under that system, the provincial governments were liable to make pre-negotiated quotas of payments to the central government.

The provincial governments retained the fiscal revenue above the quotas for local expense. Over time, within a fast-growing economy that system experienced a growing problem of leaving too much new revenue resources in the hands of the local governments, who had various information advantages over the central government in the revenue-sharing negotiation and revenue collecting process. The 1994 fiscal reform aimed to deal that problem by modernising China's fiscal federalism and balance the need for centralised control of fiscal resources and governing efficiency at the local level.[9]

The essential feature of the post-1994 fiscal regime is the "tax-sharing system". As shown in Table 5, different fiscal revenues are categorised under the central or local governments' coffers. Two main sources of tax revenues, domestic value-added tax and income tax (on enterprises and individuals), are collected and shared by the central and local governments.

The 1994 fiscal reform drastically rebalanced the fiscal revenue collection in favour of the central government. The central government's share of national fiscal revenue jumped from 22% to 55.7% from 1993 to 1994, and has since remained between 45% and 55% (Figure 3).

Two facts are crucial to understand the fiscal power of provincial governments in this regime. First, in 1993, 12 of the 30 provinces had a general budget surplus and the sum of all provincial general budget revenues exceeded their expenditures by a small margin (1.3%). After the 1994 fiscal reform, all provinces except for Fujian, which only managed to keep its budget in surplus for a few more years, started to incur huge budget deficits. These deficits have been between 54% and 87% for all provincial revenues (Figure 4).

Second, to make up for these deficits, provincial governments became heavily dependent on the central government's fiscal transfers

---

[9] For a more detailed presentation of the reform's rationale, background and early effects, see Vivek B. Arora and John Norregaard Arora, "Intergovernmental Fiscal Relations: The Chinese System in Perspective", *IMF Working Paper*, 1997; Ehtisham Ahmad, Li Keping, Raju J Singh and Thomas J Richardson, "Recentralisation in China?", *IMF Working Paper*, 2002.

Table 5: General Public Budget Revenue

Central Government	Local Governments
Central tax revenues	**Local tax revenues**
Domestic value-added tax (75% till April 2016, 50% since then)	Domestic value-added tax (25% till April 2016, 50% since then)
Corporate income tax (60%)	Corporate income tax (40%)
Personal income tax (60%)	Personal income tax (40%)
Unshared part of corporate income tax on enterprises subordinate to the central government	—
Business tax on railway and head offices of banks and insurance companies	Business tax (other than that on head offices of banks and insurance companies)
Consumption tax and VAT from imports minus rebates of consumption tax and VAT for exports	Deed tax
Resource tax on offshore petroleum resources	Resource tax (other than that on offshore petroleum resources)
Consumption tax	House property tax
City maintenance and construction tax (from railway and head offices of financial institutions)	City maintenance and construction tax (for all others)
Central share of stamp duty on security transactions	Stamp duty (on other taxable dealings)
Tariff	Urban land use tax
Ship tonnage tax	Land appreciation tax
Vehicle purchase tax	Tax on vehicles and boat operation
Other central taxes	Farm land occupation tax
—	Tobacco tax
—	Other local taxes
Central non-tax revenues	**Local non-tax revenues**
Profits of enterprises subordinate to central government	Profits of enterprises subordinate to local government
Special program receipts	Special program receipts
Charges for administrative and institutional services	Charges for administrative and institutional services
Penalty receipts	Penalty receipts
Other non-tax receipts	Other non-tax receipts

Notes: (1) The central government share of stamp duty on security transactions had been 97% till 2015 and has changed to 100% since 2016. (2) Items in the shaded cells are subject to tax sharing. (3) Value-added tax is levied on added value of sales while business tax is on gross sales. Before 2014, VAT mainly applied to the sale of goods while business tax was to the sale of services. From January 2012 to May 2016, VAT was extended to replace business tax first in selected service sectors or provinces and eventually to all major service sectors. Business tax was officially relinquished in October 2017. The columns in gray tint indicate the tax items shared between central and local governments, with specified percentages.

Source: Based on information from China's National Bureau of Statistics.

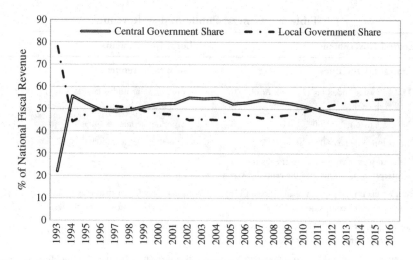

Figure 3: Intergovernmental Shares of National Fiscal Revenue
Source: China's National Bureau of Statistics.

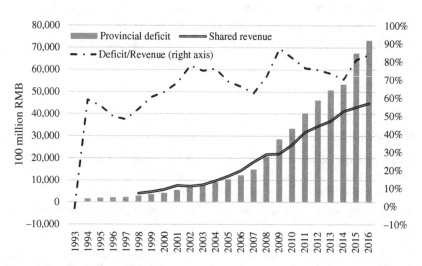

Figure 4: Provincial Budget Deficit and Central Government's Shared Revenue
Source: China's National Bureau of Statistics.

to finance nearly 50% of their expenditures.[10] The rest of the fiscal gap has been filled by proceeds from land sales and debt-financing.[11] These monies, which used to be part of the "extra-budget" revenue, are now counted in the "budget for government-controlled funds", which is separated from the general public budget revenue listed in Table 5.[12]

Since 1994, most of the central government's fiscal revenue has come from the shared revenue of value-added tax and income tax, which accounted for 61% to 88% of central government's total fiscal revenue in various years. As displayed in Figure 4, till 2008, the central government's portion of shared tax revenue was more than enough to cover all the fiscal deficits incurred by the provincial governments.

Given its importance, the contribution of a provincial economy to the central government's shared tax revenue is a good proxy of a province's fiscal power in the system. Applying the tax-sharing rules described in Table 5, we estimated each provincial economy's shared tax contribution and its percentage in the total shared tax revenue, displayed in columns C and D, respectively, in Table 6.

For comparison, the same table also shows each provincial economy's total GDP (column A) and fiscal balance (column B). The last column (E) ranks provinces' *net fiscal position*, which is the sum of values in columns B and C in descending order.

---

[10] Christine Wong and Richard Bird, "China's Fiscal System: A Work in Progress", in *China's Great Economic Transformation*, ed. Loren Brandt and Thomas G. Rawski, New York, Cambridge University Press, 2008, pp. 429–466.

[11] Bai Chong-En, Hsieh Chang-Tai and Song Zheng Michael, "The Long Shadow of a Fiscal Expansion", pp. 129–181.

[12] Since January 2011, all levels of governmental budgets are accounted separately in "General Public (Finance) Budget" and "Budget for Government-controlled Funds". The former refers to "income for the government finance through participating in the distribution of social products" in the current fiscal year, while the latter involves debt financing or sales of public assets such as land ["*caizheng bu: quanmian quxiao yusuanwai zijin, zhengfu xing shouru quanbu naru guanli* (Ministry of Finance: Replacing All Extra-budget Funds with Budget for Government-controlled Funds Management)", *People's Daily*, 10 February 2012].

Table 6: Top 12 Provincial Economies by Net Fiscal Position (2000, 2005, 2010 and 2016)

	A	B	C	D	E
	GDP	Fiscal Balance	Contribution to Shared Tax Revenue	% of Total Shared Tax Revenue	Net Fiscal Position
2000					
Guangdong	10741	−170	775	13.6%	605
Shanghai	4771	−123	526	9.2%	403
Jiangsu	8554	−143	509	8.9%	366
Zhejiang	6141	−89	446	7.8%	357
Shandong	8337	−149	429	7.5%	280
Beijing	3162	−98	315	5.5%	217
Fujian	3765	−90	191	3.4%	101
Tianjin	1702	−53	139	2.4%	86
Hebei	5044	−167	210	3.7%	43
Liaoning	4669	−222	262	4.6%	39
Henan	5053	−199	205	3.6%	6
Hubei	3545	−154	155	2.7%	1
2005					
Guangdong	22557	−482	1524	12.9%	1042
Shanghai	9248	−229	1220	10.3%	991
Jiangsu	18599	−351	1163	9.8%	812
Zhejiang	13418	−199	964	8.2%	765
Beijing	6970	−139	667	5.6%	528
Shandong	18367	−393	804	6.8%	410
Fujian	6555	−160	342	2.9%	181
Tianjin	3906	−110	283	2.4%	173
Shanxi	4231	−300	384	3.3%	84
Hebei	10012	−46	486	4.1%	22
Liaoning	8047	−529	497	4.2%	−32
Hainan	919	−83	41	0.4%	−41
2010					
Guangdong	46013	−905	3422	13.1%	2518
Shanghai	17166	−429	2467	9.5%	2037
Jiangsu	41425	−834	2791	10.7%	1957
Zhejiang	27722	−599	1984	7.6%	1385

(*Continued*)

Table 6: (Continued)

	A	B	C	D	E
	GDP	Fiscal Balance	Contribution to Shared Tax Revenue	% of Total Shared Tax Revenue	Net Fiscal Position
Beijing	14114	–363	1723	6.6%	1359
Tianjin	9224	–308	611	2.3%	303
Shandong	39170	–1396	1696	6.5%	300
Fujian	14737	–544	743	2.9%	200
Shanxi	9201	–962	819	3.1%	–142
Hainan	2065	–310	110	0.4%	–201
Liaoning	18457	–1191	924	3.5%	–267
Ningxia	1690	–404	90	0.3%	–314
2016					
Shanghai	28179	–513	5646	8.2%	5134
Guangdong	80855	–3056	6200	9.0%	3145
Beijing	25669	–1326	3956	5.7%	2630
Jiangsu	77388	–1861	4245	6.1%	2384
Zhejiang	47251	–1672	3355	4.8%	1683
Tianjin	17885	–976	1095	1.6%	120
Fujian	28811	–1621	1215	1.8%	–406
Hainan	4053	–739	231	0.3%	–508
Shandong	68024	–2895	2275	3.3%	–620
Ningxia	3169	–867	107	0.2%	–759
Shanxi	13050	–1872	758	1.1%	–1114
Chongqing	17741	–1774	601	0.9%	–1173

Notes: (1) Contributions to shared tax revenue in 2000 and 2010 are calculated using provincial budget revenues from VAT, corporate income tax and personal income tax following the tax-sharing rules in Table 5. (2) Inferred from a government policy on 2016 VAT reform,[13] the part of VAT contributions in 2016 are estimated by using the estimated VAT contributions in 2014 minus the difference of provincial business tax revenues between 2014 and 2016. (3) Units: 100 million renminbi (current year value).

Source: Compiled and estimated from data of China's National Bureau of Statistics.

---

[13] As announced by the State Council's "Transitional Arrangement for Adjusting Division of VAT Revenue between the Central and Local Governments after Full-Scale Implementation of Converting-Business-Tax-to-VAT Trial Reform", the division of VAT tax revenue in a transitional period of 2–3 years should use the revenue shares in 2014 as the base year [State Council *Gazette* (2016), no. 26].

Fiscal Power and Its Political–Economic Implications

Some observations can be obtained from the results in Table 6. First, the number of provincial economies that hold positive net fiscal positions has fallen from 12 in 2000 to 10 in 2005, 8 in 2010 and to 6 in 2016.

Second, Liaoning, Hebei, Henan and Hubei lost their rank with positive net fiscal positions during 2005–2010 while the top eight provincial economies in 2000 continued to maintain their positive net fiscal positions and stay on the top eight list in 2010.

Third, between 2010 and 2016, the same provincial economies remained in the top five positions and maintained positive net fiscal positions. These provinces are Guangdong, Shanghai, Jiangsu, Zhejiang and Beijing. It is notable that Tianjin barely made it to the positive range (0.8%) in 2016. Shandong, which used to be in the league of positive fiscal positions, dropped out of the ranking table in 2016.

Fourth, comparing the list to the ranking of GDP sizes in Table 3 tells us that the largest provincial economies are not necessarily the largest contributors to shared tax revenues. Of the top five provinces, Guangdong, Jiangsu, Shandong, Zhejiang and Henan, which stayed as the largest economies by size through 1995–2016, only Guangdong, Jiangsu and Zhejiang have also been among the top five largest tax contributors.

Finally, the weights of the few largest net fiscal contributors in total shared tax revenue appeared to be lower in the later years.

How do these changes impact the distribution of fiscal power? To evaluate the effects, Table 7 presents indicators that describe fiscal power concentration. The indicators in the first three rows measure the distributions of fiscal contributions to the shared tax revenue. All the indicators (CR-4, CR-6 and HH index) rose slightly from 2000 to 2005, but fell a bit more during the years 2005–2016. The indicators in the second three rows present the distributional trend of provincial GDP. The pattern of changes — first rising in 2000–2005 and then falling in 2005–2016 — is similar between fiscal contributions and GDP through these years.

Table 7: Concentration of Fiscal Power and GDP

Concentration Measure		2000	2005	2010	2016
Of total shared revenue	CR-4	39.6%	41.2%	40.9%	28.9%
	CR-6	52.7%	53.7%	49.9%	35.4%
	HHI	0.0624	0.0632	0.0629	0.0283
Of total GDP	CR-4	33.7%	38.9%	37.4%	36.8%
	CR-6	43.7%	49.9%	47.9%	46.7%
	HHI	0.0507	0.0620	0.0590	0.0574
Of total positive net fiscal position	CR-4	69.1%	72.1%	78.5%	88.1%
	CR-6	88.9%	90.8%	95.0%	100.0%
	HHI	0.1493	0.1527	0.1809	0.2269

Source: Author's calculation.

The lower values of these concentration indicators in later years, however, have to be interpreted carefully. The last three rows in Table 7 measure the concentration of *positive* net fiscal positions, which have taken into account the size of fiscal deficits incurred at the provincial level. By these measures, all indicators (CR-4, CR-6 and HH index) have risen sharply, suggesting that fiscal power has become more concentrated in a few provincial economies.

The more equal distribution of fiscal contribution in recent years is consistent with the convergence of provincial economic development since 2005. In contrast, the increase in concentration of net fiscal positions has been driven by the drastic rise of provincial fiscal deficits after the central government rolled out a four trillion renminbi fiscal stimulus package as a policy response to the shock of the 2008 global financial crisis. As shown in Figure 4, after the fiscal stimulus was launched, total provincial fiscal deficits sharply rose in 2009 to exceed the total provincial contribution of the shared tax revenue for the first time. The deficits continued to grow faster than the shared tax revenue since then. By 2015 and 2016, the total local government deficits reached 63 billion renminbi and 73 billion renminbi, respectively, about one-third higher than the total shared tax revenue contributed by the local economies.

As estimated by Bai, Hsieh and Song, only about a quarter of the four trillion stimulus spending appeared in government budget balance sheets.[14] The rest of the stimulus spending was financed by the off-balance-sheet companies (i.e. local government financial vehicles). This newfound financing power has allowed the local governments to continue to raise off-balance-sheet funds to finance spending (mainly in local investment projects) even after the fiscal stimulus package ended. According to Zhang and Zhu, the officially published debt stock of local governments reached 18.58 billion renminbi in 2017, as compared to 8.83 billion in 2012.[15] The implicit debt stock was estimated to be 23.57 billion renminbi in 2017, relative to 6.84 billion renminbi in 2012. These figures provide the background for the rapid rise of local government deficits since 2008.

Since the manageability of the enormous public debts has increasingly become a policy challenge to China's top policymakers, running large deficits is likely to be perceived negatively when provincial performance is evaluated by the central government. The increasing concentration of fiscal power in the top few provincial economies that hold net positive fiscal positions therefore has important implications in intergovernmental political–economic relationship.

In conclusion, both the concentration of provincial economic sizes and the concentration of provincial contributions to the central government's coffer follow a similar pattern: the distribution became more concentrated during the decade 1995–2005 but has since been moderated in the later years (2006–2016). This reflects the changes of convergence trend of provincial economic development between the first and second decades covered by this study.

Since the 1994 fiscal reform, all provincial economies have run increasingly large deficits on the balance sheets of their general public

---

[14] Bai Chong-En, Hsieh Chang-Tai and Song Zheng Michael, "The Long Shadow of a Fiscal Expansion", pp. 129–181.

[15] Zhang Ming and Zhu Ziyang, "*Zhongguo zhengfu zhaiwu guimo jiujing jihe*" (How much is the real size of government debts in China), *Caijing (Finance & Economics)*, 29 July 2018.

(finance) budget and therefore become more dependent on central government's transfers and debt finance or land sales through the (local) government-controlled funds. The huge fiscal stimulus package after 2008 tremendously accelerated debt finance among the local governments. Against this backdrop, the national fiscal power has become more concentrated in a few provincial governments that managed to maintain positive net fiscal positions or make net contributions to the state coffer.

Chapter 13

Housing Policies and China's Economic Development Agenda

LI Bingqin*

Introduction

Since the 1980s, housing has become one of the most important public concerns and field of reform in China. This is because housing used to be a welfare item in the Central Planning era, which started in the early 1950s and ended in the 1970s. During this period, new housing supply was very limited, but the population grew from 400 million to 956.2 million. Not only did people live in overcrowded conditions, the majority of the population lived in dilapidated houses. As part of the transition from Central Planning to market economy, housing reform played a pivotal role in facilitating the transformation of the labour market and the economy as a whole. At the same time, increased housing supply became an important means to improve living conditions. However, the path to improvement is not steady. New issues emerge as cities grow.[1] In recent years, housing has become a financial asset subject to rampant speculation. The land for housing and housing construction also became important sources of

---

*LI Bingqin is an Associate Professor and the Director of Chinese Social Policy Program at the Social Policy Research Centre, University of New South Wales.
[1] Wu Fulong, "Commodification and Housing Market Cycles in Chinese Cities", *International Journal of Housing Policy*, vol. 15, no. 1, 2015, pp. 6–26.

revenue for local governments.[2] These changes raised new challenges to housing affordability in China. In this chapter, the author tries to establish the logic behind China's housing affordability programs and the variations in local responses. In the following sections, the overall challenges of housing in China are discussed as well as a highlight of the key challenges. Then, the logic behind China's housing policies that try to address housing affordability issues is explained. We will then examine how different cities in China react to the national policy guidelines, which will include finance, governance and the local outcomes.

Housing Affordability Issues in China

One of the most challenging issues of urban housing in China is affordability. Figure 1 shows that prices for owner-occupied houses have

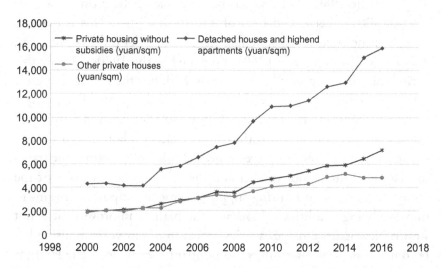

Figure 1: Average Price of Owner-occupied Houses by Types of Dwellings (yuan/sqm)

---

[2] Pan Jiun-Nan, Huang Jr-Tsung and Chiang Tsun-Feng, "Empirical Study of the Local Government Deficit, Land Finance and Real Estate Markets in China", *China Economic Review*, vol. 32, 2015, pp. 57–67.

increased significantly since 2000, with higher end apartments increasing fourfold. The fact that higher end houses grew the fastest highlights that the demand for better quality housing increased by fourfold. Also, the price of subsidised houses more than doubled over time.

However, such a broad-stroke data series can be misleading to paint a picture of China's housing affordability issues. Policies that try to address such issues at the national level may also cause problems locally. To gain a better understanding of the overall situation in China, it is important to note that there are a large number of cities in China that differ greatly by various standards. Broadly speaking, cities can be viewed by top-down-imposed administrative criteria and market criteria:

1. Administratively, by the end of 2016, there were 657 cities in China, including 4 municipalities, 15 subprovincial cities, 278 prefecture-level cities and 360 county-level cities. In cities above the prefecture level, at the end of 2015, 121 cities had 1–3 million people living in the urban districts, and 13 cities had 3–5 million people. Also, 13 cities have a population of more than 5 million people.[3]

2. Cities are often categorised by "tiers" according to a range of criteria. For example, economic competitiveness, attractiveness to investors, etc. These are often done by private ranking agencies. It is considered to be an important exercise for cities that try to break through the ranks set by the administrative criteria and to some extent part of city branding.

The market ranking helps show the relative position of each city in comparison to other cities and what they may aspire to. Figure 2 shows the medium house price for second-hand housing in 262 cities in 2017, compiled by the Housing Big Data Joint Laboratory and the Institute of Financial Strategy of the Chinese Academy of Social Sciences in

---

[3] National Bureau of Statistics of China, "*Tongji ju: 2016 Nianmo zhongguo changzhu renkou chengzhen hua lu da* 57.4%" (Bureau of Statistics: At the end of 2016, the urbanisation rate of permanent residents in China reached 57.4%), 2017, at <http://www.chinanews.com/gn/2017/07-11/8274405.shtml> (accessed 28 May 2018).

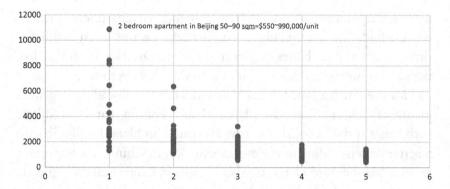

Figure 2: Medium House Price, Second-hand (from First- to Fifth-tier Cities, End of 2017) Price (US$/m²) (262 cities)

Source: Housing Big Data Joint Laboratory, the Institute of Financial Strategy of the Chinese Academy of Social Sciences (2017), and First Finance and Economic News (2017).

2018. When we sort the house price data according to the city ranking made by the First Finance and Economic News in 2017, we can see the distribution of medium prices of a second-hand two-bedroom apartment (50–90 m²) in each tier of cities. We can see that on average, cities that are ranked better are connected to the world economically (tier 1 > tier 2 > ⋯ > tier 5) and have on average more expensive houses. The house prices are also more dispersed than other cities. Relatively speaking, first-tier cities in the coastal areas, such as Beijing, Shanghai, Shenzhen and Guangzhou, were ranked the highest. First-tier cities in the inland provinces, such as Chongqing, Changsha and Xi'an, and newly emerged first-tier cities such as Dongguan have relatively lower prices.

If we examine the house price over time, Figure 3 shows the price changes of newly built privately owned houses in 36 cities in the country since 2015. We can see that the price growth in the most expensive cities in 2015 such as Shenzhen and Shanghai slowed down in the past year or so. At the same time, the house price in inland cities which were at the bottom of the price level had increased faster since then. It is important to note that the chart demonstrated the price increase. Apart

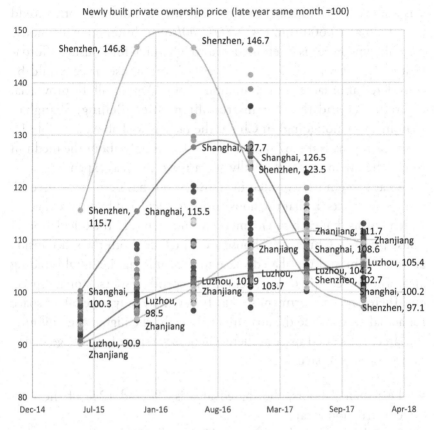

Figure 3: House Price Changes over Time in 36 Cities

Source: Housing Big Data Joint Laboratory, the Institute of Financial Strategy of the Chinese Academy of Social Sciences, "2017 China urban house price ranking", 2017, at <http://www.zfdsj.org/report/shownews.php?lang=cn&id=50> (accessed 28 May 2018).

from the city of Shenzhen, all other big cities' actual house price continued to grow, but at a slower pace. The *S*-shaped lines in Figure 3 also shows that house price fluctuated in almost all 36 cities in the past four years.

If we examine the average price level, according to Xu (2018), in 2017, among the 35 major cities in the country, only 6 cities' average house price was less than US$1,600/m² (~CNY10,000/sqm), reduced from 10 in 2016. In 2017, the contracted price of a newly built house was $6,921 (CNY43,839). In a more central location, the price could be as high as $9,600/sqm (~CNY60,000/sqm). Internationally, house price income ratio[4] is often used as a rough guide for housing affordability. On the whole, if the ratio is 5–7, the house price would be considered affordable to medium households. Among all the provincial capital cities and the four metropolitan cities (Beijing, Shanghai, Tianjin and Chongqing) in China, the ratio is well above 7 (Table 1). Only Changsha is it 6.67 (less than 7).[5] This is only about the medium price. The urban centre is usually at least two times as expensive.

What is often not counted in statistics, but has been recognised by some researchers, is that the house price is calculated by square metres, which means that each square metre would count. In the calculation of house prices in China, the "house area" includes both the space inside an apartment and the shared space in the building, i.e. total building area. The shared space may include the corridor, stairs, storage space, etc. Therefore, an apartment sold as 100 m² may only have 60 m² space for actual areas inside the apartment. Usually, the higher the building, the larger the shared space as there will be extra space for garbage shafts, utility rooms, lift shafts, etc.

- Less than 7 floors, the shared area is 7% and 12% of the total construction area;
- 7–11 floors, shared area is 6%–10% of the total construction area;
- 12–33 floors, shared area is 12%–24% of the total construction area.

Apart from the shared space inside the building, public space such as communal gardens, public toilets and public service spaces that would be within the boundary of the estate will all be added to the house

---

[4] House price income ratio = total housing price/household disposable income = (average transaction price of new commercial housing × urban household average area)/(per capita disposable income of urban residents × urban household average population).

[5] Xu Qian, "35 *Ge zhongdian chengshi fangjia shouru bi chulu*" (House price to income ratio in 35 key cities have been released), 2018, at <http://www.creb.com.cn/index.php?m=content&c=index&a=show&catid=13&id=41336> (accessed 28 May 2018).

Table 1: Housing Big Data Joint Laboratory, the Institute of Financial Strategy of the Chinese Academy of Social Sciences (2017)

	Cities	2017 Average Price of Newly Built Private Property (P)	2017 Urban Household Disposable Income (I)	P/I 2017	P/I 2016	P/I Changes
1	Shenzhen	57348	52938	39.64	40.42	0.78
2	Sanya	25877	33638	28.16	23.5	4.66
3	Shanghai	47865	62596	27.98	24.29	3.69
4	Beijing	43839	62406	25.7	21.35	4.35
5	Xiamen	34375	50019	25.15	24.21	0.94
6	Fuzhou	21636	40973	19.33	18.09	1.24
7	Zhuhai	23056	47386	17.81	16.01	1.8
8	Haikou	13651	33320	14.99	11.7	3.29
9	Hangzhou	22987	56276	14.95	12.14	2.81
10	Shijiazhuang	13257	32929	14.74	13.04	1.7
11	Nanjing	21601	54538	14.5	13.85	0.65
12	Tianjin	15670	42949	13.35	13.26	0.09
13	Zhengzhou	12058	36050	12.24	11.16	1.08
14	Hefei	12666	37972	12.21	13.96	-1.75
15	Ningbo	18280	55656	12.02	10	2.02
16	Taiyuan	10287	31469	11.96	12.38	-0.42
17	Suzhou	18621	58806	11.59	12.66	-1.07
18	Wenzhou	16013	51866	11.3	12.03	-0.73

(Continued)

Table 1: (*Continued*)

Cities		2017 Average Price of Newly Built Private Property (P)	2017 Urban Household Disposable Income (I)	P/I 2017	P/I 2016	P/I Changes
19	Guangzhou	16959	55400	11.2	12.19	-0.99
20	Xuzhou	8848	30987	10.45	9.05	1.4
21	Langfang	10500	37474	10.25	12.38	-2.13
22	Chongqing	8993	321 93	10.22	8.65	1.57
23	Nanchang	10418	37492	10.17	10.13	0.04
24	Xian	10124	38536	9.62	7.33	2.29
25	Nantong	11108	42756	9.51	8.23	1.28
26	Kunming	10096	39788	9.29	7.94	1.35
27	*Jinan*	11713	46642	9.19	8.23	0.96
28	Chengdu	9697	38918	9.12	8.14	0.98
29	Qingdao	11067	47176	8.59	7.57	1.02
30	Wuhan	10031	43405	8.46	8.69	-0.23
31	Wuxi	11945	52659	8.3	7.09	1.21
32	Changzhou	11207	49955	8.21	5.97	2.24
33	Lanzhou	7138	32478	8.04	8.79	-0.75
34	Guiyang	6677	32186	7.59	7.09	0.5
35	Changsha	8559	46948	6.67	5.92	0.75

Source: Xu Qian, "35 Ge zhongdian chengshi fangjia shouru bi chulu" (House price to income ratio in 35 key cities have been released), 2018, at <http://www.creb.com.cn/index.php?m=content&c=index&a=show&catid=13&id=41336> (accessed 28 May 2018).

price. Adding all the extras, it means that buying one square metre of housing space in China would have only 60% for actual living space.[6] In this sense, the actual living conditions of the urban residents in China would be less spacious than the official statistics show.

Housing Rights in China — National Level

The term housing rights can have multiple meanings in Chinese: (1) rights to shelter (*zhufang quanli*) and (2) tenure rights (*fangwu shiyong he suoyouzhe quanyi*). There is no formal guarantee of rights to housing in China as there is no housing law to stipulate such rights. However, there are some laws and regulations to protect parts of the rights: "Real Estate Management Law", "Land Management Law", "Building Law", "Property Rights Law", "Construction Engineering Quality Regulations" and "Demolition Compensation Regulations". But these laws can only be classified as part of the affordable housing policy system. There is no overarching legislation to guarantee basic right to shelter. Also, because the laws and regulations were treated as policy documents and changed frequently, they cannot be qualified as a strict legislation system.[7] An attempt to legislate housing security was initiated in 2008. However, protecting housing rights was not as straightforward and the increasingly diverse forms of housing tenure and the rapid changes in housing protection system made the legislation particularly difficult to pin down. In March 2018, a draft was finally completed and it was submitted for the national government to discuss. Once passed, the new legislation would be able to guarantee all residents a house to live in either through subsidised ownership or subsidised renting.

---

[6] Zhao Jianjun, "*Gongtan mianji de zhexie mimi ni zhidao ma?*" (Do you know these secrets of the shared space?), 2017, at <http://finance.qq.com/original/MissMoney/MM00416.html> (accessed 28 May 2018).

[7] Tang Hongmiao and Feng Yanjun, "*Dangdai zhongguo zhufang quan de shixian lujing — yi baozhang xing zhufang zhidu wei zhongxin de fenxi*" (The Path to the Realisation of Housing Rights in Contemporary China: An Analysis of the Housing Security System), *Social Science Front*, vol. 5, 2017, pp. 237–247.

However, the lack of explicit legislation on housing rights does not mean that people do not enjoy any housing rights in China.

Earliest social housing in China

During the period of the Republic of China (1911–1948), the state recognised the right to housing. Slogans such as "Settled Living and Safe Employment" (*anju leye*), "Everyone Has A Room" (*Juzhe You Qi Wu*), "One Person One Bed", and "Guaranteed physical health and pleasant life" were raised by the national government. A large-scale housing rights movement (rent reduction) and Home Owners' Associations to protect ownership emerged. There were also housing charity sales by non-governmental organisations. In some cities, such as Nanjing, Beijing and Xian, a small number of low-rental housing was produced by either the national government or the military force.

Sacrificing home ownership to meet housing needs

During the Central Planning era (1953–1978), there were improvements in the rights to shelter, but the ownership rights were invaded as a result. The State Council considered that it was necessary to build housing for urban employees without housing, and established a whole set of principles for funding, managing, allocating and reallocating houses. It was required that "the central government ministries, the People's Committees of provinces, autonomous regions, and municipalities should pay due attention to the investment in construction of houses when allocating construction, and spend part of the funding for urban employees who in need of housing annually. The accrued bonus funds could also be partly contributed to the construction of housing for employees." This marked the beginning of the employee housing welfare system, which provided publicly owned housing through means-tested in-kind allocation and low rental charges.

However, the housing welfare system turned out to be overambitious. According to the sketchy statistics, in 1949–1956, more than 81 million m² of housing (building area) was constructed and the total investment was CNY4.4 billion. In the first four years of the first five-year plan (1953–1957), 65.15 million m² were constructed, and the investment was CNY364 billion, accounting for 9.3% of the total capital construction investment. Despite increased supply, the housing need was far from being satisfied. According to the National Bureau of Statistics, in September 1956, in the 99 cities across the country, the waiting list had 1.1 million, and another 1.4 million entered the list in 1956. If all the housing needs were to be satisfied, 44% of the total investment in construction in 1956 would be devoted to housing.[8] If the state spent so much money on housing, the speed of industrialisation would be seriously compromised. To find quick solutions to the problem, homeowners were stripped off their owners' rights and forced to open up their houses and shared rooms to other families in need.[9]

Housing marketisation reform — separating housing with employment

The reform of China's urban welfare housing system commenced in the early 1980s. Since then, a market-based housing system, including a variety of housing tenure forms[10] and private ownership — such as commercially built and government-subsidised ownership — gradually became the dominant form of housing tenure in Chinese cities. By 2011, over 85% of urban households nationwide owned residential property. Due to fast rising housing prices, the rate of owner occupation was lower in large coastal cities, such as Shanghai (71%), Beijing (71%) and Shenzhen (76%), and higher in inland cities such

---

[8] Zhang Qun, "*Ju you qi wu: Zhongguo zhufang quan wenti de lishi kaocha*" (Home Ownership: An Historical Investigation of China's Housing Rights), 27 November 2013, at <http://news.ifeng.com/history/zhongguoxiandaishi/special/maozedongshidaizhufang/detail_2013_11/27/31615212_0.shtml> (accessed 28 May 2018).

[9] Wang Yaping, "Public Sector Housing in Urban China 1949–1988: The Case of Xian", *Housing Studies*, vol. 10, no. 1, 1995, pp. 57–82.

[10] The term tenure means the financial arrangements under which someone has the right to live in a house or apartment. The most frequent forms are tenancy, in which rent is paid to a landlord, and owner-occupancy in which the person owns the house for his/her own use.

as Urumqi (>90%) where housing was more affordable.[11] Meantime, a private rental market also re-emerged in the 1980s, becoming the most important source of housing for rural-to-urban migrant workers and new graduates.[12] By the early 1990s, China began to experiment with an individual savings fund system to aid home ownership, since the earlier reform aimed at privatising public housing had not worked. In 1991, Shanghai first introduced a Housing Provident Fund (HPF) modelled on Singapore's Central Provident Fund, which is a compulsory savings scheme that allows savers to draw against a special housing account for the purpose of buying housing. In 1992, the practice was extended to more cities, including Beijing, Tianjin, Nanjing and Wuhan. The Fund functioned as a savings mechanism designed to help people purchase housing, whereby participation into the fund was made compulsory for all urban employees and their employers. Further, a subsidised rental system and a subsidised home buying system were also gradually set up in Chinese cities. In essence, as entitlement to the various forms of housing subsidies was designed to be means-tested, these measures functioned as new forms of social assistance.[13]

Before 1998, the Chinese government provided housing to urban employees via its public work unit or *danwei* (单位) system, which included government agencies, public institutions, and state-owned and large collective urban enterprises. This housing system was called the "welfare housing system" (*fuli fenfang zhidu* 福利住房制度), and housing allocated through it was thus regarded as "welfare housing"

---

[11] These statistics did not include the migrant population who did not hold a local household registration. Chinese Family Financial Investigation and Research Centre, *Zhongguo jiating jinrong diaocha baogao* (*Household non-financial assets, in China household finance survey report*), China, South-western University of Finance and Economics Press, 2012.

[12] Chen Jie, Yang Zan and Wang Yaping, "The New Chinese Model of Public Housing: A Step Forward or Backward?", *Housing Studies*, vol. 29, no. 4, 2014, pp. 534–550.

[13] Gu Junqing, Sun Lan, and Shi Meicheng, "*Zhongguo zhufang gongjijin zhidu xianzhuang yu fazhan*" (Current Situation and Development of the Chinese Housing Provident Fund System), *China Real Estate Development Report No. 3*, China Social Science Literature Publishing House, 2006, pp. 173–183.

(*fulizhufang* 福利住房). From the late 1990s, however, urban employers were no longer obliged to allocate welfare housing to their employees, with the exception of some public-sector employees, such as civil servants and university staff members, who maintained that entitlement. This was nonetheless not the end of public housing support in China. A new social housing security system (*zhufang baozhang tixi* 住房保障体系), also referred to as the housing welfare system (*zhufang fuli tixi* 住房福利体系), was gradually established after 1998. The old public housing allocation system will be referred to here as the "welfare housing system", while the new social housing protection system will be referred to as the "housing welfare system".

By 2005, the government's housing support system had two key elements: subsidised rental housing and subsidised private home ownership.[14] Between 1999 and 2008, nationally, only 4.5 million apartments were built between 60–100 m² as part of that Scheme.[15] Further pressure was added as the private market was not yet able to catch up with the housing demand, which was inflated by the Chinese government's strong limits on employer-allocated housing. Despite its limited supply, China's housing reform gradually improved the housing conditions of the lowest income groups, and the links between forms of employment and housing allocation or housing benefits were finally severed. The introduction of subsidised ownership allowed more people to buy housing with government subsidies and the support of the HPF.[16] The housing welfare system no longer favoured people

---

[14] Li Bingqin, "How Successful are China's Public Housing Schemes?", in *China's Social Development and Policy: Into the Next Stage?*, ed. Litao Zhao, London and Routledge, 2013, pp. 115–140.

[15] The most used indicator is "total square metres completed" in a given period of time. However, this data cannot reflect the actual housing supply as the house size can vary greatly. Therefore, in this chapter, the author instead uses "number of dwellings constructed". Given that one household is only entitled to one home in the Economic and Comfortable Housing Scheme, the number of dwellings constructed roughly shows how many households actually benefited from this housing scheme.

[16] Deng Lan, Shen Qingyun and Wang Lin, "The Emerging Housing Policy Framework in China", *Journal of Planning Literature*, vol. 26, no. 2, 2011, pp. 168–183.

according to their employment and political status, and instead introduced means-testing to assign housing entitlements more equitably.

Separating housing with household registration — towards more inclusive housing policies

Apart from being tied to one's work unit, housing — like other welfare entitlements — was tied to one's birth place. The concept of welfare entitlement based on birth place in China is associated with the Household Registration system (*hukou* 户口). Starting from the 1950s, only people holding an urban *hukou* were able to receive welfare benefits in cities. In essence, the *hukou* system functioned as a labour control device. Attaching welfare housing to one's *hukou* and work unit created barriers for people to move between jobs, between cities, and between rural and urban areas.[17] As explained in earlier sections, during the first two decades of the reform era, housing reforms were able to sever the link between urban employment (with regard to the employment status, sector and form of employment) and entitlement to housing welfare, fostering greater flexibility in the urban labour market by allowing talent to move between jobs and cities. The *hukou* system, however, remained in place and continued to tie the entitlement to housing welfare to one's birth place. Throughout the 1980s and the 1990s, the *hukou* was actively used to prevent rural workers from entering cities for work. After China jointed WTO, migrant workers were encouraged to move into cities. During 2003–2014, a series of social policies were introduced to improve rural migrant workers' access to social insurances and welfare. However, housing assistance in large cities was not included in the round of reforms during this period.

Partly in response to these insights, in 2008, the Central government introduced a new form of subsidised public rental housing

---

[17] Yeung Chi-Wai Stanley and Rodney Howes, "The Role of the Housing Provident Fund in Financing Affordable Housing Development in China", *Habitat International*, vol. 30, no. 2, 2006, pp. 343–356.

Table 2: Types of Subsidised Housing in China

Low rental housing (*lianzu fang*)	Owned by government, institutional landlords and rented to low-income households at low rents
Public rental housing (*gongzu fang*)	Government or institutional landlords provided rental housing with subsidies. The rent is a percentage of the market rate. Subsidies are provided by the government
Economic and comfortable housing (*jingji shiyong fang*)	Subsidised owner-occupying houses
Double-controlled commercial housing (*liang xian fang*)	Commercial housing with size and price capped by the government
Anju Commercial housing	Subsidised ownership under the National Anju Project
Purpose built resettlement housing	Resettlement housing for people whose houses are demolished as a result of urban construction

(*gongzufang* 公租房)[18] targeted at low to lower-middle income groups, including migrant workers. One of the conditions for eligibility is for tenants to have continuing employment. This programme is separate from the low-rent housing (*lianzufang* 廉租房) programme, which targets only those who are recipients of the Minimum Livelihood Guarantee (or *dibao* 低保). Low-rent housing (*lianzufang* 廉租房) is meant to be built or bought by local governments in the private housing market (though new housing cannot be bought under this scheme) and allocated directly to applicants (Table 2). Rent levels are set at a very low level.[19] In contrast, public rental housing (*gongzufang* 公租房) is built by private developers with

---

[18] Earlier literature refers to public rental housing as *lian zufang* (廉租房); this was because *gong zufang* (公租房) did not exist. The term *gong* (公) in Chinese means "public", while *lian* (廉) means "cheap".

[19] Zhu Yapeng, "Policy Networks and Policy Paradigm Shifts: Urban Housing Policy Development in China", *Journal of Contemporary China*, vol. 22, no. 82, 2013, pp. 554–572.

government financial and land subsidies.[20] As stated before, the targeted tenants are low to lower-middle income groups and, in principle, also migrant workers. The standard size of this public rental housing is limited, and apartments are only equipped with basic standard facilities. Many cities have capped the floor size at 13 m² per person, and the total size to a maximum of 50 m². Overall, the aim of the two schemes is to ensure this type of housing targets the truly low-income households.

It is reported that in the draft of the new Housing Security Law, the constraints of household registration will be further reduced and it will be easier for rural-to-urban migrants to gain access to subsidised urban housing in cities. One of the problems as raised by academics in legal studies is that the policies related to housing and housing protection are often very vague and contain such terms as encourage and promote, which are not the right approach towards housing security.[21] On the other hand, given the vast population and varied local circumstances of the country, it is very difficult at the central level to come up with detailed prescription of housing policies. The experience with reforms in various social policy fields so far shows that the attempt to universalise welfare or social protection at the national level often resulted in no enforceable policies at some parts of the country. As a result, most social policies are guidelines at the national level and subject to be operationalised locally. As a result, one cannot expect the Housing Security Law in the making to be very detailed as well. It may set some principles and limits to set the bottom lines. As a result, even with the new housing legislation, it is still important to follow how local governments react.

---

[20] Nie Chen, "7 China's Housing Policy", in *China's Social Policy: Transformation and Challenges*, ed. Ngok Kinglun and Chan Chak Kwan, vol. 16, 2015, pp. 103–126.

[21] Tang Hongmiao and Feng Yanjun, "*Dangdai zhongguo zhufang quan de shixian lujing — yi baozhang xing zhufang zhidu wei zhongxin de fenxi*" (The Path to the Realisation of Housing Rights in Contemporary China: An Analysis of the Housing Security System), *Social Science Front*, vol. 5, 2017, pp. 237–247.

Central–Local Relations in Housing Policymaking in China

In principle, housing policies are made centrally in China. The policymaking bodies include the Central Government and its functional departments: the National Development and Reform Commission, the Ministry of Housing and Urban–Rural Construction, Ministry of Finance, Ministry of Land and Resources, the Nation Administration of Taxation, People's Bank (the central bank of China), and the Ministry of Public Security. Among them, the Ministry of Housing and Urban–Rural Development, the Ministry of Finance, and The Ministry of Land and Resources are the government departments that form the core body of policy formulation for affordable housing. The Ministry of Housing and Urban–Rural Development is a specialised department responsible for housing protection. It is in charge of carrying on the housing system reform, regulating the real estate market order, supervising the real estate market and ensuring the housing of low-income families in urban areas. In terms of affordable housing, the Ministry of Finance makes policies on housing finance. The Ministry of Land and Resources will make land policies. These three departments negotiate with each other to determine the housing, finance and land supply of affordable houses. Without strong financial and land support, it is very difficult for housing policies to be made.

Locally, the governments and the corresponding functional departments — such as the Bureau of Land and Resources, Municipal Construction Commission, Planning Bureaus — are the core policymakers. The local government operationalize the central policies to fit into local circumstances and implements the policies. Similar to the relationship between central government departments, local housing policies made by the departments on housing construction and planning are also subject to local governments' land and financial support. Table 3 uses local rental housing as an example to show the different conditions published by city governments. What we can see is that the requirements are very different from each other.

Table 3:   Low-Rental Housing Entry Requirements by City (2018)

	Shanghai		Shenzhen	Beijing	Chongqing
Age			18+		
Household registration	Shanghai ≥3 years; housing district ≥1 year	Shanghai ≥3 years; housing district ≥1 year	Shenzhen	Beijing	Chongqing
	3 and 3+ households	<3 or poverty because of illness			
Current housing conditions	≤7 m² per capita Difficulties not caused by selling or transferring properties to others within 5 years	≤7 m² per capita Difficulties not caused by selling or transferring properties to others within 5 years	Do not own houses and not receiving other forms of housing benefits	≤7 m² per capita Difficulties not caused by selling or transferring properties to others within 5 years	6 m² per capita 3+ HH ≤7 m² per capita
Entry requirement	Household income (monthly per capita, yuan) ≤3,300	≤3,630	People receiving minimum income guarantee (≤920)	≤580	People receiving minimum income guarantee for more than 6 months

	Single-person household annual ≤6,960 / Two-people household annual ≤13,920	Single-person household annual ≤25,000 / 2+ HH annual ≤40,000	1 person HH ≤150,000 / 2 person HH ≤230,000 / 3 person HH ≤300,000 / 4 person HH ≤400,000
Household income			
Household wealth (per capita, yuan)	≤120,000	≤132,000	
Threshold for subsidies			
Basic subsidies	≤2,000	≤2,200	
70% of basic subsidies	2,000–2,800	2,200–2,080	
40% of basic subsidies	2,800–3,300	3,080–3,630	
Level of subsidies	15 m²/person	15 m²/person	15 m²/person, max 50 m²

Note: Basic subsidies in Shanghai are set according to the location.

Source: Local government websites.

Central–local relations in housing finance

An interesting phenomenon in the Chinese housing system is that despite the relatively clear housing policymaking responsibilities, for many years, there is no clear division of financing responsibilities between central and local governments on the actual supply of affordable housing. In most cases, the central government makes the policy or expresses its policy stance and just waits for the local governments to come up with resources to deliver (Table 4).

As there are many different forms of housing subsidies either in kind or in cash, it is very difficult to tell exactly how much each level of the governments have devoted to housing. This is particularly difficult to calculate when the land can be a form of subsidy and the land price is set by the local governments. Therefore, it is very difficult to tell exactly how much money has been devoted to the construction and subsidies of all different types of affordable housing. However, some government auditing data on some affordable housing schemes may help us get a rough idea about the financial arrangements between the central and local governments.

City and urban district governments in the housing sector in China

The Chinese governments have multiple layers: central, provincial, prefecture, city/county and district. Different layers of the government have different responsibilities. As housing is highly localised, local governments above the city level are mainly echoing central government policies, and the actual implementation will fall on the shoulder of city and district governments. The role of city and district governments has several perspectives:

• Land supply in cities is controlled by city governments. In most cities, the district government also has control over land supply. The overall land quota for construction is set by the national plan, but local governments manage the stocks of land and decide how much land is leased each year for what types of houses. They also decide the rent/price level of subsidised houses.

Table 4: Central-local Spending on Housing Benefits (in millions)

Central + Local	2015 Spending (CNY)	2015 Spending (USD)	% of Total Spending	Increase from 2014 (%)
Housing protection projects	**488.1**	766	0.96	11.3
Total spending	**535.3**	84.0	0.79	
• Regeneration of shanty towns	158.2	24.8	0.23	46.8
• Public and low-rental housing	144.2	22.7	0.21	-13.2
• Renovation of rural dilapidated housing	52.8	8.3	0.08	40.6
• Subsides for affordable housing	52.5	0.8	0.01	3
• Others	127.6	20.0	0.19	4.6

Central	Central government spending by area (CNY)	Central government spending by area (USD)		Central government spending by projects (CNY)	Central government spending by projects (USD)
Housing protection projects	254.8	40.0	Housing regeneration and supporting infrastructures	146.4	22.98
• Urban	217.9	34.2	Centrally owned state enterprise housing regeneration	2.07	0.32
• Rural	36.8	5.8			

Local	Local public finance spending
Housing protection projects	233.3	36.6

Source: Ministry of Finance of China, at <http://zhs.mof.gov.cn/zhengwuxinxi/gongzuodongtai/201603/t20160303_1860922.html> (accessed 28 May 2018).

- Local governments set housing regulations, e.g. home ownership, promotion or speculation restraint policies, subsidies for home buying and rentals.
- Demolition policy is mainly formulated by local governments.
- The space and time for development are mainly dominated by local governments.
- The city government can have guidance of local real estate development, e.g. set the proportion of subsidised housing as part of commercial housing in estate development.

Some of these tasks such as land supply and pricing are delegated to district governments, depending on the sources of housing. Sometimes, city and district governments work together. The power relationship between the two layers can vary by city.

In terms of the governance of housing policy implementation, four subsystems contribute to the system at the local level (Figure 4).

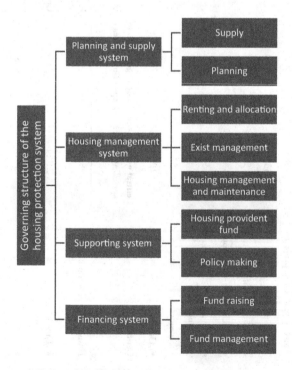

Figure 4: Housing Governance Structure

Despite the central government's expressed intention to improve housing conditions for the people, the establishment of an affordable housing system would depend on local governments' planning, financing and governing abilities. After all, the local government's willingness is crucial in realising any housing policy that the higher authorities have introduced. However, the local governments' willingness to provide affordable housing is related to the incentives that the local governments are facing in different domains of the economy and the society. Therefore, understanding the positioning of welfare housing in the economic, social and political domains in China would help understand the motivation of local governments.

• In the authoritarian government hierarchy, where local government officials report to the higher-level authorities, housing policy would be subject to what is prioritised in the government official's performance evaluation[22] and what may bring in more local revenues. Since the economic reform, local government officials were more likely to get promoted according to their economic performances, such as GDP. Such a priority can affect the behaviour of local governments in housing policies. Throughout the housing reform from 1970s to early 2000s, welfare housing was presented as "burdens" to enterprises and local governments. The marketisation reform was to relieve the burdens to allow enterprises, in particular, the state-owned or collectively owned enterprises to compete in the market. Private ownership can inject resources into the market and boost the local economy. To encourage home ownership, both central and local governments have stopped being housing providers (only played a very limited role to maintain existing housing stocks) and also minimised housing subsidies.[23]

---

[22] Zhou Li-an, "Governing China's Local Officials: An Analysis of Promotion Tournament Model", *Economic Research Journal*, vol. 7, 2007, pp. 36–50; Li Hongbin and Zhou Li-an, "Political Turnover and Economic Performance: The Incentive Role of Personnel Control in China", *Journal of Public Economics*, vol. 89, no. 9–10, 2005, pp. 1743–1762.

[23] Chen Junhua, Guo Fei and Wu Ying, "One Decade of Urban Housing Reform in China: Urban Housing Price Dynamics and The Role of Migration and Urbanisation, 1995–2005", *Habitat International*, vol. 35, no. 1, 2011, pp. 1–8.

- Real estate development was identified as a means to achieve high economic growth at the turn of the century. To this day, the real estate sector contributed significantly to the local government budgetary income. When the housing market is booming and the sales of commercial housing grows fast, the growth rate of fiscal revenue will follow within a couple of months. When the sales decline, it will also affect the fiscal revenues. Such a relationship also affected the behaviour of the regulators. When the housing market is cooling down, they would take actions to stimulate the property market to speed up the sales of commercial housing for rapid financial replenishment. This is also why in 2016, the government decided to stimulate the housing market. The idea was to sell off the existing housing stock in order to reduce local government debts. In 2016, 14 provinces and municipalities' land sales were more than 30% of the total revenue, of which 6 provinces and municipalities accounted for more than 50% of land transfer fees. In prefecture-level cities, for 169 government funds accounted for more than 50% of public finance revenues and for 44 out of the 169 prefecture-level cities, the government funds accounted for more than 100% of public finance revenues.[24] As the primary source of government funds was land lease revenues, Figure 5 shows that even in smaller cities land revenues were crucial to local governments' debt repayment, which would in turn affect the house prices.

- As the economy becomes more prosperous, the demand for better social services also emerged. The central government was keen to connect the tracks (*jie gui*) with the international society both economically and achieve social development.[25] More and more

---

[24] 21st Century Economic Report, "Local governments should not excessively dependent on the real estate industry", 2017, at <http://epaper.21jingji.com/html/2017-08/14/content_68415.htm> (accessed 28 May 2018).

[25] Zheng Lin, "Insight into UK China Articulation Programmes and Internationalisation: What has Changed in the Last Few Years?", in *Transnational Higher Education in the Asian Context*, London, Palgrave Macmillan, 2013, pp. 32–48.

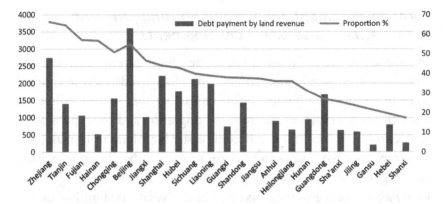

Figure 5: Proportion of Local Government Debt Paid with Land Revenues

new social roles were reassumed by the state and are expected to be taken up by the local government (e.g. education, social protection, community service provision and infrastructure investment). However, responsibilities did not come with corresponding funds. Such uneven distribution of revenue and responsibilities forced local governments to look for new ways to find money to deliver services. At the same time, housing was not recognised as a statutory right. The local governments have all the incentives to reduce land supply and funds to public housing projects and focus on supporting items that are legally binding and growth driven.[26]

Despite these considerations, if housing provision or subsidies are considered to be beneficial to achieving the economic goals, local governments would be interested in providing. This has been best exemplified in the policy towards the migrant population and the implementation of providing social housing.

---

[26] Zou Yonghua, "Contradictions in China's Affordable Housing Policy: Goals vs Structure", *Habitat International*, vol. 41, 2014, pp. 8–16.

Local development agenda and housing provision to migrants — a selective development?

In contrast to the situation in large cities, local governments in small cities were keen to urbanise farmers. This change reflected the national strategy for labour mobility control: to use smaller — or medium — size cities as reservoirs to control rural migration and the expansion of large cities.[27] As a result, it has become easier for migrants in small cities to receive an urban *hukou* and in turn to access urban housing welfare. As there was no national-level government policy change on granting local *hukous*, local governments have themselves devised initiatives. For example, the city of Changsha in Hunan Province and Hangzhou in Zhejiang Province introduced a points system by which a person has to work and live in the city and contribute to the social insurance schemes for a certain number of years before qualifying for permanent residency.[28] In 2003, Shanghai also introduced a town equivalence scheme (*zhenbao* 镇保) that aimed to integrate farmers from Shanghai suburban districts and counties, who had lost their land due to urban expansion, into the urban social insurance schemes.[29] Contribution and entitlement levels in these social insurances, however, were set at a lower level than those of other urban citizens of Shanghai Municipality. Other municipalities and cities across China also introduced similar systems, which were later extended to all rural-to-urban migrant workers, including those from beyond their administrative boundaries. But yet again, none of these local variations covered housing.

The problem faced by rural-to-urban migrants in the housing sector, even those under new *hukou* arrangements, was straightforward: they

---

[27] Wang Feng and Zuo Xuejin Zuo, "Inside China's Cities: Institutional Barriers and Opportunities for Urban Migrants", *The American Economic Review*, vol. 89, no. 2, 1999, pp. 276–280.

[28] Wang Fei-Ling, "Reformed Migration Control and New Targeted People: China's Hukou System in the 2000s", *The China Quarterly*, vol. 177, 2004, pp. 115–132.

[29] Xu Ying, Tang Bo-sin and Chan H. W. Edwin, "State-led Land Requisition and Transformation of Rural Villages in Transitional China", *Habitat International*, vol. 35, no. 1, 2011, pp. 57–65.

were not entitled to any form of housing welfare. Even workers living in an employer-provided accommodation became homeless as soon as they were laid off. Workers whose employers did not provide accommodation or who were self-employed resided with friends and relatives, built temporary accommodations in abandoned sites, rented dilapidated housing in inner cities and in "villages in cities" (*chengzhongcun* 城中村),[30] or lived in the peri-urban accommodation provided by suburban farmers. Their housing conditions were usually very poor.[31] Migrant tenants were considered to be troublesome by urban residents, especially when they crowded into shared properties in urban residential neighbourhoods. They were accused by neighbours of not engaging with local residents and of not respecting local rules. This was coupled by their high level of mobility, which was seen as a threat to neighbourhood safety.[32] To respond to these public complaints, some local governments (including some communities in Shanghai) banned group renting, making it even more difficult for migrants to find housing and settle down more permanently in urban residential neighbourhoods.[33]

Another group of urban dwellers who also found themselves facing housing constraints were university graduates. From the start of the reform era to the turn of the 21st century, university graduates had been regarded as highly qualified talent, and they could legally work in a city once they found an employer willing to sponsor them. With the help of their employers, they could receive a local *hukou* once all

---

[30] Villages in cities are rural villages turned into enclaves as the peri-urban villages became urbanised. Since "villages in cities" are convenient for urban commuting, local villagers often become landlords for migrant workers.

[31] Wu Weiping, "Migrant Housing in Urban China Choices and Constraints", *Urban Affairs Review*, vol. 38, no. 1, 2002, pp. 90–119; Wu Weiping, "Sources of Migrant Housing Disadvantage in Urban China", *Environment and Planning A*, vol. 36, 2004, pp. 1285–1304; Li Bingqin and Mark Duda, "Employers as Landlords for Rural-to-Urban Migrants in Chinese Cities", *Environment and urbanization*, vol. 22, no. 1, 2010, pp. 13–31.

[32] Zhang Yingli, "Public Security Problems and Solutions of Group-renting Housing", *Journal of Jilin Public Security Academy*, vol. 6, 2011, p. 15.

[33] Li Bingqin, "How Successful are China's Public Housing Schemes?" pp. 115–140.

administrative requirements were satisfied. However, from the early 2000s, the number of university graduates increased dramatically as a result of the expansion of access to higher education. At the same time, employers began to put more value on work experience when hiring,[34] which meant they were increasingly less willing to sponsor new graduates. Unemployment among university graduates started to become a growing social problem in urban China.[35] Many new graduates, particularly those based in large cities, such as Beijing, Shanghai, Guangzhou and Shenzhen, usually remained in these cities in the hope of finding a sponsor. Being unemployed or facing a precarious employment situation, these graduates became a part of the so-called "floating" population, to which rural migrant workers were said to belong.[36] As such, they also did not have access to urban welfare benefits — including housing — and thus also had to live in overcrowded conditions in peri-urban slums or in shared apartments in urban residential neighbourhoods.[37]

Local government responses to migration

After 2003, the Detention and Eviction Stations (*shourong qiansong zhan* 收容遣送站) were converted into Social Assistance Centres (*shehui jiuzhu zhongxin* 社会救助中心). Migrant workers without accommodation who registered at these centres were meant to be accommodated and provided with food and bathing facilities. If they wanted to return home but did not have the means, these centres were to provide them with a free train ticket to do so. These temporary shelters are funded by local governments through the local branches of

---

[34] Bai Limin, "Graduate Unemployment: Dilemmas and Challenges in China's Move to Mass Higher Education", *The China Quarterly*, vol. 185, 2006, pp. 128–144.

[35] Bai Limin, "Graduate Unemployment: Dilemmas and Challenges in China's Move to Mass Higher Education", pp. 128–144.

[36] John Giles, Park Albert and Zhang Juwei, "What is China's True Unemployment Rate?" *China Economic Review*, vol. 16, no. 2, 2005, pp. 149–170.

[37] Ian G. Cook, Gu Chaolin and Jamie Halsall (2013), "China's Low Income Urban Housing", *Asian Social Science*, vol. 9, no. 3, 2013, p. 7.

the Ministry of Civil Affairs, and thus constitute a new form of social assistance. Various housing programmes have also been put in place by local urban governments to provide more stable accommodation for rural migrant workers. In the early 2000s, for example, Tianjin Seaport and the city of Changsha provided heavily subsidised dormitories for migrant workers. These dormitories, however, were built in peri-urban areas, which made them inconvenient for migrant workers due to the long commute to work. The dormitories were also not designed for family living, which discouraged migrants from bringing their family members along. As the usage of these dormitories proved to be low, local governments became less enthusiastic about directly providing housing to migrants.[38]

In other cities, such as in Hangzhou, Shijiazhuang, Chongqing and Qingdao, various forms of state–employer partnerships were established to build and manage dormitories targeting low-income migrant workers. In such arrangements, employers either refer workers to private estate management companies hired by the state to manage this type of housing, or else employers directly rent housing estates and assume responsibility for allocating accommodation and for building maintenance.[39] Services — such as cleaning and maintaining public and indoor spaces, facilities and dormitories, canteen catering, social events, and so on — are either provided by employers or by a self-governing body of migrant workers.[40] These public–private partnerships reduced the government's administrative burden of direct allocation and management of housing for migrant workers, and created a range of efficiencies for both employers and local governments. For employers, having their workers living in one place allowed for better employee

---

[38] Li Bingqin and Zhang Yongmei, "Housing Provision for Rural–Urban Migrant Workers in Chinese Cities: The Roles of the State, Employers and the Market", *Social Policy & Administration*, vol. 45, no. 6, 2011, pp. 694–713.

[39] David Bray, "Building 'Community': New Strategies of Governance in Urban China", *Economy and Society*, vol. 35, no. 4, 2006, pp. 530–549.

[40] Wang Ying, "Self-Governance for City Residents and Changes in Community Management Styles", 2000, at <http://www.ids.ac.uk/ids/civsoc/final/china/chn5.doc> (accessed 19 May 2016).

management, including arranging group commuting between these dormitories and the work place, dining facilities and social events. Similarly, when a dormitory compound is built for an entire industrial park, local governments could then organise public transport accordingly. Employers and local governments consider these practices to be good for building worker solidarity, cultivating enterprise culture and improving the efficiency of enterprise operations.[41]

The counter argument is that these dormitories are part of an exploitative labour regime that aims to discipline and control labour.[42] More broadly, dormitory regimes in China have been found to be exploitative and a sign of local governments standing on the side of capital to achieve greater market share for the companies involved.[43] On the whole, these work-based dormitories are designed to meet the needs of employers, not workers. However, in the author's own research, it was found that when properly managed, this type of housing is not only beneficial to the state and to employers, but has also benefits for employees. This is because the quality of the accommodation offered by employers (except for those in the construction sector) is usually better than the private rental properties available to rural migrant workers; for example, they have reliable electricity and water supply. This type of housing is also particularly useful for new migrant workers who are not familiar with their urban environment. What we also observed is that not all employers were skilful and knowledgeable

---

[41] Li Bingqin and Zhang Yongmei, "Housing Provision for Rural–Urban Migrant Workers in Chinese Cities: The Roles of the State, Employers and the Market", pp. 694–713; Fang Lee Cooke and He Qiaoling, "Corporate Social Responsibility and HRM in China: A Study of Textile and Apparel Enterprises", *Asia Pacific Business Review*, vol. 16, no. 3, 2010, pp. 355–376.

[42] Anita Chan and Zhu Xiaoyang, "Disciplinary Labour Regimes in Chinese Factories", *Critical Asian Studies*, vol. 35, no. 4, 2003, pp. 559–584.

[43] Pun Ngai and Jenny Chan, "Global Capital, the State, and Chinese Workers: The Foxconn Experience", *Modern China*, vol. 38, no. 4, 2012, pp. 383–410; Cheng Yu-shek Joseph, Kinglun Ngok and Huang Yan, "Multinational Corporations, Global Civil Society and Chinese Labour: Workers' Solidarity in China in the Era of Globalization", *Economic and Industrial Democracy*, vol. 33, no. 3, 2011, pp. 379–401.

dormitory managers, for example, they might prioritise labour control to community building in dormitories, which can be damaging to labour morale in the longer term.[44] This demands the state play a more active role in guiding, regulating and monitoring the behaviour of employers. Furthermore, such work-based housing can only cover workers during the period they are employed. Local governments thus have to keep in mind that it is not possible to rely on such work-based housing as the ultimate solution to the housing needs of rural migrant workers.

Local governments receive Central government subsidies to finance the development of public rental housing and are required to devote all capital gains and at least 10% of local land revenues to its construction. The Central government's target was for urban housing welfare to benefit 6.6% of urban households by the end of 2015. Of that 6.6%, 62.7% was expected to live in public rental housing.[45] The target changed over time in line with housing market conditions. By 2010, the percentage of people benefiting from some kind of housing welfare had already reached 7% of the urban population.[46] However, rapidly rising housing prices also resulted in a growing number of people needing support to purchase housing. The official target number of people covered by at least one type of housing subsidy was also raised to 20% of the total urban population by the end of the 12th Five-Year Plan Period (2011–2015).[47] By the end of 2015, 36 million subsidised homes were to be constructed. For the 13th Five-Year Plan

---

[44] Li Bingqin and Zhang Yongmei, "Housing Provision for Rural–Urban Migrant Workers in Chinese Cities: The Roles of the State, Employers and the Market", pp. 694–713.

[45] Xinhua Newsnet, "Cheap Rental Housing Security Plan, 2009–2010", 2 June 2009, at <http://news.xinhuanet.com/fortune/2009-06/02/content_11476918.htm> (accessed 27 Mar 2016).

[46] Han Xiping and Zhou Lingling, "*Baozhang xing zhufang ruhe shixian fenpei zhengyi*" (How to Achieve Distributive Justice via Affordable Housing), *People's Forum*, no. 8, 2015, pp. 70–77.

[47] Joseph Casey and Katherine Koleski, "Backgrounder: China's 12th Five-Year Plan", US–China Economic and Security Review Commission, 2011, at <https://195.35.109.44/gifiles/attach/11/11798_US%20China%20Econo.pdf> (accessed 19 March, 2016).

(2016–2020), the targeted share of people receiving housing welfare subsidies was set to reach 35% by 2020.[48]

Although the Central government had stipulated in 2010 that all migrants should have access to public rental housing, in practice, this has been subject to local government discretion. Often only those moving within their home province are eligible, while those from other provinces are excluded from this type of housing. The equal integration of migrants across the country requires agreement between provinces, something very difficult to achieve without Central government permission and coordination.[49] In 2015, attempts to facilitate interprovincial welfare benefit transferability were only trialled with subsidised home-buying.[50]

On the whole, local governments have responded differently to the stipulation to allow migrant workers — particularly those from outside the provincial borders — to have access to local public housing schemes. The different responses are closely related to the stage of economic development of each province and to the structure and strength of the local economies.[51] Starting in 2005 the economic growth centre

---

[48] Hu Angang, "*Cong 'shisanwu' guihua kan weilai wu nian geren hongli*" (Personal benefits from the 13th Five-Year Plan), 2016, at <http://news.cri.cn/2016310/112f48d5-8e40-b389-c200-8d644e579a48.html> (accessed 31 May 2016).

[49] Shi Shih-Jiunn, "Towards Inclusive Social Citizenship? Rethinking China's Social Security in the Trend towards Urban–Rural Harmonisation", *Journal of Social Policy*, vol. 41, no. 4, 2012, pp. 789–810.

[50] By 2015, four cities — Wuhan, Changsha, Hefei and Nanchang — had started to explore the possibility of allowing people to buy houses using the HPF accumulated in a different province. The benefits would only be transferrable between these four cities. It may still take years to achieve a higher degree of integration, even if the experiments in these four cities turn out to be successful. Zhou Fang, "*Zhongbu sicheng youwang gongjijin yidi maifang, shifang wen loushi xinhao*" (Four Central Cities are expected to allow home-buying with HPF from other cities, signalling stability of the property market), *First Financial Daily*, 26 February 2015, at <http://finance.sina.com.cn/china/20150226/010421593589.shtml> (accessed 27 Mar 2016).

[51] Li Bingqin, Chen Chunlai and Hu Biliang, "Governing Urbanization and the New Urbanization Plan in China", *Environment and Urbanization*, vol. 28, no. 2, 2016, pp. 515–534.

in China shifted from the east to the west and then to the central provinces.[52] At the same time, the more developed coastal areas began to upgrade their economies towards more service-oriented or higher value-added enterprises.[53] Low-end skilled manufacturing largely moved inland. Contrasting economic strategies led to contrasting attitudes towards public housing. In cities like Shanghai, Guangzhou and Shenzhen, rural-to-urban migrant workers had no access to public rental housing, which was usually reserved for young white collar migrant workers, who were more likely to already hold an urban *hukou*. However, in the western cities of Chengdu, Chongqing and Guiyang, public rental housing was open to rural migrants, though only to those from within the same province,[54] thus demonstrating the continued link between housing welfare entitlements and the place of birth.

In mid-2014, the *hukou* system was finally reformed to eliminate the differential treatment between rural and urban populations. A single national Resident Registration (*jumin hukou* 居民戶口) system was established. This system provides individuals with an identity card, which does not categorise people by place of birth, and hence allows for all permanent residents — in principle this includes rural migrant workers — in any particular place to enjoy equal access to social insurances and welfare. Permanent residency in urban areas, however, is still determined by local governments, which in turn allows them to continue to exercise discretion in specifying the details of entitlement. For example, cities have used length of residency and length of stable employment as a way to favour those migrants deemed desirable to

---

[52] He Canfei and Wang Junsong, "Regional and Sectoral Differences in the Spatial Restructuring of Chinese Manufacturing Industries during the Post-WTO Period", *GeoJournal*, vol. 77, no. 3, 2012, pp. 361–381.

[53] Wei YH Dennis and Ingo Liefner, "Globalization, Industrial Restructuring, and Regional Development in China", *Applied Geography*, vol. 32, no. 1, 2012, pp. 102–105.

[54] Shen Yang, "Why Does the Government Fail to Improve the Living Conditions of Migrant Workers in Shanghai? Reflections on the Policies and the Implementations of Public Rental Housing under Neoliberalism", *Asia & the Pacific Policy Studies*, vol. 2, no. 1, 2015, pp. 58–74.

become local residents, and to exclude non-resident permit holders.[55] Again, Shanghai and Beijing made it particularly difficult for rural migrants to settle down permanently. For example, both cities introduced an age requirement for migrants seeking permanent residence in these cities (younger than 45 in Beijing; five points for people aged 50–60 and two more points for each year younger in Shanghai).[56] Meanwhile, medium-sized cities introduced policies to favour certain kinds of skilled migrants and actively excluded low-skilled workers.[57] Paradoxically, by granting this discretionary power to local governments, the new *hukou* system has helped legitimise some of the exclusionary local practices that earlier would have been considered to contravene existing national policies.

Since 2015, in major cities, housing has been actively used in megacities, such as Beijing, Shanghai and Shenzhen, to drive away "low-end" migrants in order to satisfy the goal of economic upgrading. Many houses in the cities were labelled as informal housing or unsafe housing. At the peak, Beijing started to drive out migrant workers living in peri-urban areas, which caused serious public outcry in China and internationally.

Local housing protection policy implementation

On paper, the housing protection system looks good. It provides multiple layers of housing protection for people from different income groups. When people's income grows, they would be able to continue enjoying housing support as they graduate from renting to owning. In

---

[55] Zhou Rui, "Pushing the Door of Heavy Household Registration", *Rule of Law and Society*, vol. 11, 2014, pp. 64–65.

[56] "*Beijing jifen luohu menkan gao, weilai 5 nian zuiduo huiji 148 wan ren*" (Beijing settlement threshold is high over the next five years and up to 148 million people could apply), *China Economic Weekly*, 22 December 2015, at <http://www.chinanews.com/gn/2015/12-22/7681314.shtml> (accessed 27 December 2015).

[57] Li Bingqin, "China's *Hukou* Reform: A Small Step in the Right Direction", *East Asia Forum*, 2015, at <http://www.eastasiaforum.org/2015/01/13/chinas-hukou-reform-a-small-step-in-the-right-direction/> (accessed 31 May 2015).

theory, a large proportion of the population should be able to receive one form of protection or another.

However, in practice, as discussed earlier, local governments want to maximise their own revenues which are largely dependent on housing sales and land lease. As pointed out by Tan and Lou,[58] in addition to the local policymakers and implementers, for-profit organisations — such as banks, real estate speculators, property management companies, construction and building material suppliers, real estate agencies, and foreign-funded institutions — all played active parts in the implementation of affordable housing policies. Commercial banks provide loans for real estate developers. The huge loans supported real estate development. Real estate speculators hoarded properties to push up the housing price. Property management companies were often part of the real estate developers and charged high service fees to make more money out of the residents. Construction companies and companies that supply building materials benefited from a prosperous construction industry and housing market. Real estate agents also benefited from active market trading. Along this network of interests, affordable housing is often not delivered. In the face of huge economic interests, such a network of businesses tries to avoid administrative orders and supervision of the central policymakers. The local government departments were often on the side of business interests as the latter could bring in cash flow for the local government. The local governments formed an alliance with businesses to sell and speculate and for fiscal and business gains, focusing on high-end residential buildings for construction and ignoring the low-cost housing market. Local governments also implemented the affordable housing policies in a very flexible manner and often delayed implementation or altered policies. As a result, the implementation of affordable housing policies was hijacked for further pushing up real estate prices and prompting the producer network to

---

[58] Tan Lingyan and Lou Chengwu, "*Baozhang xing zhufang zhengce guocheng de zhongyang yu defang zhengfu guanxi*" (The relationship between the central and local governments in the process of affordable housing policy), *Journal of Public Management*, vol. 1, 2012, pp. 52–53.

become the core network affecting the implementation process of affordable housing policies.

With such a motivation structure, the housing outcomes were not optimistic. Take Beijing as an example; in 2007, Beijing had 13.8 million urban population. By the end of November 2007, 217,000 families in Beijing benefited from low-cost housing or affordable housing policies. Suppose there were 2.65 people per household, the housing protection policy in Beijing would have benefited 4.2% of the population only. According to data released by the National People's Congress Research Team in October 2009, the national funding for affordable housing construction was only 25% of the targeted amount. The data obtained is that in 2009 the targeted number of completion of low-rental housing was 1.77 million units, but only 650,000 units were built. In 2010, the 5.8 million units of affordable housing construction target were completed. Another 10 million units of affordable housing were planned for 2011 and only 30% were built before May. Since late June 2011, local governments started to show off their performance. In Liaoning and Shanxi, approximately 90% of the houses started to be constructed. In Shaanxi Province, the total number of projects started was 101.1% of the target number of projects. However, observers remained to be suspicious of the data.[59]

Since 2012, there were major changes in the affordable housing construction. The government decided not to use economic growth as the only indicators for evaluating the performance of local government officials. The completion rate of affordable housing became a part of the performance evaluation. However, this generated another problem. According to the data published by the Auditing Office, around 128,700 public housing units were not occupied because of poor infrastructure access and another 272,400 units were left unoccupied because the houses were built too far away. The reason was that the local

---

[59] Tan Lingyan and Lou Chengwu, "*Baozhang xing zhufang zhengce guocheng de zhongyang yu defang zhengfu guanxi*" (The relationship between the central and local governments in the process of affordable housing policy), pp. 52–53.

officials were keen to deliver the quantitative results, but did not try to take into account the people's needs. Their focus was on finishing more units to meet the targets. But little considerations were given to what people really want. Also, the best locations are reserved for more expensive houses.[60]

Conclusion

After more than 30 years of reform, China has developed a multilayered affordable housing system that offers subsidised rental housing and home ownership to the urban unemployed and to lower and middle-income groups. Housing welfare reforms have successfully reduced the housing poverty inherited from the pre-reform Central Planning System.

However, housing affordability problems have emerged as a result of rising market house prices. The housing welfare system aims to benefit a large proportion of the population through subsidised rental and home ownership, in order to serve as a safety net for urban residents at different income levels.

As discussed in this chapter, the housing affordability issue has deteriorated over time. This has much to do with the local governments' unwillingness to implement affordable housing policies.

The reform since 2012 changed the incentives of the local officials by making affordable housing construction an evaluated item in the local government officials' performance. However, the results are still not satisfactory. Housing affordability has not been improved, but at the same time, public housing vacancy has become an emerging issue. Such outcomes show that there is further need to improve the regulation and governance of affordable housing supplies. So far, local governments still focus on what the central government assess and what may help them maximise the local interests.

---

[60] China Economy Net, "Why does public housing vacancy become more and more serious?", 2017, at <http://views.ce.cn/view/ent/201706/28/t20170628_23910600. shtml, 28 June 2017> (accessed 28 May 2018).

The experience of the affordable housing in China shows that the future of affordable housing will lie in the growing interaction between the housing suppliers and the people. So far, in the equation of the local governments, affordable housing is still a centrally decided task that needs to be completed without costing other businesses, i.e. the higher end of the housing markets, which will bring in revenues and serve the interests of the whole circle of production alliance. People's need for affordable housing was rarely a crucial part of the equation, albeit when "people" become an equivalence to "desired labour", the motivation would be different.

Acknowledgement

This research was supported with funding by United Cities and Local Governments (UCLG) and developed in the framework of the Global Report on Local Democracy and Decentralisation (GOLD V) on the localisation of the SDGs and the Right to Adequate Housing, which will be published in Fall 2019. For more information, please visit http://www.uclg.org.

The author is also grateful for EAI at NUS for the opportunity to present and receive comments of the work.

Chapter 14

Global Value Chains and China's Export Miracle

XING Yuqing*

Introduction

In 2017, China exported $2.2 trillion goods to the world market, the largest among all nations. Until 1978, it exported a mere $9.8 billion less than 0.5% of the export volume in 2017. After almost four decades of rapid economic growth since China launched the revolutionary economic reform, it has surpassed Germany, Japan and the United States and emerged as the largest exporting nation. "Made in China" products are now ubiquitous in markets of both developed and developing countries, ranging from labour-intensive products, such as T-shirts, shoes and toys, to high-tech products, such as mobile phones, laptop computers and digital cameras. "Made in China" products have become indispensable for millions of foreign consumers. For some consumers in the United States, it seems even impossible to live without "Made in China" products.[1]

Before China was opened to the rest of world, it was an isolated and centrally planned economy. Self-sufficiency was not only just a political

---

*XING Yuqing is affiliated with the National Graduate Institute for Policy Studies, Minato-ku, Tokyo, Japan. Email: Yuqing_xing@grips.ac.jp.
[1] S. Bongiomi, *A Year Without "Made in China": One Family's True Life Adventure in the Global Economy*, Wiley, 2008.

slogan but also a national development policy. Why are Chinese products so competitive and popular in the global market today? What are the major forces driving the worldwide expansion and diversification of its manufacturing exports? Many academic scholars and Chinese observers have tried to answer the questions from various aspects. A plethora of articles analysing the drastic growth of China's exports have been published in academic journals, magazines and newspapers. According to these studies, fundamental factors determining significant growth and worldwide expansion of China's exports include: (1) abundant labour endowment and corresponding comparative advantage in labour-intensive products[2]; (2) reforms of domestic institutions, such as the transition to a market-oriented economy, the adoption of export-led growth strategy and unilateral trade liberalisation[3]; (3) improved market access for China's exports through institutional arrangements, namely the WTO membership, bilateral and multilateral free-trade agreements and the abolishment of multifiber arrangement[4]; (4) exchange rate regime adopted by the Chinese government and undervalued currency[5] and (5) massive inflows of export-oriented foreign direct investment.[6]

---

[2] G. F. Adams, B. Ganges and Y. Shachmurove, "Why is China So Competitive? Measuring and Explaining China's Competitiveness", *World Economy*, vol. 29, no. 2, 2006, pp. 95–122; Y. Wang, "Cheap Labor and China's Export Capacity", in *China as the World Factory*, ed. K. H. Zhang, Routledge, 2006, pp. 69–82.

[3] Z. F. Hu and M. Khan, " Why is China Growing So fast?", *IMF Staff Papers*, vol. 44, no. 1, 1997, pp. 103–131; J. Y. Lin, F. Cai and Z. Li, *The China Miracle*, The Chinese University Press, Hong Kong, 2003.

[4] L. Branstetter and N. Lardy, "China's Embrace of Globalization", *NBER Working Paper 12373*; E. Prasad, "Is the Chinese growth miracle built to last?", *China Economic Review*, vol. 20, no. 1, 2009, p. 103.

[5] B. Naughton, "China in the World Economy", *Brookings Papers on Economic Activities*, 1996, pp. 2273–2344; J. Marquez and J. Schindler, "Exchange Rate Effects on China's Trade", *Review of International Economics*, vol. 15, no. 5, 2007, pp. 837–853; W. Thorbecke and G. Smith, "How Would an Appreciation of the Renminbi and the East Asian Currencies Affect China's Exports?", *Review of International Economics*, vol. 18, no. 1, 2010, pp. 95–108.

[6] K. H. Zhang and S. Song, "Promoting Exports: The Role of Inward FDI in China", *China Economic Review*, vol. 11, 2000, pp. 285–396; J. Whalley and X. Xin, "China's FDI

With a population of more than 1.4 billion, China is naturally endowed with comparative advantage in labour-intensive products. Assuming other factors determining global competitiveness are equal across countries, relatively low labour cost should grant Chinese exports an edge over its competitors. Without any doubt, trade liberalisation since 1990s in terms of tariff reductions and trade facilitations has substantially improved the market access of Chinese exports. Comparative advantage and trade liberalisation arguments, however, mainly emphasise production costs and barriers to cross-country flows of goods and fail to take into consideration the critical role performed by the organisation structure of modern trade in promoting China's exports, in particular its successful penetration into high-income countries. Those studies actually leave many important questions unanswered.

For example, without foreign brands, could China export as many shoes and toys as it does today? Why has China turned into the No. 1 laptop computer exporter even if it has no comparative advantage in technology-intensive products? Whenever Apple launches new cutting-edge products, such as new models of iPhone and iPad, the shipment of Apple products from China to the rest of the world increases and continues to grow along with the rising popularity of Apple products. Who should be given credit for the increase — innovative American company Apple, or assembler Foxcon, a Taiwanese company located in mainland China that has been banking on cheap Chinese labour?

In classic models of Ricardo and Heckscher–Ohlin, comparative advantage represents the sole factor determining competitiveness and trade patterns. Today's trade, nonetheless, is not "wine for clothes". The proliferation of global value chains (GVCs) has transformed trade in goods into trade in tasks.[7] Many firms located in various geographic locations jointly deliver ready-to-use products to consumers of the global market. Comparative advantage of an individual country alone

---

and non-FDI Economies and Sustainability of High Chinese Growth," *China Economic Review*, vol. 21, no. 1, 2010, pp. 123–135.

[7] G. M. Grossman and E. Rossi-Hansberg, "Trading Tasks: A Simple Theory of Offshoring", *American Economic Review*, vol. 98, no. 5, 2008, pp. 1978–1997.

cannot decide the competitiveness of products manufactured and traded along GVCs. Brands, global distribution networks and technology innovations, which are owned by lead firms of GVCs, typically multinational enterprises of developed countries, perform dominant roles in determining winners and losers of the global market.

GVCs are particular relevant to Chinese exports, as about half of its manufacturing exports are assembled with imported parts and components, and most of the so-called "Made in China" products available in the world market either carry brands owned by multinational enterprises (MNEs) or are distributed by global retail giants such as Walmart. In this chapter, we attempt to interpret China's export boom in the context of GVCs. We argue that GVCs have been functioning as a vehicle for Chinese exports entering international markets, especially markets of high-income countries. By successfully plugging into GVCs, Chinese firms have been able to bundle their low-skilled labour services with globally recognised brands and advanced technologies of MNEs, and then sell them to consumers of international markets. GVCs are actually a catalyst for "Made in China" products; strictly speaking, China's value-added is embedded in its manufacturing exports being bought and consumed in various nations. Continuous technology innovations, aggressive promotions on brands and the worldwide development of distribution networks by lead firms of GVCs constantly expand and create new demand, which in turn lift the demand for tasks performed by Chinese firms integrated with supply chains and eventually enhance China's exports.

To establish the argument, we first examine tasks performed by Chinese firms in GVCs of various goods. The analysis starts with the iPhone case, which has been exclusively assembled in China, then extends the coverage to high-tech products, where China has emerged as the No. 1 exporter in the world, and finally expand the scope to all products by examining the role of processing exports.

Assembly and processing are typical segments of value chains and belong to low value-added tasks. Processing exports not only reveal tasks Chinese firms performed, but also provide a direct measure of exports associated with GVC participation. We use the intensity of processing exports in China's bilateral trade to argue that GVCs help "Made in China" products successfully penetrate the world markets, especially the markets of high-income countries, such as the United States, Japan and Germany.

Spillover Effects of GVCs

A GVC comprises a series of tasks necessary for delivering a product from its inception to final consumers of international markets, including research and development, product design, manufacturing parts and components, assembly and distribution, all of which are carried out by firms located in various countries.[8] According to governance structures, GVCs can be classified into producer-driven and buyer-driven value chains. Producer-driven chains are generally developed by technology leaders in automobiles, aircraft, computers, semiconductors and other capital-intensive industries; buyer-driven chains are typically developed by large retailers, branded marketers and branded manufacturers.[9] In the context of the property-rights model, the characterisation of ownership allocation along value chains can also depend on incentives to integrate suppliers and the elasticity of demand faced by final good producers.[10]

Lead firms, either technology leaders, brand marketers or larger retailers, play central roles in organising all tasks of GVCs, such as product design, outsourcing manufacturing activities, product distribution and retailing. Value chains without lead firms, or where the relations between firms are simply market-based and not bound by contacts, cannot generate any externality or organisation effects on GVCs participants, in particular firms from developing countries.

---

[8] G. Gereffi and F. Karina, "Global Value Chain Analysis: A Primer", Center on Globalization, Governance and Competitiveness, Duke University, 2011.
[9] G. Gereffi, "International Trade and Industrial Upgrading in the Apparel Commodity Chain", *Journal of International Economics*, vol. 48, 1999, pp. 37–70.
[10] Pol Antràs and D. Chor, "Organizing the Global Value Chain", *Econometrica*, vol. 81, no. 6, 2013, pp. 2127–2204.

Technology advancement, unprecedented liberalisation in trade and investment, and profit-seeking behaviours of MNEs have been driving the emergence of GVCs in the last decades.[11] Today, most of the manufacturing commodities are actually produced and traded along value chains. GVCs have also been extended into business processes and management, such as software development and maintenance, and voice services. Like an invisible hand, GVCs have interconnected national economies. The economic integration through value chains is fundamentally market-driven and tends to be more stable and effective than that led by institutional arrangements or defined by conventional arm-length trade. The theory of international trade suggests that specialisations according to comparative advantage improve the efficiency of resource allocations, and hence the welfare of trading nations. Compared with conventional specialisations on industries or products, specialisations on tasks defined by value chains further refine specialisations among nations and enhance the efficiency of resource allocations, consequently raising the productivity and economic growth of all economies involved.

Here, we would like to emphasise spillover effects of GVCs at the micro-level and discuss how the spillover effects generated by intangible assets of lead firms, such as brands, distribution networks and technology innovations, help Chinese firms overcome entry barriers of international markets and achieve dramatic global expansion. Cheap labour is often addressed as a comparative advantage of Chinese firms. It seems that as long as they could manufacture products competitive at costs, they would be able to sell their products and compete in the global market. As a matter of fact, the competition in the global market is much more complicated than this kind of simple reasoning. Production costs are just one of the many factors determining the success in international markets. As barriers to entry in manufacturing fall, intangible assets such as brands and global distribution networks

---

[11] OECD, *Interconnected Economies: Benefiting from Global Value Chains*, Paris, OECD, 2013.

have turned into major hurdles to firms of developing countries which strive to take part in the world market.[12]

Generally, consumers of developed countries tend to be brand oriented and have high willingness to pay for particular brands. Brands are one of the critical factors determining consumers' choices.[13] Due to asymmetric information, consumers regard brands as an assurance of product quality. Switching costs may also undermine consumers' willingness to substitute preferred brands with new alternatives. Consumers' biases to particular brands grant advantage to incumbent producers and raise barrier to new entries. For instance, branded clothing constitute the majority of European clothing market with around 80% market share, and only 20% is left to private labels and non-branded clothing.[14] Despite more than three decades of high growth, Chinese firms have not nurtured a significant number of globally recognised brands. So far, only one Chinese brand Huawei is on the list of 2014 global brand chart. Creating and sustaining global brands require lavish advertising budget and global promotion campaigns, which is beyond the capacity of most Chinese firms at the early stages of their development. Owners of global brands usually lead buyer-driven value chains.[15] By plugging into buyer-driven value chains as assemblers, part producers or original equipment makers (OEMs), Chinese firms are able to circumvent the disadvantage in brands and take advantage of consumers' preferences towards international brands. Compared with non-branded products with equal or relatively low cost, labels of international brands strengthen the competitiveness of "Made in China" products and enhance their appeal to consumers. Preferences of brand-oriented

---

[12] R. Kaplinsky, "Globalization and Unequalization: What Can Be Learned From Value Chain Analysis?", *The Journal of Development Studies*, vol. 37, no. 2, 2000, pp. 117–142.

[13] B. J. Bronnenberg, J. H. Dube and M. Gentzkow, "The Evolution of Brand Preference: Evidence from Consumer Migration," *American Economic Review*, vol. 102, no. 6, 2012, pp. 2472–2508.

[14] Copenhagen Economics, *Unchaining the Supply Chain: How Global Branded Clothing Firms are Contributing to the European Economy*, 2012.

[15] G. Gereffi, "International Trade and Industrial Upgrading in the Apparel Commodity Chain", pp. 37–70.

consumers are implicitly transformed into the demand for "Made in China" products. Without any doubt, China's exports would fall substantially if foreign brands attached were taken away.

In addition, to a large extent, new and fast-growing markets have been nurtured by technology innovations and product inventions. Revolutionary innovations in information and communication technology (ICT) have given rise to a variety of new products, such as laptop computers, smartphones and tablets, thus dramatically stimulating consumers' demand beyond traditional commodities. In 2012, ICT goods emerged as one of the top products traded globally. The world imports of ICT goods rose to US$2 trillion, about 11% of world merchandise trade and exceeded trade in agriculture and motor vehicles.[16] If not all, most of the intellectual property of ICT products are owned by MNEs of developed countries. Compared with established MNEs, Chinese firms do not have comparative advantage in high-tech products. Constrained by limited human resources, insufficient investment in research and development, and relatively short learning-by-doing history, they face challenges to market products with their indigenous technology and compete with incumbent technology leaders. The global expansion of value chains, on the other hand, offers an alternative for Chinese firms to participate in markets of high-tech products and benefit fast-growing demand of these products, regardless of their disadvantages. By participating in the value chains of high-tech products and specialising on low value-added segments, such as assembly and production of low-tech components, Chinese firms are able to join value creation processes of high-tech products and grow together with lead firms. The unit value added of the segment may be relatively small, for instance, assembly adds only $6.5 per iPhone,[17] the sheer size of the world market implies a huge growth potential and economies of scale. Being a part of value chains, Chinese firms can enjoy the spillover

---

[16] UNCATD, "Global Imports of Information Technology Goods Approach $2 Trillion", 2014, at <www.uncatad.org> (accessed 11 May 2015).

[17] Y. Xing and N. Detert, "How the iPhone widens the United States Trade Deficit with the PRC", *ADBI Working Paper 257*, Asian Development Bank Institute, 2010.

effect of lead firms' technology innovations. It is imperative to clarify that the spillover emphasised here differs with that defined in conventional literature on technology and productivity growth. It refers to an opportunity of joining and benefiting from markets of high-tech products, where Chinese firms have neither necessary technology nor comparative advantage. As a matter of fact, China's leading positions in exports of laptop computers, digital cameras, mobiles and other similar ICT products have been achieved via specialising on low value-added task-assembly of those products rather than indigenous technology innovations.

Finally, selling products in world markets requires global distribution networks. The existence of basic marketing and distribution infrastructure is a prerequisite for supply and demand to be interconnected with one another. The buyer–seller links between exporters and overseas buyers are important channels for the diffusion of knowledge and information.[18] In any value chain, lead firms are buyers and responsible for marketing and distribution. They set up product standards and instruct suppliers upstream of chains about what is to be produced. Through such contacts, suppliers learn the nature of the potential market and lead firms exercise direct quality control and often transfer valuable design, packaging and production know-how to suppliers.[19] Hence, the required buyer–seller relations for exporting commodities to foreign markets are naturally built in GVCs. For firms without their own global distribution networks, joining GVCs can mitigate information deficiency, reduce transaction costs and facilitate market access. Taking advantage of GVC's spillover effects in distribution networks, Chinese firms involved in GVCs have not only entered the world market successfully but have also been free of concerns on marketing their products to consumers in dispersed geographic locations. For example, Walmart, the largest retailer in the world, imports $50 billion

---

[18] M. L. Wgan and A. Mody, "Buyer–seller Links in Export Development", *World Development*, vol. 20, no. 3, 1992, pp. 321–334.

[19] G. Gereffi, "International Trade and Industrial Upgrading in the Apparel Commodity Chain", pp. 37–70.

of goods from China annually. The retail networks of Walmart provide essential marketing and distributions infrastructure for "Made in China" products to be sold in the United Stated and other foreign countries where there are Walmart stores. Chinese suppliers use the retail networks as a vehicle to reach consumers of the United States and other foreign markets.

GVCs and the Global Expansion of China's Exports

GVC and mobile phone exports

We will take a few representative goods as examples to intuitively illustrate the contribution of GVCs to the global expansion of Chinese exports. We start with the famous iPhone. Since the launch of the first-generation iPhone, China has been the exclusive exporter of iPhones. In 2009, it exported 11.3 million iPhones valued at $2.02 billion to the United States.[20] The iPhone is a high-tech product invented by the American company Apple. That China exports iPhones to the United States, where iPhone was invented, appears inconsistent with the classic theory of comparative advantage. The iPhone clearly belongs to the category of high-tech products, where China has no comparative advantage in comparison with the United States. The strange trade pattern, however, can easily be explained by GVCs.

On the back of each iPhone, there is a statement "Designed by Apple in California Assembled in China". The message unambiguously reveals that Chinese firms assembling iPhones are part of the value chain led by Apple. Because of the participation in the iPhone value chain, China can export iPhones to the United States market. The phenomenon of exporting iPhones to the United States and other foreign markets has nothing to do with China's indigenous technology capacity. It is mainly driven by the extension of Apple's value chain into China. What China exports via the iPhone is the service of low-skilled

---

[20] Y. Xing and N. Detert, "How the iPhone widens the United States Trade Deficit with the PRC", 2010.

labour but advanced technology. It is the iPhone supply chain that provides an opportunity for Chinese workers to sell their low-skilled services to all users of iPhones. The international production fragmentation of the iPhone enables Chinese firms to be one of the beneficiaries of Apple's technology innovations, thus promoting the export of China. In 2015, China shipped 31.85 million iPhones valued at $7.52 billion to the United States. Compared with 2009, the iPhone exports to the United States more than tripled. Unambiguously, the significant increase was driven by the rising popularity of the iPhone, which is the result of Apple's innovations and marketing activities, not China's comparative advantage in labour-intensive products. China's monopoly in iPhone export and the rapid growth of its exports represent a typical case where GVCs have successfully promoted China's exports.

Not only does China benefit from the value chain of Apple, it has been integrated into the value chains of all major global mobile phone makers like Motorola, Nokia, Apple and Samsung, which have either built their production facilities or outsourced the production of their phones to Chinese OEMs, thus transforming China into the largest production base for mobile phones. At its peak, Samsung, the No. 1 mobile phone maker in the world, assembled over 60% of its mobile phones in China before it started to relocate the production facilities to Vietnam in reaction to rising Chinese wages.[21] The participation in the value chain of mobile phones enables China to benefit from the spillover effects of those MNE activities. Whenever marketing activities and technology innovations of those firms raise the demand for their mobile phones, China could ride the wave and increase its mobile phone export to international markets. Hence, it is the GVCs that helped China emerge as the largest exporter of mobile phones in the world.

The rise of the Chinese mobile phone industry is very impressive. In 2000, China exported 22.8 million mobile phones to overseas markets. After its entry into the WTO, mobile phone export had grown

---

[21] J. Lee and H. Lim, *Mobile Asia: Capitalisms, Value Chains and Mobile Telecommunication in Asia*, Seoul National University Press, 2018.

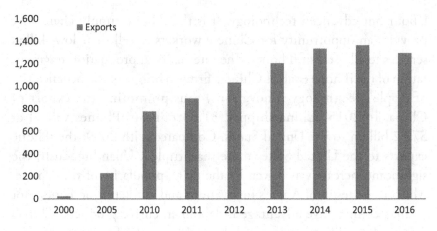

Figure 1: Chinese Export of Mobile Phones (in million)
Source: UNCOMTRDE.[22]

exponentially. By 2010, the volume surged to 776 million, making China the No. 1 exporter in the world (Figure 1). Up until now, the operating systems and core chips used in mobiles phones remain the intellectual property of foreign multinational enterprises, such as Apple, Google, Samsung and Qualcomm. Indigenous Chinese firms have not developed necessary technology in those areas yet. The technological deficiency, however, has not hindered the drastic expansion of China's mobile phone exports, because most of the Chinese firms specialised in the assembly of mobile phones rather than design, marketing or manufacturing core components.

During the period 2000–2010, intense competition and continuous technological innovations resulted in the reshuffling of global lead firms in the mobile phone industry. Motorola, the inventor of the mobile phone, exited the sector and sold its mobile phone business to the Chinese company Lenovo; Nokia filed bankruptcy; and Apple and Samsung have emerged as new lead firms, dominating the global

---

[22] UNCATD, "Global Imports of Information Technology Goods Approach $2 Trillion", 2014.

market. The growth momentum of China's mobile phone export, however, was not disrupted, because the competition is about the leadership of mobile phone technology, such as from 3G to 4G, not about where assembling task should be located. No matter which firm leads, China remains a dominant assembly base. In 2012, China's mobile export reached a new milestone and exceeded the one billion mark, and further rose to 1.3 billion in 2016. Sturgeon and Kawakami[23] ascribed the unprecedented achievement of the Chinese mobile phone industry to three trends: (1) a worldwide boom in mobile phone demand; (2) the rise of China as the primary location for mobile phone production; and (3) the emergence of China as the largest single market for mobile phones. Clearly, brands, technology and distribution networks of global leading mobile phone makers had driven the drastic expansions of China's mobile exports. In recent years, indigenous Chinese firms have nurtured a few mobile brands, such as Huawei, Xiaomi and OPPO, which have become more and more popular, and been competing head to head with Apple and Samsung in international markets. Huawei, the largest telecommunication equipment maker of China, has even rolled out the mobile phones with in-house-designed CPU. The success of those Chinese firms has surely contributed to the rise of the Chinese mobile phone industry. However, before the emergence of those indigenous brands, the growth of China's mobile export was mainly driven by value chains led by foreign MNEs.

GVCs and high-tech exports

Mobile phones are a specific product. Its dependence on GVCs may not be sufficient enough to conclude the indispensable role of GVCs in facilitating the constant growth of China's exports. Now, we expand the coverage of products into the high-tech category, which includes biotech, life science, optical, computer and information technology,

---

[23] T. J. Sturgeon and M. Kawakami, "Global Value Chains in the Electronics Industry: Was the Crisis a Window of Opportunity for Developing Countries?", *Policy Research Working Paper 5417*, The World Bank, 2010.

electronics, integrated circuit and other high-tech products, and investigate the linkage between GVCs and China's high-tech exports. With a population of 1.4 billion, it is not surprising that China has dominated the global market of labour-intensive products such as shoes, toys, garments, and so forth. It is astonishing, however, that only a few decades later China has apparently grown into the world's No. 1 exporter of high-tech products, surpassing the United States, the European Union and Japan. Furthermore, the United States, an undisputable technology leader, has been running trade with China in advanced technology products (ATPs). Statistics published by the U.S. Census Bureau indicate that, in 2017, U.S. trade deficit with China in ATP grew to a record high of US$127 billion, accounting for 34% of its trade with China.

China was not a major player in the global market for high-tech products; labour-intensive products dominated its exports. In 1997, China exported $9.8 billion high-tech products, accounting for a merely 5.3% of its overall exports. In 2003, it surged to 103.7 billion, more than ten times that in 1997; 10 years later, the number further rocketed to $660 billion, about 30% of China's total exports, resulting in a drastic transformation of China's export structure, from labour- and resource-intensive to relatively high-tech-intensive (Figure 2). The dramatic sophistication of China's exports in such a short time has caught the attention of academic scholars. For example, Rodrik[24] shows that China's export bundle had achieved the sophistication of a country with an income level three times its own. He argued that this special phenomenon cannot be explained simply by China's comparative advantage and natural endowments, but that the Chinese government's policies contributed substantially to the rapid upgrading of its export sophistication. Berger and Martin[25] also suggest that China's dominance in a few high-tech products such as laptop computers and mobile

[24] D. Rodrik, "What's So Special About China's Exports?", *China & World Economy*, vol. 14, no. 5, 2006, pp. 1–19.

[25] B. Berger and R. F. Martin, "The Growth of Chinese Exports: an Examination of the Detailed Trade Data", International Finance Discussion Papers No. 1033, The Federal Reserve Board.

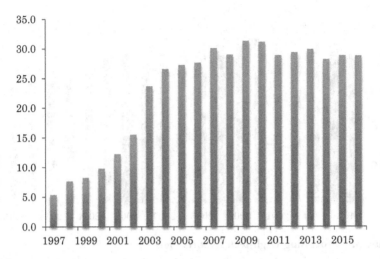

Figure 2:   China's High-tech Exports as the Share of Total Exports (%)
Source: Calculated by the author based on the Data of Chinese Customs Office.

phones can be partially attributed to the success of China's industrial policy and the sharp fall in the United States' high-tech investment.

It is true that China's R&D investment and industrial policy have significantly enhanced the technology capacity of the Chinese industry. However, it is difficult to imagine that, in less than two decades, those factors alone could drive China's high-tech exports to rise more than 600 times and even leave the United States behind. China's remarkable success in high-tech exports is mainly due to its participation in the GVCs of high-tech products, in particular information technology products, such as mobile phones, digital cameras, laptop computers and personal computers. The dominance of processing exports in the production of high-tech exports is undisputable evidence.

Most of the high-tech exports belong to processing exports, which are made of imported parts and components. Processing exports with imported intermediate inputs is a necessary task of GVCs. Typically, Chinese firms engaging in processing exports first import necessary parts and components from abroad, then assemble those imported intermediate inputs into ready-to-use products according to the

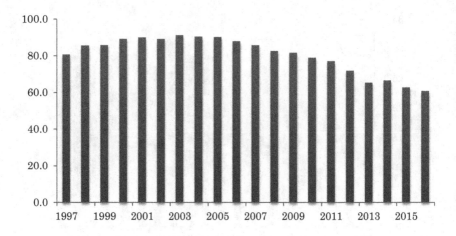

Figure 3: Processing High-tech Exports (%)

Source: The author's calculations are based on the Data of the Chinese Customs Office.

specifications given by foreign contractors. Some locally made parts may be used in the manufacturing of processing exports. However, it is the imported intermediate inputs, not locally produced parts, that determine technology specifications of high-tech exports.

In 1997, China exported $9.7 billion high-tech products, 80% of which belonged to processing exports. In 2003, the annual high-tech export surged to 103.7 billion, and the corresponding share of processing exports further grew to 91%. In other words, almost all high-tech exports were produced and traded along GVCs. The share of processing exports in high-tech exports declined in recent years. But, it now remains dominant. In 2016, processing exports consisted of a 60% of Chinese high-tech exports (Figure 3).

In addition, most of the ICT products made in China are assembled for global makers and sold under foreign brands. For instance, China is the No. 1 exporter of digital cameras. Japanese brands such as SONY and Nikon have monopolised the global market of digital cameras. It is very rare to find Chinese brand digital cameras in international markets. Most of the Japanese brand digital cameras are actually made/assembled in China. In other words, Chinese digital camera makers are downstream firms of the value chains led by the Japanese companies and simply perform an assigned manufacturing task. China is also the No. 1 exporter of laptop computers, and more than 90% of laptop computers available in international markets are actually made in China. In 2017, China exported 141.4 million laptop computers. However, of the top 6 laptop brands, accounting for 80% of the global laptop computer shipment in 2017, there was only one Chinese maker Lenovo with a 20% share, most of which came from the Chinese domestic market. In other words, most of the exported laptops from China were manufactured for foreign personal computer makers, such as Apple, HP and Dell, lead firms in the computer industry. Hence, the rapid expansion of laptop computers made in China is largely attributed to its active participation in the GVCs of laptop computers.

GVCs and China's overall exports

High-tech exports consist of about 30% of Chinese exports. Extending the coverage to all Chinese exports, we can also find a clear footprint of GVCs in fostering the growth of China's exports. Processing exports exists in almost all manufacturing products and has been a major export modality used by Chinese firms. It had contributed significantly to the overall growth of Chinese exports. During the high-growth period of 1995–2007, processing exports accounted for more than 50% of China's total exports. At the peak, the share was 57% (Figure 4). After the global financial crisis, the share of processing exports gradually declined because of the rising wage and the appreciation of Chinese Yuan.[26] In 2014, processing exports still comprised 37.7%, more than one-third of the total Chinese exports.

Processing exports can be divided into pure assembly exports (PAEs) and mixed assembly exports (MAEs). PAE refers to processing exports manufactured with only imported materials, which are supplied by foreign contractors, and Chinese firms do not provide any payments for receiving the materials. They receive assembly fees after delivering

---

[26] Y. Xing, "Rising Wages, Yuan's Appreciation and China's Processing Exports", *China Economic Review*, vol. 48, no. C, 2018, pp. 114–122.

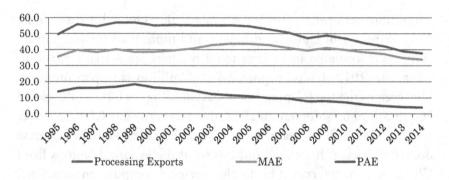

Figure 4: China's Processing Exports (%)
Source: Author's calculations using the data provided by the Chinese Customs Office.

finished products to foreign contractors. In PAE, Chinese workers' contribution is purely low-skilled labour services. MAEs are processing exports made with imported materials by Chinese firms, which purchase those materials from foreign markets. A small share of domestically produced intermediate inputs is generally used in the manufacturing of MAE. Figure 4 also shows the dynamic changes of PAE and MAE. It is noteworthy to emphasise that the share of PAE started to drop after 1999 and its growth turned to negative in 2008. By 2014, PAE fell to $90.7 billion, less than 4% of China's exports. This significant contraction of PAE suggests that many firms had exited the pure assembly sector. PAE is more vulnerable than MAE to wage increases and the appreciation of the yuan. PAE products are made exclusively with imported parts and components and require only low-skilled labour services from Chinese firms. PAE processing fees, which are invoiced in US dollars, are the only source of revenue for those firms. Wage increases and the appreciation of the yuan automatically squeeze PAE profit margins, resulting in an exodus of both domestic and foreign-invested firms from PAEs, the lowest value-added segment of GVCs. Now, MAE represents the major modality of processing exports. In 2014, it amounted to $794 billion, about 33.9% of China's total exports.

Processing exports is a direct measure of the participation in GVCs. However, the decline in the share of processing exports may not necessarily imply that the degree of Chinese firms' participation in GVCs fell. With significant technological progress, Chinese firms have improved their production capacity and have been able to product many parts and components which should have been imported before. More and more domestically made intermediate inputs have been used for manufacturing exports. According to Xing,[27] the domestic value added of Chinese exports rose to 73.2% in 2009 from 62.9% in 2000. As long as Chinese firms export their products via GVCs, their involvement in GVCs remain the same. If there are more Chinese firms participating in GVCs with their domestically made parts and components, it means Chinese firms as a whole enhance their involvement in GVCs. For instance, now there are 198 Chinese firms selected as Apple suppliers, suggesting that Chinese firms' participation in the value chains of Apple has been strengthened.[28] In addition, for buyer-driven GVCs, such as value chains led by H&M and Walmart, Chinese suppliers can use all domestic materials to manufacture products purchased by those lead firms. In this case, processing exports cannot capture the participation of Chinese suppliers in the buyer-driven value chains.

GVCs and exports to high-income nations

The United States is the largest market for Chinese goods. More than 20% of China's exports ended in the United States market in 2017. Japan is the second largest market for Chinese goods. In general, the markets of high-income countries are more important than that of low-income nations. On the other hand, consumers of high-income nations tend to be brand-oriented and prefer products with advanced technology, in which Chinese firms generally have no comparative advantage. It is more challenging for Chinese firms to sell their products in

---

[27] Y. Xing, "Measuring Value Added in PRC's Exports: A Direct Approach", *ADBI Working Paper 493*, Asian Development Bank Institute, 2014.
[28] S. Grimes and Y. Sun, "China's Evolving Role in Apple's Global Value Chains", *Area Development Policy*, vol. 1, 2016.

developed than developing countries. GVCs offer an alternative path for Chinese firms to penetrate the markets of high-income countries. Once Chinese firms plug themselves in GVCs, they can take advantage of brands and distribution networks established by lead firms.

A few studies[29] show that China's processing exports mainly end up with markets of the United States, Japan and European Union. By definition, processing exports are synonymous with GVCs. The significant presence of processing exports actually underlines a vehicle role of GVCs in facilitating "Made in China" products to enter high-income countries. Using bilateral trade data, we find that processing export had been a dominant form of Chinese exports to the United States, Japan and Germany. Specifically, processing exports comprised about 65% of China's exports to the United States on average and even exceeded 70% during the period of 1996–1999. Before 2005, processing exports to both Japan and Germany grew rapidly, much faster than ordinary exports. As a result, the share of processing export to Japan rose to 59% in 2005 from 43% in 1993, while that of Germany increased to 62% from 54%. In recent years, shares of processing exports gradually declined from the peak but remained more than 50% for the United States and Japan (Figure 5).

Concluding Remarks

In about four decades, China has emerged as the No. 1 exporting nation from an isolated centrally planed economy. This significant achievement is a miracle. While most of the literature emphasises the role of China's open door policy, comparative advantage in labour-intensive products, exchange rate regime, foreign direct investment and trade liberalisation in the process of transforming China into the

---

[29] A. C. Ma and A. V. Assche, "China's Role in Global Production Networks", 2011, at SSRN <http://ssrn.com/abstract=2179940>; Y. Xing, "Processing Trade, Exchange Rates and China's Bilateral Trade Balances", *Journal of Asian Economics*, vol. 23, no. 5, 2012, pp. 540–547.

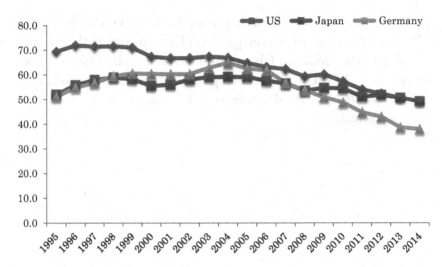

Figure 5: The Intensity of China's Processing Exports in its trade with the United States, Japan and Germany

world's largest exporting nation, this chapter argues that, besides those factors, GVCs have played a critical role in facilitating the growth of Chinese exports and its penetration into international markets. Only GVCs can explain why China — a country without comparative advantage — has grown into the No. 1 high-tech exporting nation and run a huge trade surplus with the United States in advanced technology products.

GVCs have been functioning as an effective vehicle to transport Chinese goods into almost every corner of the global market. By participating in GVCs of various manufacturing products, Chinese firms have benefited tremendously from the spillover effects of brands, technology and international distribution networks established by lead firms of GVCs. They can bundle low-skilled labour services with globally recognised brands and advanced technology and then sell them to global consumers.

The high-intensity of processing exports in high-tech products and China's bilateral trade with high-income countries clearly indicate that

Chinese companies have been deeply involved in GVCs led by foreign MNEs and have taken advantage of GVCs to penetrate the international markets. "Made in China" products sold under foreign brands remain part of GVCs. The declining share of processing exports does not necessarily mean the dependence of Chinese exports on GVCs has been weakened.

Appendix

敬悼缅怀 黄公朝翰教授

郭益耀

　　我认识黄朝翰教授超过半个世纪。今年6月中, 黄夫人简丽中教授从新加坡传来噩耗, 无异晴天霹雳, 悲痛之际, 感慨人生无常, 天地悠悠, 怆然涕下。

　　那还只不过三个月之前, 即3月3日星期六上午10时, 他们夫妇俩亲自驱车到我们下榻的泛太平洋酒店 (Pan Pacific Hotel) 接我与内子王晓瑚前去新加坡的东陵俱乐部 (Tanglin Club) 吃早餐。那也只是去年的10月28日的事, 他们伉俪俩短暂访问香港, 应邀在舍下畅饮叙旧, 并在毗邻的 "三希楼" 晚膳。我特选这家以川菜佳肴著称的餐馆, 主要原因是深信黄简伉俪他们俩久居狮城, 谅必乐于享用类似南洋偏辣的菜肴, 尽管他们不见得完全了解乾隆皇帝所指 "三希" 为何物也。

　　晚餐后, 我们两对夫妇乘电梯前往三希楼所在的科达中心大楼地库停车场取车, 就在准备上车送他们回去之前, 丽中弟媳没留意到停车场内一个下陷还不到两英寸的小石阶, 扑通一声, 摔倒了。让大家惊恐万分, 庆幸并无大碍。当时车库内灯火通明, 心想丽中何以失足, 匪夷所思。晚餐时, 我只自备几瓶德国啤酒, 以便冲刷特辣的 "霸王辣子鸡" 下肚, 并无其他烈酒, 而且主要由我与朝翰两人对饮, 丽中则着重与晓瑚欢谈儿女家事, 几乎滴酒不沾，绝对清醒，讵料居然不堪那小石阶折腾。看来莫非是朝翰更为适应南洋的辣餸，因此巴蜀的麻辣也可等闲视之乎。

提起德国啤酒，倒让我想起当年第一次与朝翰见面的情景。那是1967年秋天的事。我应邀参与香港大学一个由英国的勒伍豪姆基金 (Leverhulme Foundation) 赞助举办的学术研讨会，并提交一篇我生平第一次以英文撰写的有关 "毛泽东与刘少奇之间的经济政策争论" 的论文。当时朝翰也在场。他听完我的英语发言后，诙谐地说我的德语口音很重，我也就幽默地回应了他一句说，自己沉湎德国啤酒佳酿六年，潮洲乡音不改，鬓毛也未衰白，英雄本色也。这一则趣话，我在拙作《游学江湖六十载：心影、忆趣、反思（另类儒林外史）》（新加坡世界科技出版社2017年8月出版）一书中（页230）也谈到了。

那之前一年，即1966年底，我刚从德国取得博士学位，回新亚书院任教（1963年香港中文大学成立，新亚成为中大的创校成员学院之一）；而朝翰也于同一年稍早获得伦敦大学博士学位，应聘为他的母校香港大学的经济系讲师，英语响当当，了不得。

尽管英德两语难以沟通，但论岁数与学历，朝翰与我的关系，胜似同斋，更何言彼此从出道以还，志同道合，专注研究中国当代的政治经济学问题。实际上朝翰比我还小不到两岁。去年我八十伞寿时，也盛情邀请他们夫妇俩来港参与寿宴，而且嘉宾中也不少是朝翰认识的少林级别的 "功夫熊猫"（Gongfu Panda），只可惜朝翰身不由己，当时又必须飞往神州大地参访讲学。

说起 "功夫熊猫"，更让我深切怀念朝翰的才华，热泪盈眶，情不可抑。尤其是丽中弟媳传来噩耗时，也附上朝翰临终前在病榻上写的一篇短文，其中竟然还提到我的那本上引的《游学江湖六十载》回忆录，并将拙作书名翻译为 Gongfu Panda Roaming Around for 60 Years, 书名翻译的真是妙趣横生，让人五体投地。那篇短文实际上也可说是朝翰的绝笔书，因为这是他今年5月中因健康违和被送往医院调理时，应邀为他自己所创办的东亚研究所举办的讨论 "中国经济现代化与结构改造" 的国际会议（5月25日）所写的 "答谢词"。让人意想不到的是，无巧不成事，东亚所的这个国际会议也正是特别为了纪念这位学贯中西、令人敬重、专注研究中国政治经济学的学坛巨擎的黄朝翰教授而举办的。其不让人呼天嗟叹乎，命运弄人至此，譬如贝多芬的"命运交响曲"；尽管心灵深处，我忘不了朝翰的万卷"中国研究"论文，字里行间，处处是贝多芬"乐圣"的"英雄交响曲"，响彻云霄。真可谓广陵散于今绝矣，长叹息。

我想借网上一位音乐专家评审贝多芬"命运交响曲"的话，来概括朝翰的治学造诣与风格。这位专家说，这首交响曲是最能代表贝多芬艺术风格的作品，它结构严谨，手法精练，层次清晰，富有强烈的艺术感染力。而贝多芬对音乐感觉之精准，实为人间罕见，故称之为"乐圣"并不为过。我想将这段话中的"贝多芬"改为"黄朝翰"，恰到好处。我也想到朝翰诸多有关中国政治经济横空崛起的论文，或气势恢弘，或行云流水，也不亚于"乐圣"的"英雄交响曲"吧。

诚然，我从踏足粉笔生涯，专注讲解"中国经济"这门课程以来，第一部只字不遗地阅读的专书便是朝翰1973年出版的《中国土地改革与农业制度转型》。关于这一点，我在《游学江湖六十载》一书中也提到了（见页414-5）。其后的几十年，从1971年朝翰举家移师南海狮城算起，尤其是他掌管东亚所以后所发表的专著和论文，以及为新加坡政府出谋献策的行政简报和背景资料，我绝大多数都仔细拜读了，深受启发，受益匪浅，难以言喻（见页410）。感触之余，我也在想，朝翰著作等身，对中国经济研究的创作，论质论量，都绚丽夺目。如果他当年留在香港，而不转战星洲的话，能有如此灿烂的辉煌成绩吗（也见页415）？

记得朝翰近年，也可说是他最后发表的一批论文中，有一篇是刊载于新加坡《海峡时报》（2017年3月7日）的评论性文章，题为"中国领导全球秩序的神话"。该篇文章中说，美国总统"特朗普（的上台）标志着美国经济开始没落的拐点"。看到这一点时，我正好也完成了一篇当时准备提交给正要在马来西亚的槟城州举办的第一届"文明对话"的槟城论坛（2017年3月25-26日）的长篇论文，题为"一带一路大战略与'远交近攻'的春秋智慧----兼谈东盟的定位问题和特朗普总统的新亚太政策的可能影响"。我看到朝翰的论点时，特感激动，因为这与我自己的观点不谋而合，可谓"英雄所见略同"也（如上，页400）。

　　我看特朗普今年发起中美贸易战,极尽嚣张声势之能事,实际上是色厉内荏,近日又叫嚣要让美国退出"世贸组织",以搞乱世界自由贸易与投资的秩序。显然,这一再反映了这个世界霸主的国际竞争力已经今非昔比,开始日落西山了。这一个政治经济学的全球(或全中国)视野也可说是前后贯穿于朝翰的所有论著中,可说是他治学的特色与风格。

　　殊途同归,朝翰与我都不善长,也不热衷于应用复杂繁琐的西式计量模型,去分析和观察中国经济发展与转型的诸多现实问题,更耻于与坊间所见诸多类此的"即时专家"为伍,抽离了政治、经济、社会与制度等层面的问题,大言不惭地奢谈中国经济的大是大非(也见页425)。有关这方面的问题,台湾高雄国立中山大学政治经济学系的幸翠玲教授曾于2014年6月全面性地阐述了黄朝翰教授的治学方法论及其成果,很值得一读。

　　我相信,凡是有机会浏览朝翰所著各式论文的中外学者专家,都会感佩他的见解独特精辟,行文流畅强劲,彷若出自一个少壮派的刀笔手,绝没有人会意想到他竟然猝然而去。呜呼哀哉,天不假年,其不让人锤胸悲痛乎!抚今追昔,又不禁想起了50年前,即1967年秋天在香港大学的那个"中国经济问题"研讨会上我与朝翰倾盖如故的那个情景。虽仅属"倾盖"之谊,还谈不上"知己"深交,但朝翰与丽中伉俪在1971年移师星洲前夕,却盛情邀请我参与他们在香港半山区俯瞰璀璨港海的罗便臣道寓所的惜别酒宴。此情此景,历历在目,凄怆香江,情何以堪。

2018年10月20日 定稿

Index

Printed in the United States
By Bookmasters